S0-DTD-851

# CONTEMPORARY MANAGERIAL ACCOUNTING: A CASEBOOK

JOHN SHANK
*The Ohio State University*

# CONTEMPORARY MANAGERIAL ACCOUNTING: A CASEBOOK

Prentice-Hall, Inc., Englewood Cliffs, New Jersey 07632

*Library of Congress Cataloging in Publication Data*
Main entry under title:

Contemporary managerial accounting.

    1. Managerial accounting—Case studies.   2. Account-
ing—United States—Case studies.   I. Shank, John K.
HF5635.C753        658.1'511       81-4720
ISBN 0-13-170357-9            AACR2

Editorial production supervision and interior design by Pamela Wilder
Cover design by Judy Matz
Manufacturing buyer: Ed O'Dougherty

© 1981 by Prentice-Hall, Inc., Englewood Cliffs, N.J. 07632

All rights reserved. No part of this book
may be reproduced in any form or
by any means without permission in writing
from the publisher.

Printed in the United States of America

10   9   8   7   6   5   4   3   2   1

Prentice-Hall International, Inc., *London*
Prentice-Hall of Australia Pty. Limited, *Sydney*
Prentice-Hall of Canada, Ltd., *Toronto*
Prentice-Hall of India Private Limited, *New Delhi*
Prentice-Hall of Japan, Inc., *Tokyo*
Prentice-Hall of Southeast Asia Pte. Ltd., *Singapore*
Whitehall Books Limited, Wellington, *New Zealand*

This book is dedicated to

**Richard F. Vancil**

who taught me how to write cases and how to teach cases

# Contents

# Preface

This collection of cases in managerial accounting is intended to help fill the needs of those teachers who want to supplement and extend their classroom presentations with problem exercises that are richer and more complex than those normally included in textbooks. About forty percent of the cases included are drawn from generalized experience rather than from actual business settings. These are sometimes called "armchair" cases. What these cases lack in situational detail and contextual background for a specific industry is offset, in my opinion, by their clear-cut focus on a specific issue and their relatively low level of calculational complexity. These cases still provide a degree of realism that is sufficiently higher than textbook exercises to enhance substantially the perceived "real world" relevance of the topic areas covered. These cases can be used as course supplements even by those teachers who do not feel comfortable with more open-ended case discussion or who prefer to stick closely to specific, well-defined subject areas in their courses.

The remaining sixty percent of the cases included are drawn from actual business situations. Most of the cases are disguised, because the companies involved prefer to remain anonymous, and all the cases are simplified somewhat to facilitate student preparation and to concentrate classroom discussion on specific aspects of the problem. In a very real sense, however, all such "live" cases are sufficiently complex and multifaceted that the discussion can sometimes move in directions not anticipated or researched by the instructor. This is part of the attraction of bringing actual vignettes from the business world into the classroom. One implication of this richness for the instructor is that the teaching commentaries for such cases cannot be assumed to be as definitive as are those for the armchair cases.

It is important to note that this collection of cases is not intended to be comprehensive with regard to the topic areas of managerial accounting or to be equally balanced between easier and tougher cases for those topic areas it does cover. The collection represents the past eight years of my managerial case development efforts supplemented by several cases written by others which I consider to be outstanding and which are not widely available in paperbound published casebooks. What the collection lacks in comprehensiveness and balance is, I hope, offset by the timeliness, relevance, and teachability of the cases. The collection does span a sufficiently wide range of topics and difficulty levels to make it useable as a supplement with virtually any managerial accounting course at the undergraduate or masters level, including MBA courses.

Another feature of the book is the inclusion of five technical notes dealing with cost accounting topics that many students find particularly troublesome. I have found these notes to be useful supplements to textbook material in helping students grasp the key concepts and issues. These notes can serve either as pre-reading or as summary guides.

I want to extend my thanks to the firm of Touche Ross and the following professors who have contributed cases to this collection: William Berry, Charles Christenson, Neil Churchill, David Hawkins, Felix Kollaritsch, and Warren McFarlan. I am also indebted to the following professors for case ideas that have been adapted for the collection: Robert Anthony, M. Edgar Barrett, Robert Jaedicke, and Richard Vancil. I also want to thank National Steel Corporation and particularly Mr. G. W. Humphrey, Jr. for their cooperation in the preparation of several cases for the collection. I also want to thank Ron Ledwith and Elinor Paige of Prentice-Hall for their encouragement and help with the manuscript, Pam Wilder of Prentice-Hall for her efforts in carrying the manuscript through production, and Barbara Shoemaker for typing uncounted drafts of the cases and notes.

John K. Shank
*Columbus, Ohio*

# CONTEMPORARY MANAGERIAL ACCOUNTING:
# A CASEBOOK

# part 1

# COST ANALYSIS FOR DECISION MAKING

# Calumet Steel

In December of 1977, Robert Baxter organized a meeting of his staff to discuss specific product policy decisions for Calumet Steel's production of galvanized products in 1978. Baxter was president of Calumet Steel, a division of one of the nation's largest steel manufacturers, Pohasset Steel. He was fully responsible for the profit performance of Calumet, a modern, nonintegrated, cold-finishing mill.

Reports from corporate headquarters and regional sales representatives indicated that 1978 would be a year of substantial industry sales for galvanized products. If accurate, this forecast meant that Calumet's galvanizing equipment would be operating at 100% capacity for the year. Calumet, normally supplied with hot strip steel by its sister divisions, converted strip steel into three basic product lines: cold-rolled, tin plate (for cans), and galvanized products. Galvanized products accounted for about 30% of annual production tonnage and were generally considered to be the division's most profitable items.

Faced with a capacity-constrained situation in the galvanizing area for 1978, Bob Baxter was anxious to formulate a product strategy that would maximize the profits generated by this product group. He also hoped that by drawing together various department managers for the December strategy meeting, he could get them to expand their inputs into a long-term strategy with wider application for improving the return on invested capital at Calumet.

This case was prepared by Ms. Cynthia Kerr and Professor John K. Shank as the basis for class discussion rather than to illustrate either effective or ineffective handling of an administrative situation. All numbers in the case have been disguised to protect confidential data. However, relationships among the numbers that are relevant to the issues in the case have not been distorted.

# THE MEETING

**ROBERT BAXTER:**  President

Gentlemen, I've called you together to consider our strategy for 1978 for our galvanized business. Market forecasts indicate that we should be operating our galvanizing equipment at full capacity for the year. Since galvanized products are our most profitable ones, a good strategy here is essential for improving our overall division profitability. If we're going to be capacity-constrained in this area, it will be critical for us to get as much profit as we can from this part of our operations. This involves identifying our most profitable galvanized items and assigning marketing and production priorities to these products. First, we need to get agreement on the criteria that we should be using to measure profitability. This may be the most difficult part of the planning job. We need to establish guidelines for this that are consistent with our divisional profit objectives. Our criteria can then be applied to strategy planning for situations with less favorable market conditions.

**HUGH CRUMAY:**  Sales

We couldn't ask for more favorable conditions in 1978, Robert. If we're going to capitalize on this situation, we should be loading our order book with requests for the top-profit item, light-gauge coil products. Of the four galvanized product areas, this is our obvious profit winner [see Exhibit 1]. We make over $100 gross profit per ton on these items and $89 net profit per ton—about $25 more than the profit per ton of the heavy-gauge coil product. Our light-gauge sheet products are profitable, too, but the demand for sheet products has always been low in comparison to coil products. I think we should bank on light-gauge coil business to maximize our profits during the coming year.

**DAN SULLIVAN:**  Production

Wait a minute, Hugh, I've got to question your definition of a profit winner. If we're facing an operating capacity constraint in the galvanized area, then I think the logical thing to do is maximize the volume of tons we convert into galvanized steel. If we give production priority to light-gauge products, we're just further complicating the capacity problem. We would essentially be tying up a critical production unit with material that takes 50% longer to process [see Exhibit 2]. I just can't believe that this is an optimal solution for us; even though, as you indicate, this is what our profit reports show.

**BILL MOWERY:**  Financial Planning

I think you've got a good point, Dan. I think that's one issue Bob is trying to get us to resolve this moring. It seems to me that we have to be thinking about maximizing our return on the galvanizing equipment. To do this, we do not necessarily want to maximize tons produced or profit dollars per ton. We need to stress profit per unit of our scarce resource. If hours available on the galvanizing lines is constraining our capacity, we need to act to maximize our profit dollars relative to this variable.

**GEOFFERY BITTNER:    Production Control**

You know, Bill, I agree with your logic, but I'm not sure the galvanizing lines are really the major constraint we should be considering here. The cyclicity of demand for galvanized steel only creates a galvanizing capacity problem for us about 25% of the time. Our pickle line, on the other hand, runs at full capacity 90% of the time. In fact, when demand for cold-finished steel is high, we have to purchase prepickled steel to meet the volume of orders that our finishing mills can support.

**SAM KAUFMAN:    Metallurgy**

If you're arguing that the pickle line is the major bottleneck to be considered, Geof, that leads us back to supporting profit per ton as the most meaningful profit measure for the division. From the operating standards for the four product areas at the pickle line (Exhibit 2), you can see that there is little difference between them. Since we pickle a hot band before it is cold-reduced to any given gauge, the per ton versus per hour argument disappears. All the bands are the same thickness when we pickle them. This means that we can go back to the per ton measure as the profitability determinant. The catch to this argument, in my view, is Hugh's point that profit per ton doesn't mean much if we can't sell the tons. In other words, we have to recognize the individual limitations of demand for the four product areas and incorporate these into our analysis if we hope to maximize our return.

**TOM LEE:    Cost Accounting**

You're right, Sam, but there is another problem here which we haven't considered yet. We have to focus on the costs that are relevant in determining specific profitability figures. I don't think we should consider the fixed costs that are included in the profit per ton figures. The allocations for the fixed costs are pretty arbitrary and, besides, those costs don't really change as product mix changes anyway.

**BILL MOWERY:    Financial Planning**

But, Tom, I have always had the impression that in a capacity-constrained situation, full costing is considered to be the most relevant determinant of profit. After all, if prices don't cover fixed costs when we're operating at maximum capacity, they never will.

**HUGH CRUMAY:    Sales**

We're not talking about price cutting, Bill. As I see it, we are looking for profitability criteria with the most general applicability. We are capacity-constrained in our galvanized area at the present time, but demand won't always be this great. We've got to devise a way of comparing the relative profitability of our products that is not conditional on static market conditions.

**TOM LEE:    Cost Accounting**

I still think the problem with the full cost figures is that if we determine product profitability on that basis, we are tying ourselves too closely to the fixed-cost-allocation structure of our cost system. Our fixed costs are normally allocated to individual products on the basis of a specific monthly level of operations [see Exhibit 3]. If, during a specific month, we do not operate at this level, we generate volume variances. As a result, the standard product costs generated by the system often do not reflect the actual cost of producing a given product during this period. I think we should avoid this confusion of allocated fixed costs and deal strictly with variable costs and contribution margins in our product profitability comparisons.

HUGH CRUMAY:    Sales

Tom, do you mean we should be ignoring fixed costs? I have always been a believer that we can't really measure the profitability of any product without considering all the costs associated with its production—and with its delivery, for that matter. In fact, instead of excluding some of the reported costs, we ought to be adding on some you don't include. It has always bothered me that your cost system ignores the impact of freight equalization and competitive discounts that we incur in filling specific customer orders. These extra costs are not reflected in the standard cost figures, but probably average $5 per ton for light-gauge products and $10 per ton for heavy-gauge galvanized items.

SAM KAUFMAN:    Metallurgy

I agree, Hugh, and another item like that is the additional impact of claims costs on the profitability of our galvanized products. The automotive markets we serve with our heavy-gauge items persistently file defective material claims averaging $5-6 per ton. Plus, they're always returning products to us which we have trouble reapplying to other orders. With these kinds of intangible costs associated with heavy-gauge products, I find it difficult to consider them at all profitable relative to our light-gauge products.

DAN SULLIVAN:    Production

Sam, don't be too hasty with your conclusions. I think that if we are searching for a long-term galvanized product strategy, heavy-gauge material may be the answer. My guys really like to run the heavy gauges. Also, part of the profit differential in Tom's accounting reports is because of our somewhat arbitrary decision to run heavy gauges on the more expensive 72-inch line. If we reversed it and costed out the heavy-gauge products on the 48-inch line and the light gauges on the 72-inch line, the figures in Tom's report would change a lot. The only real difference there is our choice of where we normally run the product. Also, we serve a much more concentrated market with the heavy coil products; a market that is characterized by relatively constant volume, a few predictable customers, consistent quality standards, and good steady growth.

HUGH CRUMAY:    Sales

Sam, I hate to disagree with you, but if you are attempting to characterize the markets we serve with our heavy-gauge products, you're glossing over some of their biggest drawbacks from a sales point of view. Take the automotive market, for instance. This is really our least profitable galvanized market. Short-term, it may represent guaranteed volume, but the economic cyclicity of the auto industry creates real headaches for us in the long run. The material engineering changes they have been making during the 1970s to conform to federal EPA regulations and to reduce their own manufacturing costs have not made them the most predictable customers, either. I think they will be an even less desirable market for our galvanized business in the future.

**GEOFFERY BITTNER:** Production Control

I agree, Hugh, especially if we can't allay the chronic quality problems we run into with the order mix we accept from the auto manufacturers. Most automotive items are either for exposed or unexposed applications. Calumet accepts such a high percentage of critical exposed items that we end up producing more distressed material than prime product to fill these orders. Sam hit the nail right on the head that it is a full-time job for more than one person in production control to keep track of this unacceptable material and apply it to other galvanized orders with less critical quality specifications. Any rework that we perform on this dispositioned steel incurs additional yield and processing costs on which we certainly lose money. I can't say that I feel comfortable considering the farm product manufacturers as one of our more profitable markets, either. Grain bin manufacturers represent a large portion of the heavy-gauge coil market. Their sales have been growing a steady 4% for the past few years, and they have become a more stable and sophisticated group of manufacturers. But the seasonality of their business isn't compatible with that of our other customers. Also, the critical delivery performance they require is just about beyond the capabilities of our operations.

**ROBERT BAXTER:** President

I seem to recall, also, that this is the most competitive, heavily discounted galvanized market we serve at the present time. What about the market characteristics for light-gauge galvanized products, Hugh? Do you really feel these are the most profitable markets for the division to penetrate?

**HUGH CRUMAY:** Sales

This is difficult to judge, Bob. I think that in the long run, the building and duct product markets will be extremely profitable for Calumet. Both are vulnerable to the cyclicity of the construction industry and the national economy, however. In spite of this element of risk, the dispersed customer base of the market and the excellent relations that we are establishing with some of these manufacturers have convinced me of the markets' future potential.

**DAN SULLIVAN:** Production

Are we scheming about galvanized products 5 years down the road, or are we formalizing a product strategy for next year? I am of the opinion that our efforts should be concentrated on 1978 and the market forecast for that period alone. If you take care of the short-term problems, the long run will take care of itself. To me, the profitability of catering to the light-gauge galvanized markets in 1978 is very suspect.

ROBERT BAXTER:    President

Let me interrupt, Dan, and try to tie together what we have discussed so far. I think we have surfaced some significant issues regarding profit criteria for the division, but we need to resolve these before we can begin to formulate any specific product strategies. First, the profit per ton or profit per equipment hour issue needs to be settled with respect to our galvanized products. If equipment hours are chosen as the critical measure, then a decision has to be reached about which equipment really represents the most serious bottleneck for our operation. Next, we need to agree on whether a share of the fixed costs should be included with the variable costs in determining product profitability, and whether we should try to go outside the standard cost system to associate claims costs and discounts with individual products. I'm also bothered by the fact that the profitability measure for a product is influenced by the choice of which galvanizing line we run it on. I'm not sure how to handle the arbitrariness of that. Finally, we need to worry about the investment differentials across the products. In the long run, return on investment is what we're after rather than just profits. After quantifying all of these problems, we still face the task of incorporating the intangible marketing issues into our profitability analysis. Let's break this up now and get back together next week after Tom [Tom Lee, Cost Accounting] has had a chance to get us more specific data to help clarify the points of contention.

## QUESTIONS

1    In order to gain a better understanding of Calumet's "cost above" concept [see Exhibit 4] and the comparability of products A through D, compute the costs associated with processing each product through either the 48-inch or 72-inch galvanize lines. From these calculations, evaluate the relative profit impact if the heavy-gauge products were switched to the 48-inch line and the light-gauge products to the 72-inch line.

2    Complete Exhibit 5, the product profitability matrix. The point is relative ranking across four product groups for a given profit criterion. Note that logic may enable you to avoid some of the calculations. (Which cell entries are known by logic to dominate which other cells?)

3    On the basis of information discussed during the initial planning session and the answers to the previous questions, what measures of profitability do you feel are most relevant to Calumet's operation under what specific conditions? Do you feel that one of the four product groups is more profitable than the other three?

4   Formulate a 1978 galvanized product strategy for Calumet using your own profitability criteria. Be specific about ranking the four products and outlining individual marketing/production plans for each.

5   How could the cost accounting and/or the internal reporting system(s) be improved to better highlight the viewpoint about product profitability which you feel is more appropriate?

**EXHIBIT 1**
CALUMET STEEL
Galvanized Product Profile

| Product Description | Product A[a] (.019 × 42-in.; G-60 light-gauge coil) | Product B[a] (.019 × 42-in. × 60-in.; G-60 light-gauge sheet) | Product C[b] (.040 × 42-in.; G-60 heavy-gauge coil) | Product D[b] (.040 × 42-in. × 60-in.; G-60 heavy-gauge sheet) |
|---|---|---|---|---|
| Revenue/Ton | $500 | $507 | $443 | $450 |
| Material Cost/Ton | 338 | 342 | 327 | 331 |
| Cost Above/Ton[c] | 56 | 62 | 31 | 36 |
| Gross Profit/Ton | 106 | 103 | 85 | 83 |
| Selling, General, and Administrative; Mill Overhead; and Depreciation/Ton[d] | 17 | 18 | 16 | 17 |
| Net Profit/Ton | 89 | 85 | 69 | 66 |
| 1977 Monthly Average Tons Produced | 18,000 tons | 2,500 tons | 10,300 tons | 2,000 tons |
| Potential Sales/Month[e] | 24,500 tons | 12,000 tons | 29,000 tons | 10,000 tons |
| Markets Served and Share of Produced Tons: | Steel Converters 38% Steel Service Centers 27% Building Products 25% Duct Products 10% | Steel Service Centers 90% Duct Products 8% Farming Products 2% | Farming Products 36% Appliance 24% Automotive 20% Steel Service Centers 20% | Steel Service Centers 50% Automotive 35% Appliance 15% |

[a] Processed through the 48-in. galvanized line.
[b] Processed through the 72-in. galvanized line.
[c] Cost above/ton is the standard cost above basic steel and zinc material required to produce a ton of steel.
[d] SG&A and mill overhead are absorbed on the basis of total production conversion cost (i.e., cost above and material cost/ton).
[e] Estimated competitive discount allowances necessary for attaining these sales levels (includes competitive price allowance, freight equalization, and potential customer claims costs) are as follows: product A, $9/ton; product B, $12/ton; product C, $24/ton; and product D, $18/ton.

## EXHIBIT 2
## CALUMET STEEL

| Equipment | Capital Cost (millions of dollars) | | Standard Equipment Hours Required to Produce a Finished Ton of Galvanized Steel | | | |
|---|---|---|---|---|---|---|
| | Original Cost, 1961 | Replacement Cost, 1977 | Product A | Product B | Product C | Product D |
| Pickle Line[a] | 9.8 | 28.9 | .0051 | .0052 | .0048 | .0049 |
| Cold-Reduction Mill[b] | 35.2 | 92.5 | .0102 | .0104 | .0048 | .0049 |
| 48-Inch Galvanized Line[c] | 10.0[d] | 30.1[d] | .0508 | .0586 | .0335 | .0399 |
| 72-Inch Galvanized Line[c] | 16.1[d] | 29.0[d] | .0380 | .0420 | .0191 | .0239 |

[a]Prepares hot strip steel for the cold-reduction mill by cleaning rust, scale, and other oxide contaminants from the surface and side-trimming the steel to fit order specifications.

[b]Reduces the gauge of the incoming pickled steel and imparts a special surface finish and temper to the reduced product.

[c]Cleans, anneals, and applies a zinc coating to the cold-reduced steel, converting it into galvanized product.

[d]Shearing equipment included in capital cost:
Original Cost    $2.5MM
Replacement Cost    $4.5MM

## EXHIBIT 3
### 48-Inch Galvanized Line
### Monthly Production Cost Center Budget[a, b]

| Expense Item | Fixed Cost | Variable Cost | Total Cost |
|---|---|---|---|
| Direct Labor | $ — | $ 47,892 | $ 47,892 |
| Repair and Maintenance | 46,700 | 553 | 47,253 |
| Extraordinary Maintenance | 4,510 | — | 4,410 |
| Utilities | 67,210 | 92,100 | 159,310 |
| Roll Shop | 815 | 2,456 | 3,271 |
| Supplies | 365 | — | 365 |
| Chemicals[c] | — | 8,596 | 8,596 |
| Department General | 117,400 | — | 117,400 |
| Total | $237,000 | $151,597 | $388,597 |

[a]This exhibit illustrates how the "cost above" per ton figures are generated for one particular cost center. The data here are carried forward to Exhibit 4.

[b]Costs are based on 614 monthly budgeted equipment hours. Maximum monthly equipment hours available are 695. This budget is used to determine the "cost above" portion of standard cost associated with the 48-in. galvanize line.

[c]This is a variable material cost/surface area processed that is converted by the mill operating standards into a variable cost/equipment hour.

**EXHIBIT 4**

Processing Cost Above Material Per Equipment Hour

| Equipment | Total Fixed Cost | Total Variable Cost[a] | Equipment Hours Available | 1977 Equipment Hours Budgeted | Cost/Available Hour | | | Cost/Budgeted Hour | | |
|---|---|---|---|---|---|---|---|---|---|---|
| | | | | | Fixed | Variable[a] | Total | Fixed | Variable[a] | Total |
| Pickle Line | $573,100/month | $ 120/hr | 695 | 695 | $825 | $ 120 | $ 945 | $825 | $ 120 | $ 945 |
| Cold-Reduction Mill | $438,500/month | $1,080/hr | 695 | 483 | $631 | $1,080 | $1,711 | $908 | $1,080 | $1,988 |
| 48-Inch Galvanized Line | $237,000/month | $ 245/hr | 695 | 614 | $341 | $ 245 | $ 586 | $386 | $ 245 | $ 631 |
| 72-Inch Galvanized Line | $332,200/month | $ 408/hr | 695 | 678 | $478 | $ 408 | $ 886 | $490 | $ 408 | $ 898 |

[a]Most variable costs included in cost above are expressed in terms of dollars/equipment hour. Sulfuric acid used at the pickle line is a critical variable cost of this production unit expressed separately in terms of dollars/ton produced. The magnitude of this cost is $2.20/ton produced.

13

**EXHIBIT 5**
Product Profitability Matrix

| Profit Measure | 48-Inch Galvanize Processing | | | | 72-Inch Galvanize Processing | | | |
|---|---|---|---|---|---|---|---|---|
| | Product A | Product B | Product C | Product D | Product A | Product B | Product C | Product D |
| Fully Absorbed Profit/Ton | $ 89 | $ 85 | | | | | $ 69 | $ 66 |
| Profit Contribution/Ton | $139 | $137 | | | | | $100 | $101 |
| Profit Contribution/Galvanizing Equipment Hour | | | | | | | | |
| Profit Contribution/Pickling Equipment Hour | | | | | | | | |
| Fully Absorbed Profit/ Galvanized Equipment Hour | | | | | | | | |
| Fully Absorbed Profit/ Pickling Equipment Hour | | | | | | | | |
| Profit Contribution/Ton Allowing for Discounts, Claims, etc. | | | | | | | | |
| Profit Contribution/Galvanizing Equipment Hours, Allowing for Discounts, Claims, etc. | | | | | | | | |
| Return on Investment (%) | | | | | | | | |

# Signatron Corporation

Organized in 1960 in a suburb of Boston, Signatron Corporation had succeeded by 1974 in positioning itself as a respected producer of high-quality electronic components. Included among the firm's product lines were rectifiers, thyristors, zeners, diodes, and other high-voltage assemblies. Although these products sound exotic to the layman, they represent fundamental components in such fields as minicomputers, process controllers, and communications equipment. With 1973 sales of $20 million, Signatron might appear to have been at a competitive disadvantage when compared with the component industry's "Big Three" of Texas Instruments, Fairchild, and Motorola. However, by concentrating on high performance in high-quality segments of the market, Signatron had developed into the market leader in many speciality components. This permitted the firm to maintain a price-leadership position within these segments.

Rectifiers were a significant product group for Signatron. A rectifier's function is to allow electrical current to pass in one direction while preventing movement in the reverse direction. Its action therefore is similar to that of a valve. Step 5 of Exhibit 1 shows a completed rectifier unit. The value of this product to the final OEM user is primarily determined by two characteristics; the rapidity of response in blocking current reversals and the "surge capacity" or maximum voltage level the rectifier can withstand. Unfortunately for all manufacturers including

This case was made possible by the cooperation of the Unitrode Corporation. However, the case situation described does not reflect actual decisions faced by the company. It was prepared by William J. Rauwerdink, Research Assistant, under the supervision of Professor Neil C. Churchill and Associate Professor John K. Shank as the basis for class discussion rather than to illustrate either effective or ineffective handling of an administrative situation. Copyright © 1974 by the President and Fellows of Harvard College. Reproduced by permission.

Signatron, there is currently no known method of controlling production procedures to obtain exact electrical characteristics. Each production batch differs
from other batches processed under ostensibly the same conditions. Furthermore,
within each batch, the individual units do not have precisely the same characteristics.

Over many production runs, the distribution of unit characteristics closely
resembles that of a standard "bell curve." The units at the extreme lower end of the
distribution have limited marketability and are not repairable. Although these items
were not considered to be part of the regular product line, Signatron did offer them
for sale as "seconds" for use as components in relatively inexpensive and usually
disposable items such as toys or small home appliances. No marketing effort was
devoted to these "reject" units.

The production process starts by placing a "batch of 50 silicon wafers (purchased from outside suppliers) in a furnace which has been heated to 1,200°C and
which contains a specially prepared atmosphere containing metallic gas impurities.
By altering the concentration of the impurities, certain electrical characteristics can
be induced in the wafers. However, an improvement in one characteristic is often
accompanied by a decline in another. Also, in spite of strict monitoring of the
furnace conditions, small differences in temperature and gas distribution can occur
and these variations alter the final product.

After the heat has caused some of the gas impurities to penetrate the wafers,
each wafer is cut into about 2,000 silicon chips, each approximately the size of a
ball-point-pen tip. Exhibit 1 illustrates the production sequence then followed.
First a chip is placed between two metal cylinders. Step 2 shows the chip and
cylinders after they are fused, making a "sandwich" which is then enveloped in a
glass sleeve. The glass sleeve is heated while in place, forming a molecular bond with
the silicon chip. Silver or copper "lead" [as in need] wires are then attached (step
4). Step 5 shows the finished product after it has been painted according to a color
code.

The wafers and chips are tested at numerous steps during production for
physical and electrical defects, but the first test of a unit's actual operating electrical characteristics can only be made after the unit appears in the "sandwich" form
shown in step 3 of Exhibit 1.

About 60% of all the chips produced reach this test stage. Of that percentage,
only one-third or less (i.e., 20% or less of total chips produced) are eventually sold
as part of the regular product line.

## THE ACCOUNTING

Whenever production costs are not clearly identifiable with a specific production
unit, cost accounting systems generally rely on an allocation method to assign the
costs to the units. Direct material cost, for example, is usually directly relatable to
individual units, but equipment depreciation must somehow be allocated to the
units produced on that equipment. A "fully allocated cost per unit" is deemed

necessary by most companies for purposes of valuing units in inventory and, in some cases, to create a cost base for use in determining unit pricing.

The manufacturing of the silicon "sandwich" by Signatron creates components with differing electrical characteristics and therefore differing sales values as end products, but the manufacturing costs are "joint" with respect to the batch. In other words, there is no way to specifically match any of the costs with any of the individual components produced in one batch. All that can be said is that certain costs are incurred to produce a batch which consists of rectifiers with varying electrical characteristics.

There are two common techniques used for allocating such joint costs. The first method is to divide all joint costs by the total number of salable units produced during the process. This method is often called the average or physical measure approach. It normally yields a different gross margin percentage for each end product since the allocated costs per unit are equal regardless of the sales value per unit.

A second widely used joint cost-allocation method is called the relative sales value approach. It assigns the costs to the units based on each unit's pro-rata share of the total market value of all units produced. For example, if products A, B, and C cost $800 to produce, jointly, and have sales values of $500, $300, and $200, respectively, the allocation of costs to produce B is $\frac{\$300}{\$1,000}$, or $\frac{3}{10}$ times $800 = $240. When this method is used, the gross margin percentage for all products (without considering costs incurred after the "joint" process) is always the same.

Some cost data relating to one of Signatron's major rectifier series is reproduced as Exhibit 2.

## THE PROBLEM

Helen Barnes, a recent graduate of a well-known eastern business school, was just beginning a 6 month training assignment as assistant to Signatron's sales manager for rectifiers, Jim Jacoby. He called her attention one morning to an order for 6,000 units of number 401 rectifiers which had just been received. While many of the product lines were not inventoried, rectifiers normally were. However, very few of the 401 units were currently available in inventory. To satisfy the customer's needs, the order had to be filled with units that met or exceeded the specifications of the product ordered. The customer was perfectly willing to accept rectifiers whose performance characteristics exceeded the minimum specified levels; however, the customer was not willing to pay for the extra quality.

Exhibit 3 lists sales prices and the present inventory levels for the 400 Series rectifiers, along with projected annual sales. The production distribution, which is also shown in Exhibit 3, indicates the expected level of output of each product from a typical batch. The breakdown of products per batch can be reasonably estimated because it remains fairly constant from batch to batch. This information was all available to Helen Barnes.

Jim Jacoby asked Helen whether Signatron would be better off to fill out the order with 402 rectifiers, to trigger a production run to fill the order with 401s, or to turn down the order because of the "out of stock" condition. If additional production were authorized, inventory levels of other units would obviously go up. Jacoby was concerned about this because his performance was evaluated in terms of the profits generated by the rectifier lines. Besides the chance of these rectifiers becoming obsolete in the marketplace the higher level of inventory would tie up more cash and increase the level of inventory carrying costs. Jacoby estimated these carrying costs to be about 24% of sales value on an annual basis. He liked to keep inventory at less than one month's sales to prevent the carrying costs from getting out of hand.

After discussing this order, Mr. Jacoby also asked Helen for her opinion of an offer which had recently been received from a local toy company to purchase 4,000 of the Series 400 "reject" units a month at a price of $.15 per unit. The toy company was willing to sign a firm contract calling for 48,000 units during the next year. Jacoby said the production manager was against accepting this business at what he called a "giveaway price." He had said that $.15 wouldn't even cover the out-of-pocket expenses of a unit and that no one in their right mind would tie themselves down to a long-run contract at a price which didn't even cover the variable costs. Jacoby, however, was bothered by the growing accumulation of inventory of the seconds, even though they were carried at zero inventory value (see Exhibit 3). He asked Helen whether she agreed with the production manager that he was being naive to think of the $.15 as pure profit just because of the zero inventory value assigned to these units by the cost accounting department.

## QUESTIONS

1   Compute the per unit costs for rectifiers in the 400 Series under an average costing system and under a relative sales value system.
2   What would be the dollar impact on Signatron's income statement if the order for 6,000 401s were accepted for immediate shipment:
    *a*  Under an average costing system?
    *b*  Under a relative sales value system?
    What should Helen Barnes recommend to Jim Jacoby regarding this order?
3   What should Helen Barnes recommend regarding the offer from the toy company?
4   Which method of allocating joint costs should Signatron use? Which method yields better data for decision making?

## EXHIBIT 1
### Rectifiers at a 200% Enlargement of Their Normal Size

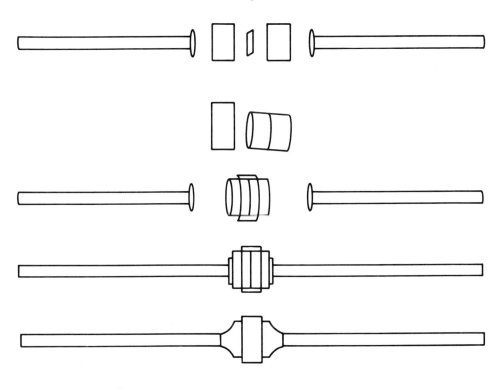

---

## EXHIBIT 2
### Product Cost Data for 400 Series Rectifiers

|  |  | *Annual Costs* |
| --- | --- | --- |
| Batch Costs |  |  |
| Direct Materials | $2,500 |  |
| Direct Labor[a] | 1,600 |  |
| Variable Overhead[a] | 2,300 |  |
| Total | $6,400 × 20[b] | $128,000 |
| Nonvariable Rectifier Manufacturing Costs[c] |  | 12,000 |
| General Factory Overhead Costs[c] |  | 60,000 |
| Total Inventory Costs |  | $200,000 |

[a]Labor and variable overhead include a total of $.05 per unit for "finishing" the product after the "sandwich" stage.

[b]Production of 400 Series rectifiers was running at about 20 batches per year.

[c]Allocated to 400 Series rectifiers based on relative sales volume.

# EXHIBIT 3
### Series 400 Rectifiers

| Product | Blockage | Maximum Voltage (volts) | Annual Sales Orders (units) | Sales Price/Unit | Current Inventory (units) | Output per Batch[a] (units) |
|---|---|---|---|---|---|---|
| 401 | .25- .74 | 300 | 100,000 | $ .40 | 3,000 | 4,500 |
| 402 | .75-1.24 | 400 | 140,000 | .60 | 10,000 | 6,000 |
| 403 | 1.25-1.74 | 500 | 100,000 | .70 | 9,000 | 4,500 |
| 404 | 1.75-2.24 | 600 | 40,000 | .80 | 8,000 | 3,000 |
| 405 | 2.25-2.75 | 700 | 20,000 | 1.00 | 5,000 | 2,000 |
| | | | 400,000 | | 35,000 | 20,000 |

[a]This column represents the average output of each product from an average batch, based on Signatron's history over the past few years. A typical batch also yielded 5,000 of the lower-quality "reject" units which Signatron offered for sales as "seconds." Demand for the "seconds" flucturated widely and was very price-sensitive. Signatron offered these units at a "scrap price of $.25 each, but sales had been very slow during the past year. An inventory of 65,000 units had accumulated. Because these units were not considered to be part of the regular product line, they were not assigned an inventory value.

# Ringo Rag Company

The Ringo Rag Company, a partnership, purchases old rags and cuts them into handy, usable sizes after they have been cleaned and graded. Main customers for these rags are garages, filling stations, oil drilling companies, suppliers of drilling equipment, etc. Major sources for these rags are textile converters, laundries, and junk dealers.

The production activity of the Ringo Rag Company is as follows. Rags purchased from junk dealers are washed and dried in special washing and drying machines. These cleaned rags and those purchased from laundries, which do not have to go through this process, move, then, to the grading department. Here, each rag is inspected and graded according to its absorbtion ability as either A, B, or C quality—A representing the best grade. Textile converters sell their spoils (rags) clean and already graded. Next, these rags are cut into squares of about 1 to 1 1/2 feet, and, at the same time, any foreign matter such as buttons, metal ornaments, buckles, etc., are removed from them. Rags purchased from textile converters do not have any foreign objects attached to them. Any leftovers which are too small for further cutting or have holes in them or are not usable for any other reason are burned. The cut rags are then packaged in 5-, 10-, 20-, and 50-pound cartons.

Prices (sales) for these rags are as follows (quoted FOB warehouse):

|  | *Carton* | | | |
| *Quality* | *5 lb* | *10 lb* | *20 lb* | *50 lb* |
| --- | --- | --- | --- | --- |
| C | $.70 | $1.30 | $2.40 | $5.00 |
| B | .75 | 1.40 | 2.60 | 5.50 |
| A | .90 | 1.70 | 3.20 | 7.00 |

This case was prepared by Professor Felix Kollaritsch of The Ohio State University.

Raw material sources and prices are as follows: Textile converters charge $6.00, $5.00, and $4.00 per cwt (hundred weight) for grades A, B, and C, respectively. Twenty percent of the quantity purchased by weight is lost during the cutting process in the form of waste, unusable parts, etc. This is referred to as "loss factor." Last month, the following quantities were purchased from a textile converter:

| | |
|---|---|
| Grade A | 43,750 lb |
| Grade B | 25,000 lb |
| Grade C | 6,250 lb |

Laundries charge $3.00 per cwt of ungraded material, and past experience indicates that from this quantity there will be a 33.33% weight loss, due to waste, foreign material, unusable quality, etc. Last month, Ringo Company purchased 60,000 pounds of material from laundries.

The highest loss factor is incurred from material purchased from junk dealers, where it amounts to 50%. Junk delaers' price for material is $1.00 per cwt; last month, the company purchased 50,000 pounds from this source. This ungraded material usually yields about 1/5 grade A, 2/5 grade B, and 2/5 grade C rags. The yield ratio of material from the laundries usually is about 1/4 grade A, 1/2 grade B, and 1/4 grade C.

Last month's output was (cleaned, cut, and boxed):

| | |
|---|---|
| Grade A | 50,000 lb |
| Grade B | 50,000 lb |
| Grade C | 25,000 lb |
| | 125,000 lb |

Last month's sales amounted to

| | | |
|---|---|---|
| Grade A | 50,000 lb | $ 7,750 |
| Grade B | 55,000 lb | 7,150 |
| Grade C | 25,000 lb | 3,125 |
| | 130,000 lb | $18,025 |

The previously described production activities, sources of materials, cost, yield, and loss factors are repesentative of normal operations. Sales usually follow production very closely, with only minor fluctuation.

The Ringo Company employs five women, each of whom gets $1.10 per hour. Last month's time cards indicate that their time was spent as follows:

| | |
|---|---|
| Grading | 1,000 hr |
| Cutting | 3,000 hr |
| Packing | 600 hr |
| | 4,600 hr total |

Two foremen are employed, each for $7,500 per year. They assist and check the women, which takes about half of their time. One-fourth of their time is spent on loading and unloading the washers and dryers, and the rest of their time is spent getting shipments ready (moving the necessary boxes to the loading zone of the building).

The two washer and dryer sets owned by the company are depreciated on a straight-line basis, and the amount of the depreciation for both amounts to $760 yearly. Each set has a capacity of 100 pounds per run, and it is estimated that each set can run about 16 times during a working day.

Other expenses for a typical year are as follows:

| | | |
|---|---|---|
| Depreciation | $2,060 | ($760 washer and dryer; $300 cutting machines and tables; $1,000 for two cars[a]) |
| Gas | 600 | (Used for the washer and dryers) |
| Electricity | 480 | (3/4 of which is attributable to the washers and dryers, 1/4 to cutting) |
| Rent | 3,600 | (Leased building[b]) |
| Detergents | 1,000 | |
| Salaries | 2,400 | (Half-time bookkeeper) |
| Gasoline and Oil | 700 | (For the cars) |
| Travel (Lodging and Meals) | 8,000 | (Half for purchasing, half for selling) |
| Miscellaneous Expenses | 1,200 | |
| Packing Material | 600 | (5- and 10-lb boxes at $.07 per box; 20- and 50-lb boxes at $.10 per box) |

[a]One car is used in selling, the other in purchasing.

[b]The building is used as follows: 1/4 for storing unprocessed rags (average about 200,000 lb), 1/4 for storing boxed rags (about 150,000 lb), 1/4 for cutting, and 1/8 each for sorting and washing and drying. A very small room is used as an office, and it is not counted in the building usage.

Mr. Ringo, one of the two partners, acts as purchasing agent and president of the company. Before going into business for himself, he was purchasing agent for a paper mill. Mr. Wall, the other partner, is the only salesman the company has. He held a similar job with a large competitor before he joined Mr. Ringo. All sales orders are local and made by phone or mail. The wives of the two partners act as part-time secretaries on an alternate basis.

## QUESTIONS

1   Which source of rags (textile converters, laundries, junk dealers) produces the highest profit?
2   If the demand for processed rags increases by 50,000 pounds per month and additional unprocessed rags could only be obtained by either offering higher prices for them or shipping them in from the outside, how much should the company be willing to pay per cwt or for shipping expenses per cwt?

# California Products Corporation

*HISTORY*

The California Products Corporation was started in 1955 by several members of the Black family. From 1955 to 1960, product I was the only product produced, and although profits were not high, they were sufficient to satisfy the family stockholders.

During 1960, the management of the California Products Corporation, mostly family members of the Black family, decided to change from absorption costing to direct costing (variable costing) upon the advice of a consulting firm. Product J was started into the production line in 1960 and product K was started in 1964.

Since 1960, the company had losses or very small profits. The profit and loss statement for 1965 (see Exhibit 1) shows that the company "broke even" during that year. At the board meeting, held shortly after the financial statements for 1965 were released, optimism was voiced concerning the future profit prospects of the company. The reasons given for this optimism were as follows:

1    Products J and K, it was believed, have overcome starting-up troubles and have finally found acceptance by the public.
2    Products J and K are both high-contribution-margin products (see Exhibit 4).
3    During 1965 some overtime had been incurred, which, it is claimed, cut into profits. It was anticipated that this would not be repeated next year.
4    The sales force had finally become convinced of the necessity of pushing product K because of its high contribution margin.

Copyright © 1978 by Professor Felix P. Kollaritsch, The Ohio State University.

24

The profit and loss statement for the year 1966 (see Exhibit 2) was anything but encouraging to the management of the California Products Corporation. The company sustained a loss during this year, and paradoxically had a considerable backlog of unfilled orders. The overtime was not eliminated, although the overall production in units of output decreased by 50,000 units (see Exhibit 5).

The board meeting which followed the release of the 1966 financial statements was unfriendly and everyone accused everyone else of inability. Without producing any evidence, the vice-president in charge of sales accused the production people of gross inefficiency. Evidence was, however, introduced which indicated that sales had to be turned down because production could not supply the goods within the normal delivery time.

The vice-president in charge of production accused the sales people of pushing the wrong product. He pointed out that all the troubles started with the introduction of products J and K. He also accused the vice-president in charge of finances of "tricky" and stated that the contribution margin (see Exhibit 4) was nothing except "fancy data" which would mislead everyone.

This meeting resulted in ill feelings among the various functional staff managers. The chairman of the board finally obtained their consent to call in a consulting firm to investigate what had happened and to suggest possible means of making the firm profitable.

An investigation into the variable expenses, shown in Exhibit 3, revealed them to be correct, and to include a charge for normally expected overtime. The prices for the products had not been changed for several years and there was no expectation that a price change was feasible in the next few years.

An investigation into the $800,000 fixed expenses, shown in Exhibits 1 and 2, showed that $430,000 was a joint fixed cost and that $370,000 was a separable fixed cost attributable to the company's products as follows:

| | |
|---|---|
| Product I | $ 60,000 |
| Product J | 200,000 |
| Product K | 110,000 |
| | $370,000 |

An analysis of the joint fixed cost of $430,000 showed them to be made up of:

| | |
|---|---|
| Manufacturing Expenses | $ 40,000 |
| Selling and Administrative Expenses | 70,000 |
| Depreciation | |
| Machine A | 100,000 |
| Machine B | 20,000 |
| Machine C | 200,000 |
| | $430,000 |

Regardless of the classification above, the full amount of $800,000 was fixed costs and had been properly classified by the company. Information gathered concerning the production process disclosed that each product had to be worked on by each of the three machines, and that each of the three products required different machine times on the various machines. (The average production capacity of the machines is given in Exhibit 6.)

It was estimated that each machine was operated about 1,750 to 1,800 hours during a normal year (practical capacity), which takes into consideration maintenance, repairs, resetting, etc. The maximum operational time one could expect from each of these machines during a given year without overtaxing them and incurring unreasonably high additional expenses was 1,900 to 2,000 hours.

## REQUIRED

Analyze the data of the California Products Corporation given above and summarize your findings in a report to the board of directors of this corporation, addressing your remarks specifically to the questions of overtime, production deficiencies and inefficiencies, the product sales mix, the costing method, the loss during 1966, and the profit potentials of the various products. Include any recommendations you might want to make and substantiate any and all of your statements with all pertinent facts and data necessary arranged and presented in proper form.

**EXHIBIT 1**
**CALIFORNIA PRODUCTS CORPORATION**
Profit and Loss Statement
Year 1965

|                      | Product I   | Product J   | Product K  | Total       |
| -------------------- | ----------- | ----------- | ---------- | ----------- |
| Sales                | $1,479,000  | $1,320,000  | $284,000   | $3,083,000  |
| Variable Costs       | 1,131,000   | 960,000     | 192,000    | 2,283,000   |
| Contribution Margin  | $ 348,000   | $ 360,000   | $ 92,000   | $ 800,000   |
| Fixed Expenses       |             |             |            | $ 800,000   |
| Net Profit           |             |             |            | $    -0-    |

## EXHIBIT 2
### CALIFORNIA PRODUCTS CORPORATION
#### Profit and Loss Statement
#### Year 1966

|  | Product I | Product J | Product K | Total |
|---|---|---|---|---|
| Sales | $1,224,000 | $1,056,000 | $568,000 | $2,848,000 |
| Variable Costs | 936,000 | 768,000 | 384,000 | 2,088,000 |
| Contribution Margin | $ 288,000 | $ 288,000 | $184,000 | $ 760,000 |
| Fixed Expenses |  |  |  | 800,000 |
| Net Loss |  |  |  | $ (40,000) |


## EXHIBIT 3
### CALIFORNIA PRODUCTS CORPORATION
#### Variable Product Costs

|  | Product I | Product J | Product K | Total |
|---|---|---|---|---|
| Materials | $2.00 | $3.00 | $2.50 | $ 7.50 |
| Labora | 1.00 | 1.20 | 1.00 | 3.20 |
| Indirect Manufacturing Expenses | .30 | .40 | .30 | 1.00 |
| Selling and Administrative Expenses | .60 | .20 | 1.00 | 1.80 |
| Total | $3.90 | $4.80 | $4.80 | $13.50 |

aIncludes reasonable allowance for normal overtime.


## EXHIBIT 4
### CALIFORNIA PRODUCTS CORPORATION
#### Contribution Margins

|  | Product I | Product J | Product K | Total |
|---|---|---|---|---|
| Sales Price | $5.10 | $6.60 | $7.10 | $18.80 |
| Variable Costs | 3.90 | 4.80 | 4.80 | 13.50 |
|  | $1.20 | $1.80 | $2.30 | $ 5.30 |

**EXHIBIT 5**
CALIFORNIA PRODUCTS CORPORATION
Products Sold
(Units)

|           | 1965    | 1966    |
|-----------|---------|---------|
| Product I | 290,000 | 240,000 |
| Product J | 200,000 | 160,000 |
| Product K | 40,000  | 80,000  |
| Total     | 530,000 | 480,000 |

**EXHIBIT 6**
CALIFORNIA PRODUCTS CORPORATION
Average Product Output Capacity per Machine Hour[a]
(Units)

|           | Product I | Product J | Product K |
|-----------|-----------|-----------|-----------|
| Machine A | 312       | 260       | 130       |
| Machine B | 364       | 208       | 156       |
| Machine C | 520       | 312       | 104       |

[a]Each machine could work at any given time on one product only.

# Morgan Steel

In July 1978, Bruce Tucker, vice-president of sales at Morgan Steel, received a letter from the purchasing agent at Illinois Drums, Inc., requesting a 5-year material contract with them. Illinois Drums is a rapidly growing firm which manufactures steel drums for storing oils, paints, and vegetable shortening. Bruce Tucker was under pressure to increase sales because Morgan Steel was operating below capacity. He thus clearly wanted the orders from Illinois Drums. In August of 1977, he had increased sales by negotiating a similar contract with State Electric. Bruce felt that analyzing the State Electric material management program would be helpful in developing a strategy for negotiating with Illinois Drums.

## BACKGROUND

Morgan Steel is located on Lake Michigan in Indiana. The company sells cold-rolled, galvanized, and tin mill products as coils and cut lengths. In 1977, sales were $516 million and net income was $1.6 million (Exhibit 1).

The Morgan plant, built in 1960, is a finishing mill and does not produce basic steel. Morgan manufactures to customer order. After accepting an order, Morgan buys hot-rolled bands (hot bands) from neighboring mills. Hot bands cost $280 per ton and it takes 100 tons of hot bands to produce 88 tons of finished products. Hot bands generally accounted for 83% of the cost of the finished product. Because the hot-band suppliers require a delivery lead time of 2 to 4 weeks

This case was prepared by Mr. James MacDonald, under the supervision of Professor John K. Shank, with the cooperation of a major steel company. All information in the case has been disguised.

Morgan keeps a 2-week hot-band inventory of high-volume items to expedite processing orders for such times.

In 1977, Morgan shipped 1.3 million tons of finished steel. The plant, in terms of 1977 product mix, has an annual production capacity of 1.5 million tons. Like most steel plants, Morgan has high fixed costs. Therefore, management is concerned with production volume and wants to maintain a high operating rate.

## MATERIAL MANAGEMENT CONTRACTS

Manufacturing companies now realize that return on assets, an important profitability measure to the investment community, can be significantly improved by reducing investment in inventories. Therefore, several large companies with competitive suppliers have instituted material management programs to reduce inventories.

In 1975, State Electric, a Fortune 500 company, developed a material management program called MSP (Material Supply Program) to enable them to carry negligible raw material inventories. To buffer against production variation which might cause stockout of raw materials, State Electric required suppliers to maintain inventory located at State's plants. Quantities on "consignment" under this plan average about 6-weeks' supply. State Electric does not pay for the inventory until items are put into production. Besides Morgan Steel, three other steel producers supply finished steel to State Electric under this program.

The main articles of the agreement between Morgan Steel and State Electric are contained in Exhibit 2. In summary, Morgan produces to blanket orders[1] and ships the items to State Electric's appliance assembly plants against releases from State Electric. State Electric, on the third of the month, submits to Morgan a list of items used during the preceding month. They pay Morgan by the eighth of the month.

Since signing the contract, Morgan has shipped an average of 850 tons of cold-rolled product to State Electric each month. To avoid breach of contract, Morgan maintains a finished-goods inventory averaging 420 tons in its own warehouse. This buffer inventory at Morgan is used to balance inventories at the State Electric plant and ensure rapid turnaround on releases by State against the blanket orders.

## THE MEETING

To develop a strategy for negotiating a material management contract with Illinois Drums, Tucker called a meeting to discuss the State Electric contract. Present at the meeting besides Bruce were Harry Linder, assistant controller; Joel Doege, Superintendent of production control; Tom Gondule, marketing analyst; and Jim Alvarez, product manager of cold-rolled steel.

---

[1]Blanket orders do not mention quantity or delivery date. They only contain product specifications.

**BRUCE TUCKER:**   Vice-President of Sales

Gentlemen, I called this meeting to evaluate our agreement with State Electric. In particular, I would like to have your views on how the system has worked so far and whether we should continue to enter into such contracts in the future. Harry, what do you think?

**HARRY LINDER:**   Assistant Controller

Well, Bruce, I don't really like the contract. State Electric is using us to warehouse their inventory. Why should we pay for *their* inventory to improve *their* return on assets when *our* return on assets is so low? Also, our 20% pretax cost of capital and other inventory costs [detailed in Exhibit 3] compared with only 3% gross profit on the sales makes me think that we're probably losing money on the deal.

**TOM GONDULE:**   Marketing Analyst

But, Harry, we signed the contract to increase volume since we weren't operating at capacity. We all know that unless we are at capacity, gross profit is meaningless. Instead, we should really look at contribution margins. I'm sure that the contribution margin of $36 per ton on the State Electric items more than covers the carrying costs of the inventory associated with the contract. [Exhibit 4 shows gross profit and contribution margins by product.]

**JIM ALVAREZ:**   Product Manager

Speaking of volume, we only expected to get 25% more sales by signing the contract and we actually got a 60% increase (Exhibit 5). If we hadn't signed the agreement, we would have been lucky to maintain our 6,400 tons per year share of State Electric business. I think we've done pretty well.

**HARRY LINDER:**   Assistant Controller

That sounds good, but Dave Field, who is in charge of shipments, was complaining about a logistics problem. State Electric doesn't send us the ticket numbers of the coils they use. They only provide us with a listing of coils used by weight. We have no way of knowing which coils have been consumed by State Electric. This causes problems in invoicing since our billing system requires ticket numbers. In some cases, it seems that State Electric has been confusing our steel with the steel from other suppliers. Also, we can't tell which coils have been kept in State Electric's warehouse over 60 days. This is important because the contract requires State Electric to pay for coils held over 60 days even if the coils have not been used.

**JOEL DOEGE:**   Production Control

We may have bookkeeping problems, Harry, but the contract has simplified production scheduling. Since we have a good idea of what State Electric will order, we can produce those products ahead of their delivery date to keep the production line full, or if we forecast a heavy month coming up. Also, with larger orders we can improve our operating performance by scheduling longer runs to minimize our setup costs.

BRUCE TUCKER:    Vice-President of Sales

Jim, you mentioned earlier that the reason we signed the State Electric con-tract was to get increased volume. Another way to increase sales volume is to discount prices. Do you have a feel for how much of a price discount would be necessary to replace our sales to State Electric? Also, doesn't price dis-counting give us more flexibility than signing a contract?

JIM ALVAREZ:    Product Manager

We should be able to replace the tonnage we supply to State Electric by giving a $10 per ton discount to some customers. I personally don't like price discounting because our competitors can easily duplicate our strategy. Price discounting leads to price wars and long-term depressed prices. On the other hand, I feel that State Electric's contract does not decrease our flexi-bility. The contract is renewable every year. If we anticipate capacity produc-tion, we have the option of terminating the contract.

TOM GONDULE:    Marketing Analyst

I don't know if I agree with you, Jim. I think it will be difficult for us to stop the process now that we've started it. I've never known a salesman to will-ingly give up any account!

BRUCE TUCKER:    Vice-President of Sales

Thank you for your comments. The discussion has been helpful to me. A lot of points were raised which I hadn't considered before.

## THE DECISION

Bruce felt he now had enough information on State Electric's material management program. However, to develop a strategy for negotiating a material management con-tract with Illinois Drums, he also obtained the following information.

Bruce learned that Illinois Drums was established in 1968. Sales and net income had been growing at an annual rate of 25% over the last 6 years. In 1977, Illinois Drums had sales of $21 million and net income of $2 million.

Due to the high growth rate, Illinois Drums was facing a working-capital shortage. To fund working capital, the company had borrowed heavily from banks. Since the banks were no longer willing to keep increasing its credit line, Illinois Drums had to reduce its working-capital requirements if it wanted to maintain its growth rate. This was the major reason Illinois Drums wanted to develop a materials program similar to that of State Electric.

In 1977, Illinois Drums bought 15,000 tons of cold-rolled steel from Jeffer-son Steel and 6,000 tons from Morgan Steel. (Exhibit 6 shows Illinois Drums' monthly steel purchases from Morgan Steel.) Jefferson Steel had declined to discuss a material management contract with Illinois Drums. Illinois Drums had indicated that if Morgan Steel would enter into a material management contract, they would stop purchasing from Jefferson and give the entire tonnage to Morgan, subject to an occasional small order just to keep open a second source of supply.

Bruce Tucker viewed a contract with Illinois Drums as a great opportunity to get additional sales. But, while the additional sales looked very good in 1978, Bruce was not sure that a 5-year commitment was desirable. He also wondered whether it would be wise to become the sole supplier to such a new company. Bruce was worried because he knew his boss would require justification for any decision.

## QUESTIONS

1   What is the total cost of carrying inventory associated with selling 850 tons/ month of steel to State Electric?

2   Did the incremental sales gain (60%) from the State Electric contract offset the additional costs of carrying the inventory at their plants?

3   If sales had only increased 25%, as expected by the product manager, would entering into the State Electric agreement have been a good idea?

4   If Morgan Steel anticipates operating below capacity next year, should the contract with State Electric be extended for another year? Why?

5   Would you enter into a material management contract with Illinois Drums? If so, what terms would you request?

**EXHIBIT 1**
MORGAN STEEL
(Thousands of Dollars)

Balance Sheet
December 31, 1977

| *Assets* | | *Liabilities* | |
|---|---|---|---|
| Cash | $ 1,824 | Accounts Payable | $ 8,847 |
| Accounts Receivable | 44,515 | Accrued Expenses | 10,075 |
| Inventories[a] | 61,221 | | $ 18,922 |
| Current Assets | $107,560 | | |
| Property and Equipment | $217,812 | Equity | 168,779 |
| Less Depreciation | $138,933 | | |
| Net Property | | | |
| and Equipment | $ 78,879 | | |
| Other Assets | 1,262 | | |
| Total Assets | $187,701 | Total Liabilities | |
| | | and Equity | $187,701 |

Income Statement
For Year Ended December 31, 1977

| | |
|---|---|
| Sales | $516,158 |
| Cost of Sales | 498,063 |
| Gross Profit | $ 18,095 |
| Selling, General, and Administrative | 6,328 |
| Operating Profit | $ 11,767 |
| Other Income | 526 |
| Income before Taxes and Depreciation | $ 12,293 |
| Depreciation | 8,954 |
| Income before Taxes | $ 3,339 |
| Taxes | 1,730 |
| Net Income | $ 1,609 |

[a]Inventories are carried on a LIFO basis. The actual value of inventories at December 31, 1977 (using 1977 standards) is $83 million.

EXHIBIT 2
Material Supply Program Agreement

*1*   State Electric will issue a purchase order to Morgan Steel. Morgan will produce and ship the ordered items to the specified State Electric plant.

*2*   Title to all items furnished by Morgan and in the State Electric storeroom shall remain with Morgan until such items have been withdrawn by State Electric and have been listed in its MSP (Material Supply Program) report. Title to them shall be deemed to have passed to State Electric on the date of each MSP report. Such report shall be submitted to Morgan by the third day of each calendar month.

*3*   State Electric will store Morgan Steel orders separately from those of other suppliers. State Electric shall also maintain insurance for the full value of all steel supplied by Morgan and shall be liable for any losses to said items.

*4*   State Electric shall, with 20 days after the submission of the MSP report, pay Morgan the amount constituting the net purchase price of all items as to which title has passed to State Electric during the preceding month. If State Electric shall pay said amount within 5 days after the submission of such report, State Electric shall be entitled to ½% early payment discount.

*5*   Morgan shall, upon reasonable notice to State Electric, have the right to take inventory of all items owned by it.

*6*   State Electric shall withdraw all items which have remained in its storeroom for more than 60 days and shall thereafter show items on its next MSP report as having been withdrawn.

*7*   State Electric will at all times have the sole authority to determine inventory levels for all items.

*8*   The terms of this agreement shall be for 1 year and shall be automatically extended in yearly increments unless terminated at the end of a term by either party giving to the other party at least 90 days' prior notice of termination.

---

### EXHIBIT 3
Inventory Carrying Cost[a]

| | |
|---|---|
| Pretax Cost of Capital | 20.0% |
| Cost of Space Occupied | |
|     Hot Bands (Outdoors) | -0- |
|     Other (Indoors) | 2.0 |
| Inventory Service Costs (Out-of-Pocket) | |
|     Insurance | 0.25 |
|     Property Tax | 0.50 |
|     Pilferage | -0- |
|     Deterioration | 0.25 |
|     Handling Labor | 0.50 |
|     Handling Machinery—Operating Cost | 2.0 |
|     Bookkeeping | 0.50 |
| Obsolescence | -0- |

[a]Yearly costs based on a percentage of the dollar value of the inventory.

**EXHIBIT 4**

Statistics on Shipments to State Electric

| Gauge (inches) | Width (inches) | Percent of Shipments | Finished Inventory (Value/Ton) | Revenue | Gross Profit/Ton[a] | Contribution Margin/Ton[a, b] |
|---|---|---|---|---|---|---|
| .0265 | 26 | 25 | $340 | $370 | $14.50 | $36.00 |
| .0265 | 29 | 35 | 340 | 370 | 14.50 | 36.00 |
| .0295 | 46 | 15 | 335 | 360 | 9.50 | 31.50 |
| .0295 | 47 | 25 | 335 | 360 | 9.50 | 31.50 |

[a]Gross profit and contribution margin assume that State Electric takes the early payment discount.

[b]Gross profit is before deducting depreciation and selling, general, and administrative expenses. Depreciation was $6.89 per ton and SG & A was $4.87 per ton in 1977.

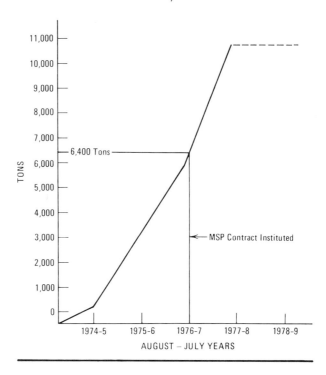

**EXHIBIT 5**

State Electric Yearly Steel Purchases

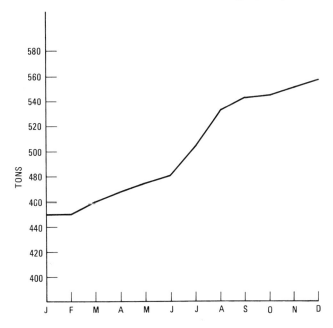

**EXHIBIT 6**

Illinois Drums' Steel Purchases from Morgan (1977)[a]

[a]Item: Cold Rolled Steel
Gauge: .043 in.
Width: 36 in.
Selling Price: $365/ton

Finished Inventory Value: $340/ton
Gross Profit: $11/ton
Contribution Margin: $33.50/ton

# Hansen Steel

George Hartman, president of Hansen Steel, a division of American Steel, was organizing his thoughts for the upcoming meeting he had called with the Tin Mill Products marketing staff and the division controller. The meeting was part of a series of general review meetings being held to develop the Five-Year Strategic Plan for Tin Mill Products (TMP) at Hansen. George felt, however, that this meeting could be especially pivotal in Hansen's five-year TMP capital reinvestment planning because Mike Lyons, division controller, was going to introduce some of the work he had been doing on "supply pricing" as applied to Hansen's TMP business. "Supply pricing," in itself, was not a new concept. But, for Hansen, it represented an approach to product strategy formulation that was different from what Hansen management had been accustomed to. Mike had told George that the results of his TMP supply pricing study could lead to some surprising conclusions about future pricing and market emphasis strategies for TMP.

## BACKGROUND

American Steel competes with five other major U.S. steel producers in the domestic tin mill products business. Industry volume in TMP is currently 6 million tons per year; American's share of this market is approximately 27 percent. Hansen is one of two tin-producing divisions of American, contributing about 30 percent of American's total TMP volume.

This case was written by Ms. Jane Stanwick under the supervision of Professor John K. Shank. It is designed for classroom discussion and is not intended to illustrate either effective or ineffective handling of an administrative situation.

TMP can be divided into three major product categories: tin plate, chrome plate, and black plate, all of which have applications in industries using metal containers. Because American expects to phase out black plate production in 1981, this case focuses on the tin plate and chrome plate product categories. Current TMP end uses include:

| *Tin Plate* | *Chrome Plate* |
|---|---|
| 1. Beer and Beverage (3-piece) | 1. Beer and Beverage (3-piece) |
| 2. Food (3 piece) | 2. Food (3 piece) |
| 3. Beer and Beverage (2-piece D & I) | 3. End Stock |
| 4. End Stock | 4. Food (2-piece Draw/Redraw) |
| 5. General Lines | |

Essentially, this categorization focuses on product use (beer, soft drinks, food, etc.) and type of can (3-piece, 2-piece, etc.). Except for one segment, D & I tin plate, historical and projected IMP market segment growth rates are negative (see Exhibit 1). Major factors contributing to the diminishing TMP market position are the aggressive introduction and penetration of two-piece aluminum cans and the industrywide practice of using lighter gauges in metal containers. Ten years ago, aluminum can manufacturers had an approximate 20 percent share of the domestic beer and beverage market which was dominated by 3-piece steel containers. In 1980, aluminum manufacturers have an 80 percent share in this market (see Exhibt 2).

## THE MEETING

**GEORGE HARTMAN:** **President**

Gentlemen, as part of our five-year planning program, we are faced with the task of developing capital reinvestment and product line pricing strategies for our TMP business here at Hansen. As you all know, prospects for overall market growth in TMP are not good, and profit margins on most of our TMP product lines have been shrinking. Because TMP represents the most energy-, capital-, and labor-intensive segment of our business, we need to direct our efforts toward improving our future TMP cost position relative to competitors, projecting our future capital requirements in TMP, and developing an overall TMP market positioning strategy through proper product pricing.

I have called this particular meeting to have Mike Lyons present some of his findings on the "supply-pricing" study he conducted on our TMP business. Mike, since the concept is relatively new for most of us, why don't you start with a definition of "supply price" and then go on to explain the methodology.

**MIKE LYONS:** **Controller**

Okay, George. "Supply price," as related to our tin mill products, is the weighted-average selling price which is needed to justify incremental investment in our TMP production facilities. If market prices are below this target selling price, capital investment to maintain TMP production capacity should be avoided. The supply price is the minimum sales price which produces a return on invested capital sufficient to justify the capital investment necessary to supply the product.

In our case at Hansen, our TMP production equipment was purchased and installed within the last 20 years. Much of this equipment is fully depreciated because we use a depreciable life of 12 years. From an historical perspective, the TMP capital investments we had to concern ourself with in the 1970s were basically of a replacement or maintenance nature. In the 1980s, however, our TMP capital-investment needs at Hansen will be somewhat steeper because the emphasis will be more toward modernization and technological upgrading to achieve full cost effectiveness. It has been estimated that the capital reinvestment rate required for the modernization of a tin plating facility which is part of a fully integrated steel concern is equivalent to about 2 1/2 percent per year of the replacement value of the tin producing equipment. With the gross replacement value of Hansen's TMP production equipment estimated at $240 million in 1980, the average capital investment required to maintain and modernize the TMP facilities would be about $6 million a year over the next 10 years, at present prices.

**DOUG DAMROW:**   Manager—TMP Sales

Wait a minute, Mike. I think I followed you through the definition of supply price, but I lost you when you started talking about capital expenditures and reinvestment rate. What are we supposed to arrive at when we do supply price analysis on our TMP business?

**MIKE LYONS:**   Controller

Sorry, Doug. I'll back up on the analysis technique. Essentially, what a supply price analysis allows you to do is back into the weighted-average selling price for TMP which is necessary to cover all the following costs:

1    The incremental or variable operating costs to produce TMP.
2    A fair share of the general overhead costs of the mill.
3    A fair share of the selling and administrative costs of the mill.
4    A return on the capital invested in TMP production facilities, including a fair share of the general support facilities of the mill.
5    The required incremental capital investments to maintain and modernize the TMP facilities.

Of course, someone might argue that some of these areas don't have to be covered by TMP revenues.

Take a look at this chart (Exhibit 3). This is an actual cash outflow statement for TMP at Hansen from 1975 to 1979. As you can see, our TMP tonnage varied little over the five-year period, averaging 476,500 tons per year. Each year, however, operating costs rose over the previous year by an increasingly larger rate; 1979 operating costs were as much as 25 percent higher than 1978 costs. S and A and other expenses rose more in line with the general rate of inflation.

The various rows of Exhibit 3 show various parts of the calculation of overall after-tax costs, including the cost of capital and the cost of incremental investment, net of the 10 percent ITC. The net result is the total after-tax *outflow* created by TMP at Hansen. Now, assuming that TMP was an attractive business for us to be in during the 1975 to 1979 period, we should have generated enough cash *inflows* to cover the discounted present value of all these outflows, which totaled $351,900,000.

To calculate the supply price for 1975, we need to know our historical price increases in TMP. We found that, on average, they increased only with the rate of general inflation (6% per year during the 1975-1979 period). This fact coupled with the understanding that every dollar of TMP revenue only increases after tax inflows by 50 cents enables us to set up the following equation for the cash inflow in years n:

$$I_n = P \times V \times (1 + i)^n (1 - t)$$

where

$I_n$ = cash inflow in year n
$P$ = supply price per ton
$V$ = volume (in tons)
$i$ = inflation rate of price increases
$t$ = tax rate

The NPV of this inflow is given by $I_n$ times the discount factor. This can be written as $I_n \cdot (1/1+r)^n$ where r is the discount rate.

From this point, in order to arrive at the supply price, it is necessary to perform the following sequence of calculations:

1  To recover all costs and earn a return on invested capital, assume that the NPV of the after-tax outflows equals the NPV of the after-tax inflows.

2  The NPV of the cash inflows is given by:

$$\Sigma I_n \cdot (1/1 + r)^n = \Sigma P \cdot (1-t) \cdot V \cdot (1 + i)^n \cdot (1/1 + r)^n$$

Assuming volume (V) is constant each year, this can be rewritten as:

$$P \cdot (1-t) \cdot V \cdot \Sigma (\frac{1+i}{1+r})^n$$

*3*    P equals the price needed at the beginning of the first year of the cash flow analysis to make the sum of the net present value of inflows equal to the sum of net present value of outflows.

I calculated the supply price that would have been required at the beginning of 1975 to cover the costs in the 1975-1979 period as shown in Exhibit 4. You can see that the requisite supply price at the outset of 1975 was $347/ ton. Our actual weighted-average net selling price at the beginning of 1975 was approximately $450/ton. So, you can see that we were well on target as far as TMP product pricing in 1975.

**GEORGE HARTMAN:**    President

That's very interesting, Mike. But all that does is give Hansen a pat on the back in hindsight for proper product pricing. How can this type of analysis be adapted for use in understanding some of our current problems such as rapidly escalating operating and capital costs and shrinking market potential due to aluminum's competition?

**MIKE LYONS:**    Controller

That's where I'd like everyone's input today. I think we can develop a supply price analysis for the 1980s based on what our market and cost projections are for the next 10 years. Let's start with sales mix, for example. Doug, what are the marketing staff's projections for TMP market mix at Hansen?

**DOUG DAMROW:**    Manager—TMP Sales

Mike, as you've mentioned before, our volume in TMP has been relatively constant over the last 5 years. I view 1980 as being a fairly representative year for TMP mix at Hansen, and I think it could be used to project the annual shipments in the 1980s. The end uses might change through the 1980s as beer and beverage shift increasingly toward aluminum 2-piece containers, but, in total, I think our volume should remain fairly constant as we pick up other nonbeer and beverage tonnage. (The projected volumes for the 1980s are shown in Exhibit 5).

**MIKE LYONS:**    Controller

Given that you feel confident using our 1980 mix as an annual forecast mix, we can look at 1980 operating costs for the mix and make some projections about how the costs will escalate during the 1980s. Year-to-date weighted-average *actual* TMP operating cost is roughly $618/net ton. This compares rather unfavorably with our weighted-average TMP *standard* cost of $530/ net ton.

To understand how operating cost should be inflated each year during the 1980s, we have to break operating cost into its components. Historically, from primary end to finishing end, three components of TMP operating cost have had the following representative shares:

1    Energy—25%
2    Labor—30%
3    All other (including hot bands)—45%

If these components are inflated at their respective projected inflation rates (see Exhibit 6), we arrive at a weighted-average annual inflation rate of 14.6 percent for operating costs.

Other nonoperating costs such as S and A and other expenses are only expected to increase at a rate of 10 percent per annum.

**GEORGE HARTMAN:**   President

What about capital expenditures for our tin mill product facilities, Mike?

**MIKE LYONS:**   Controller

I think 5 million per year is a reasonable estimate for our capital requirements for TMP facility modernization and maintenance over the next 10 years.

**GARY ANDERSON:**   Salesman—TMP

We also have to account for the tax shields we would get from depreciation and ITC. But, I'm not sure how to arrive at a depreciation charge per year.

**MIKE LYONS:**   Controller

I'm going to leave that up to you and the rest of the group here today to figure out. I will say that the depreciation expense applicable to our existing TMP facilities is approximately $3.5 million per annum. But, in addition, you will have to account for the extra depreciation being brought on yearly by $5 million of capital expenditures. Average equipment life is 12 years, and we use a straight-line method of depreciation at Hansen.

**GEORGE HARTMAN:**   President

Mike, didn't you say that we had to include price increases in our supply price analysis.

**MIKE LYONS:**   Controller

Yes, in fact, that's the only piece of information that we're missing. Doug, what do you feel is a realistic price escalation factor?

**DOUG DAMROW:**   Manager—TMP Sales

We've discussed this with our corporate marketing staff and we feel that TMP prices will rise about 10 percent per year, industrywide, during the next decade.

**MIKE LYONS:**   Controller

Gentlemen, I think we can readily develop a 10-year cash outflow statement for TMP at Hansen from 1981-1990 and back into the supply price that we'd need in January 1981 to cover all our projected costs and earn an adequate return on our invested capital during the 1980s.

GEORGE HARTMAN:    President

I'm anxious to see the results. From the points already raised in our discussion, however, the results should not be very favorable. We're already "in the red" in 1980 with actual operating costs at $618/net ton and average selling price at $600/net ton. I think we should examine some alternatives such as cost improvements in TMP manufacture and market segmentation or product mix selection strategies aimed at maximizing profits.

Mike, I think your presentation on supply pricing has been very helpful in updating our thinking on Hansen's TMP profitability. Hopefully, the results of the 1981 supply price calculation will instigate further discussion on where we see our real opportunities for profit improvement in the TMP business.

## QUESTIONS

1    Prepare a 10-year cash outflow statement for TMP at Hansen based on a volume of 477,600 tons/year. Calculate the supply price required at January 1, 1981.

2    What effect would a $20 cost improvement/ton have on the supply price for January 1, 1981? A $70 cost improvement/ton?

3    If it were possible to change Hansen's marketing mix by dropping the least profitable TMP tonnage so that weighted-average operating costs were only $570/ton, what would the new January 1, 1981 supply price be, based on the lower volume (350,000 tons/year) of TMP? (Assume that capital expenditures would still be $5 million/year).

## EXHIBIT 1
### HANSEN STEEL
TMP Market Growth Rates

*Percentage Change From Prior Year*

| | *1977* | *1978* | *1979* | *1980* | *1981* | *1982* | *1983* |
|---|---|---|---|---|---|---|---|
| *Tin Plate* | | | | | | | |
| Beer and Beverage (3-piece) | −11 | −23 | −20 | −24 | −22 | −17 | −18 |
| Sanitary (3-piece) | | No Growth | | | | | |
| D & I (2-piece) | +35 | +35 | +27 | +17 | + 9 | + 9 | + 8 |
| End Stock | −11 | −23 | −20 | −24 | −22 | −17 | −18 |
| General Lines | | No Growth | | | | | |
| *Chrome Plate* | | | | | | | |
| Beer & Beverage (3-piece) | −11 | −23 | −20 | −24 | −22 | −17 | −18 |
| Sanitary (3-piece) | | No Growth | | | | | |
| End Stock | −11 | −23 | −20 | −24 | −22 | −17 | −18 |
| Draw/Redraw (2-piece) | N/A[a] | N/A | + 5 | + 5 | + 5 | + 5 | + 5 |

[a]N/A = Not applicable.

## EXHIBIT 2
### HANSEN STEEL
Metal Cans (in billion cans)
Industry Shipments

| *Product Categories* | *1976 (Actual)* | *1980 (Estimate)* | *1985 (Forecast)* |
|---|---|---|---|
| Food Cans: | | | |
| Steel | 26.4 | 26.1 | 26.5 |
| Aluminum | .8 | 0.9 | 0.9 |
| Subtotal | 27.2 | 27.0 | 27.4 |
| Beer Cans: | | | |
| 3-Piece Steel | 6.6 | 1.1 | — |
| 2-Piece Steel | 3.8 | 5.2 | 6.2 |
| 2-Piece Aluminum | 16.5 | 24.0 | 27.7 |
| Subtotal | 26.9 | 30.3 | 33.9 |
| Soft Drink Cans: | | | |
| 3-Piece Steel | 13.4 | 5.7 | 1.5 |
| 2-Piece Steel | 1.6 | 5.8 | 5.8 |
| 2-Piece Aluminum | 4.5 | 15.5 | 24.6 |
| Subtotal | 19.5 | 27.0 | 31.9 |
| Pet Food Cans (Steel) | 3.0 | 3.0 | 3.1 |
| General Packaging (Steel-Motor Oil, Paints, Aerosols) | 6.0 | 5.0 | 5.2 |
| *Total by Metal Used:* | | | |
| Steel | 60.8 | 51.9 | 48.3 |
| Aluminum | 21.8 | 40.4 | 53.2 |
| TOTAL | 82.6 | 92.3 | 101.5 |

EXHIBIT 3
HANSEN STEEL
TMP Cash Outflows Schedule

| | 1975 | 1976 | 1977 | 1978 | 1979 |
|---|---|---|---|---|---|
| Total TMP Tonnage | 438,000 | 481,000 | 495,000 | 488,000 | 480,000 |
| Manufacturing Cost Per Ton | $ 325 | $ 330 | $ 372 | $ 431 | $ 539 |
| Total Manufacturing Cost | $142,360,000 | $158,730,000 | $184,140,000 | $210,330,000 | $258,720,000 |
| Share of Selling and Administrative Cost | 3,260,000 | 3,410,000 | 3,320,000 | 3,230,000 | 4,200,000 |
| Total Costs (pretax) | $145,620,000 | $162,140,000 | $187,460,000 | $213,560,000 | $262,920,000 |
| 1) Total Costs (After tax) (50%) | 72,815,000 | 81,070,000 | 93,730,000 | 106,780,000 | 131,460,000 |
| 2) Capital Expenditures (Net of ITC) | 900,000 | 950,000 | 1,010,000 | 1,070,000 | 1,140,000 |
| Avg. Invested Capital (Net Book Value) | 46,100,000 | 42,400,000 | 39,000,000 | 36,000,000 | 33,500,000 |
| 3) Required Return on Investment (at 12% after tax) | 5,530,000 | 5,090,000 | 4,680,000 | 4,320,000 | 4,020,000 |
| 4) Depreciation Tax Shelter | 2,470,000 | 2,390,000 | 2,090,000 | 2,060,000 | 1,710,000 |
| Total Net Cash Outflows (1+2+3−4) | $ 76,770,000 | $ 84,720,000 | $ 97,330,000 | $110,110,000 | $134,910,000 |

NPV (12%)  $351,900,000

EXHIBIT 4
HANSEN STEEL
Calculation of TMP Supply Price for 1975
(000)

1) NPV of A/T outflow stream = $351,900,000

2) NPV of after tax outflows = NPV of after tax inflows

3) Solve for P in the equation:

$$P \cdot (1-50\%) \cdot 477,000 \cdot 4.25^* = \$351,900,000$$
$$(.5)P = 173.58$$
$$P = \$347.$$

*This factor is equal to $\sum_5 (\frac{1+6\%}{1+12\%})^n = 4.25$

EXHIBIT 5
HANSEN STEEL
TMP Sales Mix 1981-1990

| Product Category | 1980(E) and Projected Annual Tonnage 1981-90 | Current 1980 End Uses | Projected 1981-90 End Uses |
|---|---|---|---|
| 1) TIN D & I | 36,000 | 2-piece beer and beverage | same |
| 2) TIN SR (Single Reduced) | 192,000 | 80% sanitary 20% miscellaneous | same |
| 3) TIN DRH (Double-Reduced, Heavy Gauge) | 16,800 | end stock for 3-piece beer and beverage | end stock for 3-piece sanitary |
| 4) TIN DRL (Double-Reduced, Light Gauge) | 26,400 | 40% pet food cans 30% beer and beverage body stock 30% sanitary | 50% pet food 50% sanitary |
| 5) CHROME SR (Single-Reduced) | 84,000 | sanitary body and ends | same |
| 6) CHROME DRH (Double-Reduced, Heavy Gauge) | 96,000 | sanitary bodies and ends | same |
| 7) CHROME DRL (Double-Reduced, Light Gauge) | 26,400 | 20% beer and beverage body stock 80% sanitary body stock | same |
| HANSEN ANNUAL TOTAL | 477,600 tons | | |

**EXHIBIT 6**
HANSEN STEEL
Components of Operating Expense for TMP

FORECAST: 1981-1990

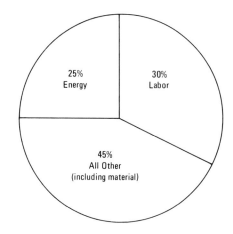

1981-1990 Projected Annual Inflation Rates:

| | |
|---|---|
| Labor | 12% |
| Energy | 17% |
| All Other | 15% |

Weighted Average Annual Inflation Rate
for TMP Operating Expenses:

| | % of Total | | Inflation Factor | | |
|---|---|---|---|---|---|
| Labor | .30 | X | .12 | = | .0360 |
| Energy | .25 | X | .17 | = | .0425 |
| All Other | .45 | X | .15 | = | .0675 |
| | | | | | .1460 |

Weighted-Average Annual Inflation Rate = 14.6%

# Olson Metals

"Well Frank, our new computer system shows that we have just finished the most profitable year in our history and we did it without raising prices," said John Olson, founder of Olson Metals Corporation to his son Frank. "We have held the price line since 1974 and now that we have gotten one major competitor almost out of the grinding and plating business, I think our strategy of process innovation to get productivity and product quality up and constant prices to keep competition out has paid off. I guess we've been both right and lucky."

"I agree, Dad," said Frank Olson. "It's been a great year but there are a couple of things that bother me. Let me look the 'financials' over and talk to you about them next week. With steel prices going up some 7% next month [August 1977] it could be the time to change our pricing strategy."

"I'll listen to what you say, Frank," said John, "but we are doing pretty well. I'd hate to see us either price ourselves out of the market or hold a profit umbrella over the heads of our competitors—and potential competitors as well. We didn't get 40% of the market by raising prices."

## COMPANY BACKGROUND

John Olson left a large corporation to start his own business in Chicago in 1951 with $2,500 of paid-in capital and a total of five stockholders. Under the title of Olson Metal Company, the firm's original job was cleaning steel castings that were

Copyright © 1978 by the President and Fellows of Harvard College. Reproduced by permission. The case was prepared by Professor Neil C. Churchill and Research Associate Ashis Gupta at a basis for class discussion rather than to illustrate either effective or ineffective handling of an administrative situation.

to be used in large generators. The company cleaned the castings, weighed them, and finally arranged them in circles so that, when placed in the generator, the generator rotor would be properly balanced. The company cleaned about 150,000 of these castings before it moved onto other activities. John Olson explained the transition as follows:

> *Our original plan, when we saw this opportunity, was to grab it, make a little money, take it out and spend it. But then we got started and didn't want to stop. We started looking around for something else to do. I knew how to do silver brazing. So we did a little of that. Then we decided we'd go into the centrifugal pump business. It took us a while to get the designs right and tool up. When we did, we sold only 10 pumps in the first year. We begin to hurt so badly that we started doing general machining just to stay in business.*

Around 1954, John found the opportunity to buy two multiple-spindle drill presses, which, although the company had no immediate use for them, looked a real bargain. In 1955, General Telephone approached Olson Metals and suggested it tool up to make mounting bars for the former's direct dialing program since Olson was the only company in the country with any surplus drilling equipment suitable for the job. This association lasted until the severe recession in 1958, when General Telephone canceled their contract and John Olson found himself in serious financial difficulties. Once more, a fortuitous set of circumstances helped him out. As John Olson explained:

> *About this time, Jones Manufacturing Corporation of Franklin Park, Illinois, received an order from John Deere to manufacture all their hydraulic cylinders. They accepted the order, but without any clear idea of where they would get the piston rods ground and plated. I was selling Jones one of my drilling machines to get enough money to meet the payroll. It so happened that I was in their offices when they were talking about the problem. When the fellow I was meeting with left his room, I thumbed through a used machinery magazine and saw a picture of a centerless grinder; called the seller up; bought the machine for $1,700; and bid on the job.*

Gradually, John Olson embarked on a planned program of buying grinding machines on the used-machine market and from war surplus. He financed his purchases largely through selling time to other companies on his machines and partly through his expanding grinding and plating operations. The capital demands were considerable. While the equipment varied in price on the used market, the basic tooling for a single machine and plating cell could amount to $75,000. The tooling is consumable over one to several years. By 1977, in the Chicago plant alone, Olson Metals employed seven people manufacturing tooling full time. In addition, it was carrying between $250,000 and $300,000 worth of consumable supplies.

While the business was not characterized by a high level of technology, it did demand high standards and tolerances of work. John Olson believed in running his business on the basis of good engineering. The tool room was a vital part of his operations, for into it went ideas obtained from the factory floor and from it came new machines and attachments to do the work better and more efficiently. "My philosophy of survival in business," said John Olson, "is simple. You've got to have some kind of advantage over others. Better skill; better machines; better financing strengths." For Olson Metals, the philosophy worked and from 1960 onward, the demand for Olson's grinding and plating services increased as fast as the company was able to provide machinery and equipment to do the job. In fact, the company added several grinding machines and plating cells every year consistently from 1960 to 1977.

In 1966, it became apparent that Olson Metals had neither the plant nor the people in Chicago to do the job. The company expanded to a small town in central Indiana which put up $25,000 as a down payment on the new plant and helped Olson Metals borrow the rest through the local banks. John Olson recalled:

> I well remember the period. I owned all the machinery that I needed to put in the plant, and I had $100,000 in cash. But even with all the town's help, I had to borrow another $100,000 before we began to get the first dollar back. The second plant had a cash flow above direct cost of $20,000 to $30,000 per month. This proved that the operating principles established in Chicago could be transferred to other locations and the tooling facility, accounting, and selling expenses did not increase proportionally. So product contribution was substantial. The problems in expansion were capital, equipment, and manpower. The capital came from the cash-basis accounting;[1] the equipment originally by rebuilding used machines, and later, essentially, by building our own. And all the manpower was trained internally. By 1969 the Indiana plant had doubled its size.

Early in 1970, Frank Olson got out of the army. About the same time, Olson Metals lost an order to a competitor who was supplied by a steel mill in California. This was an order for a very unusual product. Until then, the only company that could make this product was located in Chicago. Curious about the nature of this source of supply, John Olson decided to pay a visit to the California supplier. He

[1] At the start of business in 1951, the advantages of cash-basis accounting were recognized by John Olson. For a service-type business, where inventories are not significant, this is an accepted basis of accounting for tax purposes. On the cash basis of accounting, accounts payable, including material on hand not paid for, and accounts receivable are ignored for tax purposes. Once started on a cash basis a company can continue until the IRS forces a change. In such an event, 10% of the receivables are taxed each year for the next 10 years as an addition to the profits or loss for the year. By managing the outstanding receivables at the end of the tax year and paying all the outstanding bills, profits were held at the lower tax brackets until the 1972-1973 fiscal year when, having an IRS audit, conversion to accrual accounting was forced. Receivables in 1972 were $590,000 (see Exhibit 1), which represented a tax savings of nearly $300,000.

visited them in April 1970; was impressed with the location and their production process; and came away two weeks later with an agreement for Olson Metals to buy substantial quantities of stock under favorable terms.

John had been accumulating money and machines for a third plant and in May, Frank Olson went down to California to find a site. He found it; ground was broken in July; and the first piece of bar was ground and plated in November 1970. From May 1971, the California plant, under Frank's management, made a profit and, within one year, a second bay had to be built which doubled the size of the plant. By 1977, production levels in California were between 3,000 to 4,000 feet of bar per day.

With the start of the California venture, Olson moved, in all its locations, toward selling the "total product" to its customers rather than just providing a grinding and plating service. This permitted Olson Metals, in John Olson's words, "to go along without price increases and to maintain profit margins by selling steel. Increasingly, we have been buying, grinding and plating, and selling as a package instead of processing other people's steel" (see Exhibit 1). By 1977, John estimated that Olson Metals held between 40 and 50 % of the piston rod market. Of course, this estimate did not take into account the substantial "captive" market of OEMs such as Caterpillar and International Harvester. Using ballpark figures, John judged the size of the "noncaptive" market at approximately $20 million.

## THE FINANCIAL ANALYSIS

Since returning from a management program for smaller company executives, Frank Olson had been concerned that Olson Metals had not been "managing its margins" in the face of inflation and he had expressed this concern to George Pacl, his accountant. Taking advantage of the computer output, which showed gross margin on a product-line basis (Exhibit 2), Frank calculated that while the margin on material sales had remained at 11% from 1976 to 1977, the margin on grinding the plating had decreased from 23.5% to 13.4% on a historical-cost basis. The result was that while profits had increased substantially, the increase had come about from increased sales without proportional increases in administrative expenses and nonoperating revenue-trucking operations and occasional machinery sales. Frank had come to recognize the basically conservative nature of Olson's accounting system— it had been on a cash basis until 1973—and its underlying philosophy that "an expenditure is an expense unless convincingly demonstrated to be otherwise." Thus, Frank thought it might first prove useful to draw up a set of financial statements on a modified historical cost basis which might better capture the "economic reality" of the business and asked George to help him prepare these statements. The company had consistently "expensed" the costs of refurbishing and improving old grinding machines and producing new plating tools. This practice had increased expenses in recent years when many of the old grinding machines had been refurbished as the business expanded and new plating fixtures purchased and expensed. Frank estimated that the company had written off some $1,060,500 over the 7 years from 1971 to 1977 that, from a public corporation's point of view, might possibly have been capitalized. In modeling the historical records, Frank also decided to depreciate the machinery over 15 years instead of the 10-year life used by the company. The results of these modifications are shown in Columns (2), and (5) of Exhibits 2 and 3. Appendix A details the assumptions used by Frank in calculating the adjusted figures. Appendixes B and C indicate how the asset figures were actually adjusted. Not surprisingly, the value of the assets and the profit before taxes both increased as a consequence of these adjustments.

## REPLACEMENT-COST ACCOUNTING

While this approach helped Frank understand the basic economics of the business a bit better, it still did not come to grips with the problem of inflation. Frank knew that since 1976, the Securities and Exchange Commission had required large corporations to show the effects of inflation on their assets and profits by calculating the "replacement cost" of inventories and fixed assets and disclosing the impact of these current-value calculations on the balance sheet and, through cost of goods sold and depreciation, on the operating statement. Frank thought that what was good enough for the big guys might be helpful for his father and him in their pricing decision, so he asked George to apply this approach to Olson Metals.

Inventories—To adjust inventories, George constructed an index of steel prices and applied them to the LIFO layers of inventory beginning in 1970, the year Olson Metals went on LIFO (see Appendix D). Since LIFO costs closely approximated replacement costs on the operating statement,[2] George made no adjustment to the cost of purchased materials sold.

Machinery and Equipment—For the machinery, George prepared a list of all items still in use, mostly used machines which had been extensively reengineered and refurbished. George asked John Olson to estimate the cost to Olson Machines of acquiring these machines in their present condition as of June 30, 1977.[3] The results of the calculations are shown in Appendix E. Since the values were estimated as those at 6/30/77, no accumulated depreciation was shown on the balance sheet, although 1/15 of the reported cost was taken as depreciation on the 1976 and 1977 operating statements.

Buildings—For the buildings in California and Indiana, George obtained John's and Frank's estimates of the cost of constructing the same facilities today. In Chicago, George took John's estimates of their present market value—more on the basis of expendiency than because of the unique nature of the facilities (see Appendix F).

George was puzzled when it came to calculation of the income tax on replacement cost. On the one hand, the company only owes $393,032 in 1977 and that is

---

[2] Inventory turned over more than four times a year.

[3] This approach was used in contrast to trying to assess the replacement cost of new equipment of essentially the same capacity due to the unique nature of the equipment and Frank's and John's feeling that this approach was more sensible.

what they would pay even if they kept their books on a replacement-cost basis. On the other hand, a new company coming into the industry would pay with "replacement costs" taxes 48% of profits. Thus, George chose the latter alternative.

## THE PRICING DECISION

Frank and John Olson met in early August 1977 to discuss the results of the replacement-cost analysis. They had confirmed the news that steel prices would go up 7% later in the month and that if Olson was to change its prices, this would be the psychologically appropriate time.

John Olson believed a 6% price rise by Olson Metals would be followed by their competition. Lincoln Steel, a $300 million steel company, was their major competitior—although in John's opinion, they did plating and grinding primarily to sell more steel. John also believed that they probably sold the service side of the project at or below costs since they didn't have the equipment edge that Olson had. The other competitor, Geiger Machinery, had dropped from a 40% to a 10% market share under Olson Metals pricing policies and was not, in John's eyes, a factor in the market any more. John was hesitant, however, to raise prices more than 6%. "We have a fascinating business here," he told Frank, "I don't know if we've priced our products properly or not, according to your new theories, but we're making profits, increasing our market share, and getting rid of some of our competition. And that I like. I also think that keeping prices low has expanded the market—people won't do it themselves if they can get it done cheaply enough."

"I know it, Dad," Frank replied, "but look at the numbers. Our after-tax return on assets was 6.2% in 1976 and 10.2% in 1977—if you believe our accounting figures. On a more economically realistic basis, they were 8.9% and 11.8%. Now if a competitor would come in with the same equipment and facilities that we have, he would have to invest $13 million and the after-tax rate of return on his assets would be 2.1%. Of course, he might get some kind of a deal with a merger situation and thus have his assets and depreciation at figures closer to ours—but I don't think this is too likely. I still think the figures show that we can raise our prices by at least 9%, get our margins under control and our return on investment up to where it should be, and still not be too fat a target for others to shoot at."

"Well, I don't know, Frank," said John. "It sounds logical, and your figures show what I always said, 'we need a dollar of investment to produce a dollar of sales.' But you've put in a lot of assumptions. I would sure hate to raise prices and lose our competitive edge. We have kept our prices down and still made profits and not only kept competition away but got one of our competitors out. So what if we have a little inflation, our business is fundamentally sound. If it wasn't, the auditors would not let us keep our books the way we are doing it. I'm inclined toward 6% and no more but I can be convinced otherwise."

**QUESTIONS**

1    What do you think of the approach taken by Frank and George? How would
     you change their analysis?
2    What would you do about prices? Why?

**EXHIBIT 1**
OLSON METALS
General Information Operation

| | Fiscal Year | Purchased Material | Sales | Material (% Sales) | Profit | Ending Inventory | Inventory (% Sales) | Estimated Receivables Not Included in Audit |
|---|---|---|---|---|---|---|---|---|
| (Est.)ᵃ | 1978 | $7,546,504 | $13,975,008 | 54 | $2,475,000 | $1,638,000 | 11.7 | — |
| | 1977 | 5,260,210 | 10,994,901 | 47 | 818,816 | 1,527,071 | 13.9 | — |
| | 1976 | 2,716,654 | 6,888,069 | 39 | 415,819 | 887,910 | 12.9 | — |
| | 1975 | 3,200,477 | 7,327,815 | 44 | 403,146 | 839,925 | 11.5 | — |
| IRS | 1974 | 1,820,115 | 5,154,233 | 35 | 166,126 | 325,384 | 6.3 | — |
| Audit | 1973 | 2,124,222 | 5,156,283 | 41 | 146,938 | 325,384 | 6.3 | $1,188,000 |
| IRS | 1972 | 1,241,783 | 3,484,326 | 36 | 98,686 | 318,623 | 9.1 | 594,000 |
| Audit | 1971 | 640,192 | 2,257,031 | 28 | 59,549 | 143,901 | 6.4 | 297,000 |
| IRS | 1970 | 399,280 | 1,767,832 | 23 | 73,458 | 44,430 | 2.5 | 169,000 |
| Audit | 1969 | 274,879 | 1,713,367 | 16 | 36,843 | 48,180 | 2.8 | 135,000 |
| | 1968 | 331,011 | 1,465,325 | 23 | 70,808 | 49,681 | 3.4 | 101,000 |
| | 1967 | 294,755 | 1,153,347 | 26 | 31,365 | 40,453 | 2.7 | 68,000 |
| | 1966 | 267,295 | 1,090,274 | 25 | 31,134 | 34,142 | 3.1 | 68,000 |
| | 1965 | 243,938 | 946,580 | 26 | 50,532 | 26,438 | 2.8 | |
| | 1964 | 294,219 | 797,251 | 37 | 36,300 | 26,182 | 3.3 | |
| | 1963 | 235,228 | 715,187 | 33 | 36,088 | 8,998 | 1.3 | |
| | 1962 | 94,221 | 420,139 | 22 | 32,256 | 2,576 | .6 | |
| | 1961 | 102,857 | 363,647 | 28 | 7,131 | 1,731 | .5 | |
| | 1960 | 63,623 | 287,856 | 22 | 4,740 | 1,211 | .5 | |
| | 1959 | 138,120 | 459,197 | 30 | 33,492 | 1,266 | .3 | |
| IRS | 1958 | 96,520 | 306,059 | 32 | (10,444) | 17,572 | 6.0 | |
| Audit | 1957 | 176,186 | 500,236 | 35 | (30,956) | 29,850 | 6.0 | |
| | 1956 | 174,276 | 686,374 | 25 | 4,802 | 41,418 | 6.0 | |
| | 1955 | 129,335 | 394,593 | 26 | 7,792 | 28,908 | 7.3 | |
| | 1954 | 67,750 | 225,335 | 30 | 18,398 | 8,524 | 4.0 | |
| | 1953 | — | 111,650 | — | 516 | — | — | |
| | 1952 | — | 151,601 | — | 1,222 | — | — | |

ᵃIncludes projected price increase of 7% on steel and 6% on services.

EXHIBIT 2
OLSON METALS
Profit and Loss Statements
(in dollars)

| | Year Ended 6/30/76 | | | Year Ended 6/30/77 | | |
| | (1) Historic Cost | (2) Modified Historic | (3) Replacement Cost | (4) Historic Year End | (5) Modified Historic | (6) Replacement Cost |
|---|---|---|---|---|---|---|
| Material Sales | $3,055,217 | $3,055,217 | $3,055,217 | $5,928,705 | $5,928,705 | $5,928,705 |
| Total Cost on Material | 2,716,652 | 2,716,652 | 2,716,652 | 5,260,211 | 5,260,211 | 5,260,211 |
| Margin on Material Sales | 338,565 | 338,565 | 338,565 | 668,494 | 668,494 | 668,494 |
| Grinding and Plating Sales | 3,832,850 | 3,832,850 | 3,832,850 | 5,066,196 | 5,066,196 | 5,066,196 |
| Inventory Reduction | — | — | — | 39,523 | 39,523 | 39,523 |
| Total Factory Labor | 1,187,032 | 1,187,032 | 1,187,032 | 1,546,626 | 1,546,626 | 1,546,626 |
| Total Employee Benefits | — | — | — | 500,413 | 500,413 | 500,413 |
| Total Operating Expenses | 1,746,243 | 1,637,840 | 2,039,140 | 2,065,680 | 1,967,386 | 2,358,786 |
| Total Selling Expenses | — | — | — | 243,020 | 234,020 | 234,020 |
| Margin on Grinding and Plating | 899,575 | 1,007,978 | 606,678 | 679,934 | 778,228 | 386,828 |
| Total Margin | 1,238,140 | 1,346,543 | 945,243 | 1,348,428 | 1,446,722 | 1,055,322 |
| Administrative Expenses | 946,307 | 946,307 | 946,307 | 749,525 | 749,525 | 749,525 |
| Nonoperating Profits | 123,985 | 123,985 | 123,985 | 219,911 | 219,911 | 219,911 |
| Profit before Taxes | 415,818 | 524,221 | 122,921 | 818,814 | 917,108 | 525,708 |
| Provision for Taxes | 199,593 | 251,626 | 59,002 | 393,032 | 440,212 | 252,340 |
| Net Income from Operations | $ 216,225 | $ 272,595 | $ 63,919 | $ 425,782 | $ 476,896 | $ 273,368 |

57

EXHIBIT 3
OLSON METALS
Balance Sheets
(in dollars)

| | June 30, 1976 | | | June 30, 1977 | | |
|---|---|---|---|---|---|---|
| | (1)<br>Historic<br>Cost | (2)<br>Modified<br>Historic | (3)<br>Replacement<br>Cost | (4)<br>Historic<br>Cost | (5)<br>Modified<br>Historic | (6)<br>Replacement<br>Cost |
| **Assets** | | | | | | |
| **Current Assets** | | | | | | |
| Cash | $ 88,472 | $ 88,472 | $ 88,472 | $ 183,634 | $ 183,634 | $ 183,634 |
| Accounts Receivable | 1,184,109 | 1,184,109 | 1,184,109 | 1,164,987 | 1,164,987 | 1,164,987 |
| Inventory | 887,910 | 887,910 | 1,125,400 | 1,527,071 | 1,527,071 | 1,764,500 |
| Total Current Assets | $2,160,491 | $2,160,491 | $ 2,397,981 | $2,875,692 | $2,875,692 | $ 3,113,121 |
| **Fixed Assets** | | | | | | |
| Land | $ 92,894 | $ 92,894 | $ 92,894 | $ 92,894 | $ 92,894 | $ 92,894 |
| Buildings | 457,241 | 457,241 | 4,195,000 | 391,041 | 391,041 | 4,286,000 |
| Machinery | 648,630 | 1,604,385 | 5,506,000 | 590,568 | 1,651,046 | 5,601,000 |
| Cars and Trucks | 55,092 | 55,092 | 55,092 | 78,008 | 78,008 | 78,008 |
| Total Fixed Assets | $1,253,857 | $2,209,612 | $ 9,848,986 | $1,152,511 | $2,212,989 | $10,057,902 |
| Other Assets | 80,714 | 80,714 | 80,714 | 138,893 | 138,893 | 138,893 |
| | $3,495,062 | $4,450,817 | $12,327,681 | $4,167,096 | $5,227,574 | $13,309,916 |

**EXHIBIT 3**
OLSON METALS
Balance Sheets
(in dollars) (continued)

| | June 30, 1976 | | | June 30, 1977 | | |
|---|---|---|---|---|---|---|
| | (1) Historic Cost | (2) Modified Historic | (3) Replacement Cost | (4) Historic Cost | (5) Modified Historic | (6) Replacement Cost |
| Liabilities | | | | | | |
| Current Liabilities | | | | | | |
| Accounts Payable | $ 445,500 | $ 445,500 | $ 445,500 | $ 167,642 | $ 167,642 | $ 167,642 |
| Accrued Payroll and Taxes | 4,907 | 4,907 | 4,907 | 36,916 | 36,916 | 36,916 |
| Corporate Income Taxes | 63,766 | 80,390 | 18,850 | 372,992 | 417,766 | 239,474 |
| Others | 27,582 | 27,582 | 27,582 | 31,315 | 31,315 | 31,315 |
| Total Current Liabilities | $ 541,755 | $ 558,379 | $ 496,839 | $ 608,865 | $ 653,639 | $ 475,347 |
| Long-Term Liabilities | 1,238,315 | 1,238,315 | 1,238,325 | 1,384,776 | 1,384,776 | 1,384,776 |
| Capital Stock | 56,048 | 56,048 | 56,048 | 56,048 | 56,046 | 56,046 |
| Retained Earnings | 1,658,944 | 1,939,712a | 1,939,712 | 2,117,407 | 2,554,556b | 2,554,556 |
| Capital Required for Asset Growth | – | 658,363 | 658,363 | – | 578,557 | 578,557 |
| Capital Required for Asset Replacement | – | – | 7,938,394 | – | – | 8,260,634 |
| | $3,495,062 | $4,450,817 | $12,327,681 | $4,167,096 | $5,227,574 | $13,309,916 |

aBeginning retained earnings; $1,442,719 + .52 of net asset increase of $955,755 ($496,993).
b$1,939,712 + $476,896.

OLSON METALS
Notes on Calculation of "Modified" Historic Figures

Assumption: Capitalize $1,060,500 equally over 7 years (1971-1977) @ $151,500/year.

Effect:    *1* From expenses for each of the years 1976 and 1977, take away $151,500.
           *2* Capital additions for each of the years 1976 and 1977 will be $151,500.
           *3* Depreciating over 15 years, depreciation (additional) for 1976 and 1977 will be $60,600 and $70,700, respectively.

*Note:*   Adjust assets for capital additions (1970-1975) not recorded in books.

|                  | *1971*    | *1972*    | *1973*    | *1974*    | *1975*    |
|------------------|-----------|-----------|-----------|-----------|-----------|
| Annual Increment | $151,500  | $151,500  | $151,500  | $151,500  | $151,500  |
| Less Depreciation| 10,100    | 20,200    | 30,300    | 40,400    | 50,500    |

Aggregate for 5 years:  Capital         $757,500
                             Depreciation    151,500
Net Addition (see Appendix C)  $606,000

---

**APPENDIX B**
OLSON METALS
Schedule of Assets (Machinery Only)
(in dollars)

| Purchase Year | | Book Value at 10-year Depreciation | | Book Value at 15-year Depreciation | |
|---------------|------------|-----------|-----------|-----------|-----------|
|               |            | *1976*    | *1977*    | *1976*    | *1977*    |
| 1960 | $ 7,965   | –         | –         | –         | –         |
| 1961 | 2,445     | –         | –         | –         | –         |
| 1962 | 45,086    | –         | –         | $ 3,005   | –         |
| 1963 | 70,871    | –         | –         | 9,450     | $ 4,725   |
| 1964 | 41,835    | –         | –         | 8,367     | 5,578     |
| 1965 | 12,150    | –         | –         | 3,240     | 2,430     |
| 1966 | 9,113     | –         | –         | 3,038     | 2,430     |
| 1967 | 12,957    | –         | –         | 5,181     | 4,317     |
| 1968 | 73,919    | $ 10,885  | –         | 34,495    | 29,568    |
| 1969 | 37,109    | 7,398     | $ 4,388   | 19,792    | 17,318    |
| 1970 | 54,749    | 14,548    | 9,072     | 32,850    | 29,199    |
| 1971 | 159,255   | 67,774    | 51,848    | 106,173   | 95,557    |
| 1972 | 106,789   | 53,155    | 42,475    | 78,312    | 71,192    |
| 1973 | 48,256    | 31,460    | 26,060    | 38,605    | 35,388    |
| 1974 | 398,678   | 278,906   | 236,412   | 345,520   | 318,942   |
| 1975 | 59,415    | 49,860    | 42,823    | 55,454    | 51,493    |
| 1976 | 164,002   | 134,644   | 131,778   | 164,003   | 153,068   |
| 1977 | 52,140    | –         | 45,711    | –         | 52,140    |
|      |           | $648,630  | $590,567  | $907,485  | $873,345  |

Add back to 1976 B/S value of machinery – $907,485 – $648,630 = $258,855 (Appendix C)
Add back to 1977 B/S value of machinery – $873,345 – $590,567 = $282,778 (Appendix C)

| Difference in 1977 Reserve on 10-Year Basis | $103,774 | |
|---|---|---|
| Difference in 1977 Reserve on 15-Year Basis | 86,280 | |
| Change in 1977 Depreciation Expense | $ 17,494 | (Appendix C) |

OLSON METALS
Adjustments to and Value of Machinery

| | |
|---|---:|
| Balance Sheet Figure on 6/30/76 | $ 648,630 |
| + Capital Additions from 1971 to 1975 | |
|    at $151,500 (5 Years) = $757,500 | |
|    Less Depreciation     151,500 | 606,000 |
| | $1,254,630 |
| + Capital Additions for 1976 | 151,500 |
| | $1,406,130 |
| − Less Additional Depreciation 1976 | (60,600) |
| | $1,345,530 |
| + Add-back Depreciation (for 15-Year Depreciation) | |
|    (See Appendix B) | 258,855 |
| | $1,604,385 |
| | |
| Balance Sheet Figure on 6/30/77 | $ 590,568 |
| + Capital Additions from 1971 to 1976 | |
|    at $151,500 (6 Years) = $909,000 | |
|    Less Depreciation     212,100 | $ 696,900 |
| | $1,287,468 |
| + Capital Additions for 1977 | 151,500 |
| | $1,438,968 |
| − Less Depreciation for 1977 | 70,700 |
| | $1,368,268 |
| + Add-back Depreciation (for 15-Year Depreciation) | 282,778 |
| | $1,651,046 |
| | |
| Operating Expenses (Historic), Year End 6/30/76 | $1,746,243 |
|    Less Capital Additions for 1976 | 151,500 |
| | $1,594,743 |
|    Plus Additional Depreciation for 1976 | |
|      (See Appendix A) | 60,600 |
| | $1,655,343 |
|    Less Reduction in Depreciation on "15-Year Basis" | |
|      (See Appendix B) | 17,494 |
| Operating Expenses (Modified Historic), Year End | |
|    6/30/76 | $1,637,849 |
| | |
| Operating Expenses (Historic), Year End 6/30/77 | $2,065,680 |
|    Less Capital Additions for 1977 | 151,500 |
| | $1,914,180 |
|    Plus Additional Depreciation for 1977 | |
|      (See Appendix A) | 70,700 |
| | $1,984,880 |
|    Less Reduction in Depreciation on "15-Year Basis" | |
|      (See Appendix B) | 17,494 |
| Operating Expenses (Modified Historic), Year End | |
|    6/30/77 | $1,967,386 |

## APPENDIX D
### OLSON METALS
Replacement Cost of Inventory
(LIFO to Replacement Value in Thousands of Dollars)

| Year | LIFO Layer | Index[a] | Replacement Cost |
|------|-----------|----------|------------------|
| 1970 | $   44.4  | 1.70 | $   75.5 |
| 1971 | 99.5      | 1.56 | 155.2 |
| 1972 | 174.7     | 1.42 | 248.1 |
| 1973 | 6.8       | 1.28 | 8.7 |
| 1974 | —         | 1.21 | — |
| 1975 | 514.6     | 1.14 | 586.6 |
| 1976 | 47.9      | 1.07 | 51.3 |
| 1977 | 639.1     | 1.00 | 639.1 |
|      | $1,527.0  |      | $1,764.5 |

[a]Index developed from Olson Metals purchasing records.

## APPENDIX E
### OLSON METALS
Schedules of Machinery (Replacement-Cost Values)
(Depreciated over 15 Years)

| Purchase Year of Machinery | Estimated Market Value (Used) as of 6/30/77 |
|---------------------------|---------------------------------------------|
| 1960 | $   261,000 |
| 1961 | 7,000 |
| 1962 | 182,000 |
| 1963 | 473,000 |
| 1964 | 321,000 |
| 1965 | 203,000 |
| 1966 | 203,000 |
| 1967 | 11,000 |
| 1968 | 293,000 |
| 1969 | 183,000 |
| 1970 | 309,000 |
| 1971 | 1,100,000 |
| 1972 | 419,000 |
| 1973 | 81,000 |
| 1974 | 1,009,000 |
| 1975 | 184,000 |
| 1976 | 267,000 |
| Subtotal | $5,506,000 |
| 1977 | 95,000 |
| Total | $5,601,000 |

|  | 1976 | 1977 |
|--|------|------|
| Replacement-Cost Value of Machinery at Year End | $5,506,000 | $5,601,000 |
| Annual Depreciation over 15 Years | 367,100 | 373,400 |
| Less Depreciation Accounted for in Historic Figures | 90,300 | 118,300 |
| Additional Depreciation Expense for Profit and Loss Statement | 276,800 | 255,100 |

**OLSON METALS**
Schedule of Buildings (Replacement-Cost Values)
(Depreciated over 25 Years)

| Site of Buildings | Approximate Construction Year of Buildings | Estimated Value as of 6/30/77 | Depreciation Reserve | |
|---|---|---|---|---|
| | | | 6/30/76 | 6/30/77 |
| Chicago | 1951 | $ 800,000 | a | a |
| Indiana | 1967 | 1,670,000 | $ 601,000 | $ 668,000 |
| California | 1970 | 3,450,000 | 828,000 | 966,000 |
| | | $5,920,000 | $1,429,000 | $1,634,000 |

| | 1976 | 1977 |
|---|---|---|
| Replacement Cost Value of Buildings | $5,624,000[b] | $5,920,000 |
| Annual Depreciation over 25 Years | 225,000 | 236,800 |
| Less Depreciation Accounted for in Historic Figures | 100,500 | 100,500 |
| Additional Depreciation Expense for Profit and Loss Statement | 124,500 | 136,300 |

[a]Zero since current market cost is being used.
[b]1976 value estimated at 95% of 1977 values.

# Lewis Redi-Mix (A)

Lewis Redi-Mix is a supplier of ready-mixed concrete located in metropolitan Cleveland, Ohio. At the end of 1958 the company was completing its twentieth consecutive year of operation.

Bob Lewis founded the company in the late thirties and served as its president and maintained controlling interest of the outstanding capital stock. In the early fifties, Lewis Redi-Mix became the largest supplier of ready-mixed concrete serving the metropolitan Cleveland area. Mr. Lewis took great pride in maintaining a large and modern fleet of delivery mixer-trucks. He employed a sizable staff of drivers, yard workers, and garage personnel, and always seemed to have the capability to meet the sudden, unscheduled needs of contractors. A radio-controlled dispatching operation made it possible for office personnel to keep close track of delivery operations at all times. Company advertising emphasized the quality and service features of Lewis Redi-Mix.

In 1957, Lewis Redi-Mix experienced a financial loss for the first time in its history. The loss for the year 1958 was even greater. The nationwide economic recession of 1957-1958 played havoc with the construction industry. Suppliers of building materials such as ready-mixed concrete no longer found themselves in a seller's market.

Bob Lewis was quite disturbed by developments within the ready-mixed concrete business. A number of smaller suppliers entered the Cleveland market area during the building boom of the early fifties. With the building boom on a downhill skid, there was significant excess capacity in the ready-mixed concrete industry. Many of the smaller firms were resorting to price-cutting tactics in order

All rights reserved. Reproduction in any form without express permission from Touche, Ross and Co. is prohibited. Reproduced by permission.

64

to survive. Lewis Redi-Mix was fortunate to have been in a healthy working-capital condition when the recession began. Lewis had hoped that the construction lag would be short-lived. The company continued to stress the quality and service image of Lewis Redi-Mix without resorting to price cuts. The even greater financial loss of 1958 and discouraging forecasts of little or no upturn in building activity for 1959 was forcing Mr. Lewis to reexamine the entire operation of his business.

Late in 1958, he had attended a conference on managerial accounting techniques for decision-making purposes. One of the points frequently made at the conference was the need to analyze and segregate expenses by their variable and fixed components. The conference had stressed a concept called "profit contribution." Mr. Lewis was particularly interested in the application of the profit-contribution concept to pricing and volume decisions. Upon his return to the company, Lewis discussed the conference proceedings with his chief accountant. They decided to seek the assistance of a management consultant well qualified in the area of profitability accounting to assist in converting the full costing system of Lewis Redi-Mix to a system incorporating the concepts of profit contribution.

Exhibit 1 shows the sales, profits, and market share of Lewis Redi-Mix for 1952-1958. The consultant was particularly concerned that the market share had been declining. To him, this indicated that Lewis was suffering losses not solely due to economic conditions affecting the construction industry.

A look at the company's advertising for 1957 and 1958 revealed the same messages used during the preceding years of prosperity:

"Lewis *Quality* Concrete"

"Top-quality ingredients"

"Delivered promptly"

"Personal service"

"Don't gamble with bargain mixes"

"Lewis provides the best concrete on earth"

Bob Lewis summed up his company's marketing approach and competition as follows: "In the years of the seller's market that ended in 1956 we had all the business that we could get cement for. We waited for business to come to us. Then the concrete industry became depressed from coast to coast. It is now characterized by tough competitive practices, excess capacity, low selling prices, and lack of profit. We thought it would be temporary and wanted to maintain our image of high quality and good service. While we waited, our volume fell sharply. Our competitors cut prices and ran over us, through us, and around us. We're in a dilemma and seeking a way out.

"We aren't waiting any longer for conditions to change. We'll take prices the way they are, meet them, and learn how to make a profit at lower price levels."

Mr. Lewis then proceeded to outline the jobs he wanted done by the consultant. Among them was an analysis of cost-reduction possibilities and methods of improving efficiency. But prior to the beginning of these tasks, Mr. Lewis wanted the accounting system revised on a profitability accounting basis. He felt it imperative to begin pricing on the basis of profit contribution as quickly as possible.

Exhibit 2 is the original budget for the year 1959 prepared by the chief accountant under the company's full-cost accounting system. Based upon business forecasts and contracts for future orders already signed, sales volume was projected at 377,000 cubic yards. Mr. Lewis explained that this volume projection had been made assuming that the company would again maintain a fixed price level during 1959. For the past several years, Lewis had been selling his concrete at $13.00 a cubic yard.

The consultant's first objective was to take the original budget shown in Exhibit 2 and separate the variable costs from the fixed costs. With the help of the company's chief accountant, variable-cost data as shown in Exhibit 3 was established.

The only components other than water entering into the concrete mix were cement and aggregate (often referred to as "buckshot"). Depending upon the contractor's requirements, the concrete could be mixed with one of three sizes of "buckshot" and appropriate quantities of cement. The cost variations for each possible mixture are summarized in Exhibit 3. Other variable costs are also shown. The consultant discovered that some costs varied not only by the cubic yard, but by the number of miles the delivery site was from the plant and the number of minutes a round-trip delivery cycle required.

For budgeting purposes, the consultant wished to use a standard cost figure to project anticipated variable costs. He decided that a four-sack, small-buckshot mixture requiring a 15-mile round-trip delivery of 90 minutes best represented the average cubic yard sold.

The consultant then prepared a revised budget for 1959 based upon the projected sales level of 377,000 cubic yards. The revised budget shown in Exhibit 4 separates the variable and fixed costs, and shows a profit contribution of $1,319,500 and a net loss of $40,500. The net loss projected under the new profitability accounting system was the same as that projected under the old full-costing system.

After the new accounting system was established, the consultant turned his attention toward application of the system for pricing and volume decisions.

"Understanding the relationship between the demand for ready mixed concrete and the price that can be most profitably charged for that concrete is of utmost importance in your business," the consultant explained to Mr. Lewis. "Establishing that relationship is not an easy or precise matter, however, and can only be an approximation of ever-changing demand-price relationships. As you are well aware, your business is quite seasonal. High sales volumes are typical of spring and summer months and low sales volumes typical of winter months. An analysis of previous year's records shows that your business actually has different demand characteristics each quarter. If the projected 1959 volume of 377,000 cubic yards is broken down quarter by quarter (Exhibit 5), these seasonal effects upon profit contribution can be seen.

"In addition, we have found that there is a correlation between advanced bookings and sales. The correlation of booked yards to yards delivered in future months as of January 1 is shown in Exhibit 6. Although we did not analyze data for all months of the year, it seems likely that such a correlation could be found for each month. This information would be of great value in establishing prices for future delivery, as it would give a good estimate of capacity utilization. This is another vital factor in pricing.

"To simplify your pricing procedures when bidding on various jobs, we suggest that you use a pricing form similar to Exhibit 7. After the variable cost per yard is determined, the price at which you think you can get the job is determined and the profit contribution calculated. The pricing decision is then made based on whether you want the job at that profit contribution."

## REQUIREMENTS

1   The consultant used a standard variable cost of $9.50 for the average cubic yard sold for budgeting purposes. Show how the $9.50 figure was derived, based upon variable cost data in Exhibit 3.

2   Lewis is to submit a bid to the ABC Construction Company for 10,000 cubic yards of large-buckshot, five-sack cement to be delivered in February 1959. The delivery point is 4 miles away from the plant and a complete round trip should require 40 minutes. What should be the total bid price if a $2.50 per yard profit contribution is considered appropriate at that time?

3   Describe a general pricing objective which applies to the company and any other company which bid prices. What are the practical problems involved in achieving this objective?

4   Suppose Mr. Lewis had told you that his primary objective was to maximize total revenue. Would you agree that this was an appropriate objective?

5   Suppose the company desired to set prices by a percentage mark-on to cost to yield a target profit. Do you think this would work?

6   How would you determine the variable cost rates in Exhibit 3 for the elements of "other variable costs"?

## EXHIBIT 1
### LEWIS REDI-MIX (A)
#### Historical Sales Data

| Year | Sales (cubic yards) | Sales | Profits | Market Share (%) |
|------|---------------------|-------|---------|------------------|
| 1952 | 424,000 | $5,520,000 | $130,000 | 26 |
| 1953 | 455,000 | 5,910,000 | 240,000 | 25 |
| 1954 | 440,000 | 5,730,000 | 190,000 | 25 |
| 1955 | 515,000 | 6,690,000 | 450,000 | 23 |
| 1956 | 467,000 | 6,070,000 | 270,000 | 20 |
| 1957 | 375,000 | 4,870,000 | (50,000) | 17 |
| 1958 | 348,000 | 4,530,000 | (140,000) | 15 |

## EXHIBIT 2
### LEWIS REDI-MIX (A)
#### Original Budget for the Year 1959
#### Full-Costing System

| | | |
|---|---:|---:|
| Sales (Cubic Yards) | | 377,000 |
| | | |
| Sales | | $4,901,000 |
| Less Cost of Goods Sold | | |
| Raw Materials | $2,488,200 | |
| Delivery Expense | 801,440 | |
| Truck Repair, Maintenance, and Garage Expense | 280,540 | |
| Yard Operation Expense | 242,320 | |
| Depreciation | 248,000 | |
| Heat, Light, and Power | 112,800 | |
| Rent | 120,000 | |
| Total Cost of Goods Sold | | 4,293,300 |
| Gross Margin | | $ 607,700 |
| Less Selling and Administrative Expenses | | |
| Salaries—Sales and Administrative Personnel | $ 149,800 | |
| Wages—Clerical Personnel | 86,400 | |
| Insurance | 43,200 | |
| Licenses | 55,200 | |
| Telephone | 15,400 | |
| Associations | 7,200 | |
| Legal and Professional Expenses | 16,800 | |
| Office Supplies and Postage | 4,800 | |
| Automobile Expense | 14,400 | |
| Guard Services | 4,800 | |
| Social Security Taxes | 32,400 | |
| Employees' Welfare Fund | 32,400 | |
| Employees' Pension Fund | 21,600 | |
| Life Insurance Premium | 600 | |
| Provision for Bad Debts | 7,200 | |
| Advertising | 30,000 | |
| Total Selling and Administrative Expense | | 522,200 |
| | | $ 85,500 |
| Less Other Expenses | | |
| Taxes | $ 78,000 | |
| Repairs and Improvements—Building and Property | 48,000 | |
| Total Other Expense | | 126,000 |
| Net Profit or (Loss) | | $ (40,500) |

EXHIBIT 3
## LEWIS REDI-MIX (A)
### Variable-Cost Data

#### Raw Materials Cost per Cubic Yard

| Type of Aggregate | Cement Sack Content | | | | |
|---|---|---|---|---|---|
| | *3* | *3½* | *4* | *4½* | *5* |
| Large Buckshot | $5.60 | $6.00 | $6.40 | $6.80 | $7.20 |
| Small Buckshot | 5.80 | 6.20 | 6.60 | 7.00 | 7.40 |
| Fine Buckshot | 6.00 | 6.40 | 6.80 | 7.20 | 7.60 |

The four-sack, small-buckshot mixture with a raw materials cost of $6.60 per cubic yard represents the most frequent or average order.

#### Other Variable Costs

| | |
|---|---|
| Truck Drivers' Wages and Compensation | $.01815 per minute per cubic yard |
| Garage Workers' Wages and Compensation | .0227 per mile per cubic yard |
| Yard Workers' Wages and Compensation | .36 per cubic yard |
| Dispatching Personnel Wages and Compensation | .20 per cubic yard |
| Gas, Oil, and Grease | .00326 per minute per cubic yard |
| Tires | .0053 per mile per cubic yard |

The average delivery round trip is 15 miles and takes 90 minutes.

EXHIBIT 4
LEWIS REDI-MIX (A)
Revised Budget for the Year 1959
Profitability Accounting System

| | | |
|---|---|---|
| Sales (Cubic Yards) | | 377,000 |
| | | |
| Sales | | $4,901,000 |
| Less Variable Costs | | |
| Raw Materials | $2,488,200 | |
| Truck Drivers' Wages and Compensation | 614,510 | |
| Garage Workers' Wages and Compensation | 128,180 | |
| Yard Workers' Wages and Compensation | 135,720 | |
| Dispatching Personnel Wages and Compensation | 75,400 | |
| Gas, Oil, and Grease | 109,330 | |
| Tires | 30,160 | |
| Total Variable Cost | | 3,581,500 |
| Profit Contribution | | $1,319,500 |
| Less Standby Costs | | |
| Salaries—Sales, Administrative, and Supervisory Personnel | $ 214,000 | |
| Wages—Clerical and Yard Personnel | 172,800 | |
| Depreciation | 248,000 | |
| Taxes | 78,000 | |
| Insurance | 43,200 | |
| Heat, Light, and Power | 112,800 | |
| Licenses | 55,200 | |
| Rent | 120,000 | |
| Telephone | 15,400 | |
| Associations | 7,200 | |
| Legal and Professional Expenses | 16,800 | |
| Office Supplies and Postage | 4,800 | |
| Automobile Expense | 14,400 | |
| Guard Services | 4,800 | |
| Social Security Taxes | 10,800 | |
| Employees' Welfare Fund | 10,800 | |
| Employees' Pension Fund | 7,200 | |
| Life Insurance Premium | 600 | |
| Provision for Bad Debts | 7,200 | |
| Total Standby Expenses | $1,144,000 | |
| Less Programmed Costs | | |
| Repairs and Improvements—Building and Property | $ 48,000 | |
| Repairs and Modernization—Equipment | 72,000 | |
| Tire-Rotation Replacement Program | 30,000 | |
| Yard and Garage Supplies | 36,000 | |
| Advertising | 30,000 | |
| Total Programmed Expenses | $ 216,000 | |
| Total Standby and Programmed Costs | | 1,360,000 |
| Net Profit or (Loss) | | $ (40,500) |

## EXHIBIT 5
### LEWIS REDI-MIX (A)
Quarterly Budget for the Year 1959
Profitability Accounting System

|  | 1st Quarter (Jan-Mar.) | 2nd Quarter (Apr.-June) | 3rd Quarter (July-Sept.) | 4th Quarter (Oct.-Dec.) | Total |
|---|---|---|---|---|---|
| Sales (Cubic Yards) | 45,000 | 120,000 | 140,000 | 72,000 | 377,000 |
| Sales | $ 585,000 | $1,560,000 | $1,820,000 | $936,000 | $4,901,000 |
| Less Variable Costs | 427,500 | 1,140,000 | 1,330,000 | 684,000 | 3,581,500 |
| Profit Contribution | $ 157,500 | $ 420,000 | $ 490,000 | $252,000 | $1,319,500 |
| Less Standby and Programmed Costs | 340,000 | 340,000 | 340,000 | 340,000 | 1,360,000 |
| Net Profit or (Loss) | $(182,500) | $ 80,000 | $ 150,000 | $ (88,000) | $ (40,500) |

## EXHIBIT 6
### LEWIS REDI-MIX (A)
Historical Relationship of Booked Yards to
Yards Actually Delivered in Future Months
(As of January 1)

|  | Yards Booked on Jan. 1 as a Percent of Yards Actually Delivered in the Month |
|---|---|
| January | 90 |
| February | 85 |
| March | 75 |
| April | 60 |
| May | 50 |
| June | 40 |
| July | 20 |
| August | 10 |
| September | — |
| October | — |
| November | — |
| December | — |

EXHIBIT 7

**LEWIS REDI-MIX (A)**
Job Pricing Form

Variable Costs Per Cubic Yard

| | |
|---|---|
| Raw materials: (_____ Aggregate _____ Cement Sack) | $ _____ |
| Drivers wages, etc.: _____ minutes @ $.01815 | _____ |
| Garage workers' wages, etc.: _____ miles @ $.0227 | _____ |
| Yard workers' wages, etc.: | _____ .36 |
| Dispatching personnel wages, etc.: | _____ .20 |
| Gas, oil, and grease: _____ minutes @ $.00326 | _____ |
| Tires: _____ miles @ $.0053 | _____ |
| Total variable cost per cubic yard | $ _____ |
| Add probable profit contribution per cubic yard | _____ |
| Bid price per cubic yard | $ _____ |

Total yards _____ × bid price $_____ =

Total Bid Price    $ _____

# Prendergarth Shipping Company

Mr. William Thomas, President of Prendergarth Shipping Company, was considering what actions he should take regarding the reassignment of one of the company's vessels in May 1964. In view of the market for ships at that time, it had become evident that the possibility of selling the vessel was not a feasible one; the ship had to be assigned to where it would best serve the company's interests.

## HISTORY OF THE VESSEL

The vessel in question, the *Prendergarth Warrior,* had been purchased in October 1963. It was the only vessel purchased during the year ended December 31, 1963. In contrast with the remaining 27 vessels of the Prendergarth fleet, which were all of about 12,500 tons burden, the *Warrior* was a small ship of only 4,500 tons (the burden of a freighter is the weight of freight of a standard bulk it can carry). It had been acquired to allow the Prendergarth company to compete for the tapioca trade in the port of Balik Papan in South Borneo. The *Warrior* was making the voyage from Singapore to Balik Papan and back at a rate of 50 round trips a year at the present time. The freight rates on this commodity were satisfactory, but the harbor channel was such that only small vessels like the *Warrior* could get into Balik Papan

Copyright © 1965 by the President and Fellows of Harvard College; revised 1966. Reproduced by permission. This case was prepared by A. M. McCosh under the supervision of D. F. Hawkins and J. Yeager. Case material of the Harvard Graduate School of Business Administration is prepared as a basis for class discussion. Cases are not designed to present illustrations of either effective or ineffective handling of administrative problems. Distributed by the Intercollegiate Case Clearing House, Soliders Field, Boston, Mass., 02163. All rights reserved to the contributors. Printed in the U.S.A.

to take advantage of these revenues. The cost per dollar of revenue of operating a small vessel, fully laden, was higher than would be the case for a larger ship, were the latter able to navigate the channel.

Operating costs for the two sizes of vessel owned by Prendergarth are given in Exhibit 1. The behavior of these and other costs is discussed in Exhibit 2.

## RECENT DEVELOPMENTS

In April 1964, the port authority of Balik Papan had obtained a grant to deepen the harbor channel. The plan, which had just arrived at the Prendergarth head office, showed that ships of up to 15,000 tons would be able to use the port after the deepening operation had been completed, which was expected to be in September or October of 1964. It would therefore be possible for the larger vessels of the line to be used to serve Balik Papan. The greater carrying capacity of the larger ships should, it was thought, more than compensate for the higher total operating costs of such a vessel, since the quantities of tapioca available were substantial and the demand great. The estimated costs that would be incurred by having the larger vessel deviate from the normal route to take in Balik Papan are described in Exhibit 3. The larger vessels would have to call at Balik Papan as frequently as the *Warrior* would have called there in order to fulfill shippers' requirements. If the big ships called at Balik Papan, they would have to call twice at Singapore, once before Balik Papan and once after. This was because (1) the tapioca had to be transshipped at Singapore, (2) the large vessels were usually too full of cargo on the eastward run to get the tapioca in as well before calling at Singapore, and (3) the cargo to be moved from Singapore to Balik Papan had to be loaded.

The possibility of using both the *Warrior and* the larger vessels on this route had been considered but had been rejected because "it would slow down the big ships too much."

## ALTERNATIVE USE OF THE WARRIOR

The only feasible alternative use of the *Warrior* that Mr. Thomas was considering was on the route from Dar-es-Salaam (in East Africa) to Zanzibar. Some financial aspects of this alternative are discussed in Exhibit 4. At present, the large vessels of the line called at both of these ports, incurring port charges as detailed in Exhibit 5. The Prendergarth ships used lighters in place of docking in all the ports listed in Exhibit 5 because it was less expensive and often quicker for the amounts of cargo involved. The cargo, which consisted of dates and ground nuts from Dar-es-Salaam, and coconuts, copra, and special timbers from Zanzibar, was usually carried to the United States; the freight rates from Zanzibar and from Dar-es-Salaam to the U.S. were virtually identical.

If the *Warrior* were to be used on this alternative route, it would shuttle the cargo from one of the two ports to the other, so that the large vessel need make only one call in the area on a given run, thereby saving time and portage dues.

The portage dues incurred by the *Warrior* at the two ports would have to be considered, of course. The freight normally collected at the two ports amounted to about 3,850 tons per pair of calls.

## THE PROBLEM

Mr. Thomas was anxious to arrive at a decision between the two possible assignments of the *Warrior* within the next few days rather than wait until the problem became critical in the fall. The reason for the haste was that an opportunity had arisen to move the *Warrior* from Singapore to Zanzibar with a cargo which would not only pay for the cost of moving the ship but would also pay for the lighterage expenses that would be needed at Balik Papan until the new harbor channel was ready. As this was a very unusual cargo, it was not thought likely that a similar opportunity would arise before the fall.

Mr. Thomas was anxious to keep all the ships as active as possible, because the company had a very good reputation among shippers and had therefore been able to fill its ships all the time. This made it one of very few fully booked shipping lines in the business.

The most recent income statement of the company is shown in Exhibit 6. The year ended December 31, 1963, was considered a typical year in the company's history. Maps of the areas under review are presented in Exhibit 7.

### ASSIGNMENT

The issue in this case is pretty exotic—should the motor vessel *Warrior* be used on the tapioca run between Singapore and Balik Papan in East Asia or as a freight tender between Zanzibar and Dar-es-Salaam in East Africa? This decision hinges on a cost analysis as to which option is more profitable. One issue we will discuss in class is cost analysis when some costs vary per ton, some per day, some per mile, some per stop, and some do not vary at all. Other issues we will discuss include the importance of defining the alternatives precisely, the concept of profit contribution per unit of capacity, and the role of cost analysis in helping management to ask the right questions.

In order to help you work through this very difficult but also very important case, the following specific questions should be answered in order. These questions help you work up, piece by piece, to an overall analysis of the decision:

1   a   How much contribution can be earned by carrying 1 ton of tapioca from
        Balik Papan to Singapore, dock to dock, independent of the operating
        costs of the vessel? How much can be earned by carrying 1 ton of general
        merchandise from Singapore to Balik Papan?
    b   Given the contribution/ton figures arrived at in part a, what is the total
        contribution which can be earned on one round trip of the *Warrior*
        between Singapore and Balik Papan and return? By one of the large
        vessels?

2    Independent of the amount and type of cargo carried, what are the incremental costs of sending the *Warrior* on a round trip between Singapore and Balik Papan and return? One of the large vessels? What, then, is the total contribution *per round trip* for each of the vessel types? What is the total contribution *per year* for each of the vessel types?

3    If the *Warrior* is transferred to the East Africa route, which is the preferred port of call for the large vessels: Zanzibar or Dar-es-Salaam? What costs can be saved by having the large vessels avoid one of the two ports, and how much will these savings amount to in a year? (Answer follows.)

4    What would be the additional costs per year (portage, bunkerage, and tonnage) of using the *Warrior* on the East African shuttle run? (Answer follows.)

5    What action should Mr. Thomas take, and what would be the impact of that action on Prendergarth's profits? (*Hint:* What is Prendergarth's average profit contribution per shipping day for 1963?)

As noted above, suggested answers are provided for Questions 3 and 4 in order to cut down the amount of time for you to analyze this case. You should study the answers provided for these two questions to make sure you agree with them so that you can incorporate them in your overall analysis.

Question 3

Inspection of Exhibit 5 shows that Zanzibar has far cheaper portage dues than Dar-es-Salaam, is at least as cheap in all other cost categories, and has no lighthouse charge. Therefore, at first glance it appears that the Dar-es-Salaam port call should be eliminated for the large vessels. We must be careful, however, because cargo at the eliminated port will have to be doubled-handled, and so if Dar-es-Salaam generates more cargo, *total* cost might be lower if Zanzibar is eliminated. But Exhibit 4 shows that Zanzibar generates more cargo (2,500 tons per call vs. 1,350 tons). Therefore, without detailed calculation, we can conclude that the large vessels should call at Zanzibar.

*Cost savings by having large vessels avoid Dar-es-Salaam:*

| | |
|---|---|
| Portage | $7,750[a] |
| Lighthouse | 62 |
| | 7,812 |
| Bunkerage | 91[b] |
| Total/Trip | $7,903 saved[c] |
| Times (80 Trips) | $632,240 per year |
| or | 624,960 per year (see Note b) |

[a]12,500 tons × $.31/day/ton × 2 days = $7,750.

[b]$1.27/mile × 72 miles = $91. *Note:* It is debatable whether this is really saved since ships may travel past Dar-es-Salaam anyway.)

[c]No stevedoring, lighterage or cranage will be saved as the cargo will still have to be loaded onto a ship at Dar-es-Salaam eventually.

Question 4

*Portage and Bunkering costs*

|                                            | Dar-es-Salaam | Zanzibar |
|--------------------------------------------|:-------------:|:--------:|
| Portage                                    | 1,395[a]      | 1,170[b] |
| Lighthouse                                 | 62            | —        |
|                                            | 1,457 +       | 1,170 = 2627 |

Sea Bunkering (.73/mile × 144 mile) =                 105 (round trip)
                                                       $\overline{\text{2,732/trip}}$

Times 69 Trips[c]                                      $188,508/year

*Tonnage costs (additional):*[d]

Total Tons/Year = (1,350/trip × 80 trips) = 108K tons
Unloading Costs @ Zanzibar (.14 + .32 + .13) = .59
Loading Costs @ Zanzibar (.14 + .32 + .13)   = $\underline{.59}$
                                            1.18 × 108K tons = $127,440/year
*Additional costs:*                                         $315,948/year

[a]4,500 tons × .31/day/ton × 1 day = $1,395.
[b]4,500 tons × .13/day/ton × 2 days = $1,170.
[c]345 days (from Exhibit 1)/5 days per trip (2 in Zanzibar + 2 at sea + 1 in Dar-es-Salaam).
[d]Same tonnage must be loaded at Dar-es-Salaam per year as B.W. (Before *Warrior*), so the only additional charges are for unloading this Dar-es-Salaam cargo from the *Warrior* in Zanzibar and for reloading it in Zanzibar onto a large vessel.

EXHIBIT 1
**PRENDERGARTH SHIPPING COMPANY**
Annual Operating Costs of Vessels

|  | Costs Typical for Size of Vessel | |
| --- | --- | --- |
| *Item* | *4,500 Tons* | *12,500 Tons* |
| Payroll | $143,594 | $210,877 |
| Depreciation | 222,956 | 363,228 |
| Repairs | 40,000 | 47,500 |
| Overhead Costs | 8,225 | 16,900 |
| Stores and Provisions | 32,657 | 39,283 |
| Insurance | 36,030 | 46,750 |
| Miscellaneous | 4,750 | 5,625 |
| Total Annual Cost | $488,212 | $730,163 |
| On the average, there were 345 operating days in a year, so the cost per operating day was | $    1,415 | $    2,116 |
| In addition, bunkering costs (fuel costs) were incurred amounting to | $0.73 per mile | $1.27 per mile |

---

**EXHIBIT 2**
PRENDERGARTH SHIPPING COMPANY
Discussion of Cost Behavior

| *Cost Item* | *Behavior of Cost* |
| --- | --- |
| Payroll | Payroll expense is, in the short run, a fixed item. The complement of the ship is virtually fixed over a year, and in the course of one voyage it is completely fixed. No change in union rates is expected in the near future. |
| Depreciation | Depreciation is charged on a straight-line basis on the original cost of the vessel. |
| Repairs | This amount varies randomly. The figures shown are the average annual amounts expended in the industry on ships of the sizes indicated. |
| Overhead | This includes all expense items incurred on board the vessel, and is fixed. |
| Stores and Provisions | This varies with the payroll, and is therefore virtually a fixed. |
| Insurance | There is a fixed charge of $30,000 per ship annually, plus an annual charge of $1.34 per ton of burden. |
| Miscellaneous | Fixed. |
| Bunkerage | Fuel costs will depend on the routes being traveled, as the price of fuel varies to some extent from place to place. For calculation purposes, however, the figures shown may be taken as suitable averages. |

Since the normal terminal point of the voyages of the larger vessels was Singapore on the eastward run, and since Balik Papan was farther east than Singapore, it would have been necessary for the large vessels to make a round trip in order to call at Balik Papan. The feasibility of additional calls at Brunei, Djakarta, and other ports had not been investigated, but it was thought that these were not likely to be profitable.

The distance from Singapore to Balik Papan by the best navigable route was 480 sea miles, or 960 sea miles round trip. At the normal sailing speed of the larger vessels in these waters—16 knots—they required about 60 hours steaming time round trip, or approximately 2½ steaming days. This compares with the slightly less than 3½ days that the *Warrior* required.

The capacity of the larger vessels was such that 6,850 tons of tapioca could be carried on each voyage from Balik Papan to Singapore, as against the 3,950 tons that the *Warrior* could take. It was thought that the bookings of manufactured goods that were currently being taken from Singapore to Balik Papan by the *Warrior* would be the same for the larger vessels; there were no indications that any additional bookings could be obtained. The *Warrior* had been carrying 3,150 tons of manufactured goods on a typical voyage from Singapore to Balik Papan, at an average rate of $2.70 per ton. The difference in tonnage between the tapioca and manufactured goods was caused by the relative bulk of the two types of cargo.

The current freight rates for tapioca, amounting to $5.10 per ton for the trip from Balik Papan to Singapore, seemed likely to remain in force for a considerable time. Most of the tapioca was sent out on contracts, and there appeared to be a constant or increasing demand for the commodity. While the rate might go up in the future, it was reasonable to assume that it would not go down.

The turn-round time (the period between the ship's arrival at a port and departure from it) at Balik Papan was relatively slow. Because of the inadequacy of the cranage facilities, it would take 3 days to turn one of the large vessels as against 2½ days to turn the *Warrior*. This difference was caused by the greater amount of cargo to be moved in the larger vessels.

Because of the extensive facilities at Singapore, all ships of the size being considered could be turned around in 1 day at that port, regardless of the amounts being loaded or discharged.

The cargoes that were shipped from these ports were made up of the five commodities listed below. The rates shown were those for shipping 1 ton of the commodity from either port to the United States, and the tonnage listed was the average amount of each commodity that had been carried per voyage in all voyages in the last 6 months. The remaining capacity of the larger vessels was used by freight from other ports. The large vessels collectively called at each of the two ports 80 times a year.

| Commodity | Port | Rate per Ton | Average Tonnage |
|---|---|---|---|
| Dates | Dar-es-Salaam | $88 | 500 |
| Ground Nuts | Dar-es-Salaam | 84 | 850 |
| Coconuts | Zanzibar | 74 | 400 |
| Copra | Zanzibar | 66 | 1,600 |
| Special Timbers | Zanzibar | 65 | 500 |

The turn-around time in Zanzibar had averaged 2 days for the larger vessels, and the use of the *Warrior* would not shorten this. The turn-around at Dar-es-Salaam had been 2 days with the larger vessels; the *Warrior* could be turned in 1 day.

The sailing time between the two ports was very short, and this distance (72 miles) was such that only 1 day (2 days round trip) was involved no matter which vessel is being used. The higher speed of the larger vessels had no noticeable effect over such a short trip. It was thought that an overall savings of 3 days per voyage would be attained by the large vessels (one port call and a day of steaming in transit) if the *Warrior* were used on the Zanzibar/Dar-es-Salaam run.

If the *Warrior* were to be used as a "shuttle," it would be necessary for scheduling purposes to have the larger ships call at the same port each time. It would be impractical to try to arrange for the large ships to call at whichever port the *Warrior* had most recently served, because of complications in the booking of freight at other ports which would be called on subsequently.

The larger ships passed through the area with sufficient frequency to permit the *Warrior* to shuttle as frequently as it could.

## EXHIBIT 5
### PRENDERGARTH SHIPPING COMPANY
#### Cost of Calling at Ports

| Cost Item | Varies with: | Units | Balik Papan | Singapore | Zanzibar | Der-es Salaam |
|---|---|---|---|---|---|---|
| Portage dues | Tonnage | $/day in port/ ton burden | 0.14 | 0.20 | 0.13 | 0.13 |
| Lighterage[a] | Freight moved | $/ton of freight moved | 0.25 | 0.16 | 0.14 | 0.15 |
| Stevedoring | Freight moved | $/ton of freight moved | 0.56 | 0.32 | 0.32 | 0.32 |
| Lighthouse | Fixed | $/visit | 73.0 | 126.0 | — | 62.0 |
| Cranage | Freight moved | $/ton of freight moved | —[b] | 0.14 | 0.13 | 0.13 |
| Special assessment | | | —[c] | | | |

[a]Lighterage expense is the cost of having small barges called lighters come alongside the vessel to facilitate loading and unloading of cargo. The Balik Papan lighterage charge is for ships anchoring in the harbor channel; having lighters come out to the channel mouth would involve an additional charge of $.25 per ton. Portage due are required on entering a port and independent of the above charges.

[b]There is no cranage charge at Balik Papan because the freight is manhandled. This considerably increases the charge for stevedoring relative to other ports.

[c]All ships exceeding 8,000 tons burden were to be assessed $2,000 for each port call (in addition to portage dues). This assessment was intended to contribute to the investment in and maintenance of the new deep channel that these ships required.

## EXHIBIT 6
### PRENDERGARTH SHIPPING COMPANY
#### Income Statement
#### for the Year to December 31, 1963

| | |
|---|---|
| Voyage Revenues for the Year | $49,661,000 |
| Voyage Expenses | 33,480,000 |
| Gross Margin | $16,181,000 |
| Shore Support Expenses | 6,318,000 |
| Administrative and Other Expenses | 3,916,000 |
| Net Income before Taxes | $ 5,947,000 |
| Income Tax Expense | 3,088,000 |
| Net Income | $ 2,859,000 |

**EXHIBIT 7**
Maps of Areas Relevant to the Assignment of the *Prendergarth Warrior*

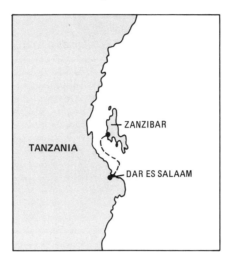

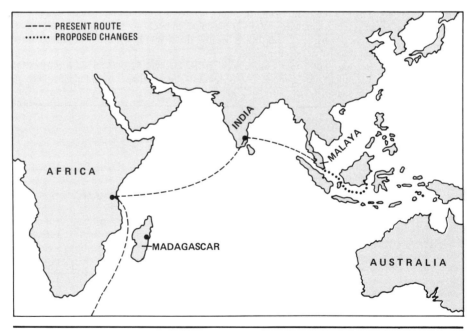

- - - - PRESENT ROUTE
· · · · · · PROPOSED CHANGES

# Majestic Motel

The Majestic Motel is open only during the skiing season. It opens on November 1 and closes the last day of February. Each of the 50 rooms in the east wing rent for $15 for single occupancy or $20 for double occupancy. The west wing of the motel has 30 rooms, all of which have a breathtaking view of the skiing slopes, the mountains, and the village. Rooms in this wing rent for $20 and $25 for single or double occupancy, respectively. The average occupancy ratio during the season is about 80%, and this ratio remains constant from month to month. The ratio of single versus double occupancy is 2:8, and it is also constant.

Last year's operating results and the operating results of the last month of that season are shown in Exhibit 1. Although February is the shortest month of the year (28 days in the year analyzed), it accounted for 75% of the yearly income ($8,738 vs. $11,643), a fact which disturbed the owners of the motel considerably. Mr. Kacheck, the manager of the motel, describes February as a typical high-season month, and points to the off-season months, which show losses each month and reduce the high profits reported during the season. He suggests to the owners, who acquired this motel only at the end of the preceding season, that to reduce the off-season losses, they should agree to keep the west wing of the motel operating year-round. The average occupancy rate for the off-season is estimated to be 20% at the least and not more than 40% at the most, for the next few years. Kacheck estimates that careful attention to the off-season clientele, and advertising in large cities close by, might gradually result in a 40% occupancy rate during the off-season. The owners, however, would have to commit at least $4,000 for advertising in each of the next 5 years ($500 for each of 8 months). There is no evidence to indicate that

This case was prepared by Professor Felix Kollaritsch of The Ohio State University.

the 2:8 ratio of singles vs. doubles would be different during the remainder of the year or in the future. Rates, however, would have to be drastically reduced. Present plans are to reduce them to $10 and $13 for singles and doubles.

The manager's salary is paid over 12 months. He acts as a caretaker of the facilities during the off-season and also contracts most of the repair and maintenance work during that time. Using the west wing would not interfere with this work, but would cause an estimated additional $2,000 per year for repair and maintenance.

Mrs. Kacheck is paid $20 a day for supervising the cleaning function and partially manning the desk. During the season, she works every day, with no day off. The clerk (desk clerk) and each maid is paid on a daily basis at the rate of $24 and $15 respectively. The payroll taxes and other fringe benefits are around 20% of the payroll. The depreciation and the property taxes would not be affected by the decision to keep the west wing open. The insurance, however, would increase by $500 for the year. During the off-season, it is estimated that Mr. and Mrs. Kacheck could man the desk. Mrs. Kacheck would, however, be paid for only 5 days a week.

The cleaning materials and supplies and half of the miscellaneous expenses are considered a direct function of the number of rooms occupied. The other half of the miscellaneous expenses are fixed. The linen expenses (linen is rented from a supply house) also depend on the number of rooms occupied, but are twice as much, on the average, for a double occupancy than for a single occupancy. The utilities include two items: telephone and electricity. There would be no electricity expense with the motel closed. With the motel operating, electricity expenses are a function of the number of rooms available to the public. Rooms must either be heated or air-conditioned. The telephone bills[1] for each of the four seasonal months were as follows:

| 80 Telephones @ $3.00 | $240 |
|---|---|
| Basic Service charge | 50 |
| | $290 |

During the off-season, only the basic service charge is paid. The monthly charge of $3 is applicable only to live phones.

The most disturbing part of Mr. Kacheck's proposal, in the mind of the owners, is his request that a covered and heated swimming pool be added to the motel's facilities. Mr. Kacheck believes that this would increase the probability that the off-season occupancy rate would be the higher of the two estimates given (above 30%). Precise estimates are impossible. It is felt that although the winter occupancy rate will not be noticeably affected by the acquiring of an indoor pool in the short run, in the future, Mr. Kacheck believes that such a pool will have to

---

[1] Long-distance calls by customers have been excluded, as well as the collection of amounts due for them. They have also been excluded from the amounts in the financial statements.

be built to stay even with the competition. The cost of such a pool is estimated to be $40,000. This amount could be depreciated over 5 years and would not have any salvage value after that time. $15,000 of the $40,000 is for a plastic bubble and the heating units, which would be used approximately 4 months during the winter and 4 months during the rest of the year. The only other costs associated with the swimming pool are $400 per month for a lifeguard, required by law during the rush hours; additional insurance and taxes, estimated to be $1,200 and $400 per year, respectively; and a yearly maintenance cost of $2,400. Except for the lifeguard, none of these expenses would vary substantially whether the pool were heated and covered, or unheated and uncovered. If it is covered and heated, a guard would be needed for 12 months. If it is not covered, a guard would be needed only for 5 off-season months.

## REQUIRED

Using the information provided in the case, you are asked to evaluate the various courses of action open to the owners and report the results to them, substantiaing anticipated results with quantiative information. Also advise them as to the most economical action. Further, you are to consider the form and content of the monthly reports for the motel and suggest any improvements you deem necessary to advance the usefulness of these reports.

**EXHIBIT 1**
**MAJESTIC MOTEL**
Operating Statement

|  | For the Year 19X3 | | For February 19X3 | |
| --- | --- | --- | --- | --- |
| Revenues |  | $160,800 |  | $37,520 |
| Expenses |  |  |  |  |
| Salaries |  |  |  |  |
| Manager | $15,000 |  | $ 1,250 |  |
| Manager's Wife | 2,400 |  | 560 |  |
| Clerk | 2,880 |  | 672 |  |
| Maids (four) | 7,200 |  | 1,680 |  |
|  | $27,480 |  | $ 4,162 |  |
| Payroll Taxes and Fringe Benefits | 5,496 |  | 832 |  |
| Depreciation | 30,000 |  | 2,500 |  |
| Property Taxes | 4,000 |  | 1,000 |  |
| Insurance | 3,000 |  | 750 |  |
| Repairs and Maintenance | 17,204 |  | 2,780 |  |
| Cleaning Materials and Supplies | 1,920 |  | 448 |  |
| Utilities | 6,360 |  | 1,410 |  |
| Linen | 13,920 |  | 3,248 |  |
| Interest Extension (Mortgages) | 21,716 |  | 1,810 |  |
| Miscellaneous Expenses | 7,314 |  | 1,774 |  |
| Total Expenses |  | 138,410 |  | 20,714 |
| Profit before Federal Income Taxes |  | $ 22,390 |  | $16,806 |
| Federal Income Taxes (48%) |  | 10,747 |  | 8,068 |
| Net Profit |  | $ 11,643 |  | $ 8,738 |

# R.C. Blake Co.

Brent Mullen, a mechanical engineer in the process development department of the R. C. Blake Company's Spartanburg, South Carolina, factory, was concerned about how to react to some criticism that had recently developed of a promising project in the company's solvent spread Department that he had been working on for the past several months.

The R. C. Blake Company produced adhesive tapes for the industrial and consumer markets and also manufactured a line of special adhesive products that were sold, through distributors, to hospitals. One product, a vinyl-backed finger bandage, accounted for about half of the sales of all hospital products and, while intense competition in the finger-bandage market kept profits on this item low, finger bandages were considered to be an integral part of the total hospital products line, which was noted for its overall profitability.

## THE SOLVENT SPREAD DEPARTMENT

The solvent spread department consisted of two 80-foot-long machines, the "east" and the "west" solvent spread lines. These machines applied adhesive mixed with a volatile solvent to 40-inch-wide tape backing material. The coated backing material was then passed through an oven, which made up most of the length of the solvent spread line. Elevated temperature in the oven evaporated the solvent, leaving behind the adhesive firmly bound to the backing. The resulting tape was wound on

This case was prepared as a basis for class discussion and is not designed to illustrate either effective or ineffective handling of an administrative situation. Copyright © 1977 by Professor William L. Berry, Babcock Graduate School of Management, Wake Forest University, and by Richard D. Irwin, Inc.

"jumbo" rolls, which were later rewound, slit to commercial lengths and widths, and packaged or, in the case of most hospital adhesive products, further processed: Flesh-colored vinyl material was converted into finger bandages by a special machine that applied a gauze pad, cut individual bandages between the pad, covered the adhesive area with a silicone-treated nonstick paper, and encased each bandage in a wrapper.

The east solvent spread line could have theoretically supplied more than sufficient capacity for all of the R. C. Blake's adhesive products but, due to subtle differences in product characteristics, two different solvent spread lines were needed. For example, because the flesh-colored vinyl material used to manufacture finger bandages tended to soften when exposed to the heat of the oven, finger-bandage material had to be produced on the west line, which had a supporting belt to transport the vinyl material through the oven. Also, because the vinyl would deform when subjected to pressure, an unconventional procedure was used to apply the adhesive/solvent mixture to the vinyl. The only other product manufactured on the west line was a plastic electrician's tape, which, despite its relatively low volume, was consistently profitable.

The east line handled a wide variety of cloth or paper tapes whose backings were not as flexible or sensitive to heat as vinyl. These product characteristics meant that the east line could run hotter (and thus faster) and allowed the use of a more precise method of applying the adhesive/solvent mixture to the backing than was used on the west line. Another characteristic of the east line was that there was no transport belt through the oven. Since products run on that line were able to support themselves, they simply passed over rollers spaced at about 3-foot intervals.

It took three men to operate a solvent spread line. In 1976, the department was operating about one and a half shifts. That is, a daytime crew of six men operated both lines and an evening crew of three men operated one or the other of the lines according to instructions left by the foreman. In 1976, the evening crew had operated the west line about 850 hours and the east line about 1,100 hours.

## R&D EFFORTS

Brent Mullen had been assigned the task of lowering finger-bandage costs through development of improved manufacturing methods in the summer of 1976. Since the cost of solvent spread processing amounted to about 50% of finger-bandage costs for other than materials, he felt that this was a logical place for his cost-reduction program to start. Mullen concentrated on ways to manufacture finger-bandage material on the east line and soon hit upon the idea of applying adhesive to paper coated with a silicone release agent, drying the adhesive by passing the paper through the oven, and laminating the vinyl to the paper at the end of the line. The release paper could then be removed and reused and the adhesive would remain on the vinyl. He designed and had fabricated a special fixture to perform this operation. Experimentation with this new process was successful. It was found that there were several significant benefits to the new method:

1    The paper coated with adhesive could be run three times as fast on the east
     line as vinyl could be run on the west.
2    The vinyl retained more flexibility since it hadn't been exposed to heat. This
     could be viewed as either a desirable marketing feature or as a potential to
     begin purchasing a lower-grade vinyl.
3    The amount of adhesive applied could be reduced by 12% because of better
     control of adhesive application on the east line.
4    The east solvent spread line had a lower overhead rate.

In a report to management that summarized his experiments, Mullen estimated that the annual savings from this new method of running finger-bandage
material amounted to over $80,000 (see Exhibit 1). Initial reaction to this report
was quite positive. The production and hospital products marketing departments
were convinced that Mullen's project represented some significant savings and could
also provide some product improvements.

Mr. Anthony Duncan, head of the cost accounting department, was less
enthusiastic about Mullen's innovation. In a memorandum to Mullen, he expressed
his feeling that Mullen's estimates of savings were overstated:

> . . . your reported cost reduction is largely illusory. While the reduction in
> overhead would indeed lower the standard cost of finger-bandage material,
> there would be no reduction in the amount of actual charges to the over-
> head accounts. Therefore, your savings figure has to be reduced from
> $80,851 to $43,526 because that's the net impact of the change on the
> factory as a whole.

Duncan went on to detail some undesirable potential side effects of Mullen's project:

> In a few weeks we will be calculating overhead rates for the coming year
> based on the marketing department's projections of volume. If Mullen's
> proposal is adopted, there will be a significant impact on the standard cost
> of black electricians' tape, which, as I understand it, would continue to be
> produced on the west line. Using 1976 volume on this product (170,000
> linear yards at 10 feet per minute), we get about 850 hours of production
> on the west line. At that usage, the hourly overhead rate goes up to over
> $90.00 per hour. This is more than enough to completely wipe out the
> $35,000 or so in profit made on that product. Inevitably, management
> would decide to stop producing electricians' tape and the company would
> lose that profit. Not only would that completely wipe out Mullen's
> savings, but it would completely idle the west solvent spread line. If that
> happened, most of the overhead from the west line would have to be
> picked up by the east line, causing reduced profitability for all products
> there. If that happened, the overhead rate on the east line would go up to
> about $40 per hour (based on the 3,800 total hours per year that the east

*line would have been run had we produced finger-bandage material as*
*Mullen proposes last year). For these reasons, I strongly recommend that*
*product machine assignments remain as they have been in the past.*

A few days after Mr. Duncan's memo was circulated, a meeting was held.
Attending were the plant manager, Alfred Cathcart; William Whyte, the manager
of hospital products marketing; Anthony Duncan, the head of the cost accounting department; and Brent Mullen. Mr. Cathcart opened the meeting with a review
of the problem and added that the purpose of the meeting was to determine
whether Mullen's project should be continued or scrapped.

CATHCART

Tony, I don't suppose there is any way that we could adopt Mullen's proposal and continue to assign the output to the west line so that its overhead
would still be absorbed by the finger-bandage material?

DUNCAN

Well, Fred, I gave that idea quite a bit of thought and, as I see it, there are a
couple of relevant arguments against it. First, we would be violating a couple
of pretty explicit corporate rules about overhead allocation that have been
around a long time. Second, if we start to monkey with the way overhead is
allocated in the solvent spread department, then other departments will soon
want to be doing the same sort of thing. We simply can't allow that to happen
if we want to maintain the overall integrity of our cost accounting program.

WHYTE

What you've been saying makes a lot of sense, but it seems a shame to just
discard the results of Brent's good efforts because of an arbitrary sort of
accounting convention. There must be another way to get those benefits.
After all, the product is dramatically improved and about half of Mullen's
savings are really there. Look, suppose everything goes as your scenario
suggests. Couldn't we simply get rid of the west line and use that space for
something else? And couldn't we run electricians' tape on the east line using
the new release-paper method?

MULLEN

Actually, Bill, you couldn't do either of those things. Unlike finger bandages,
electricians' tape is sold in rolls. Thus, it is wound upon itself and, unless the
adhesive is actually cured on the plastic by running it through the oven, it
would delaminate or pull off when you used the tape. In other words, half of
the time the adhesive would be on the "back" side of the tape when you
unrolled it. Your other point, about finding another use for the space now
occupied by the west line, is a good one except that the area around the
spread lines is an explosive environment because of all the vaporizing solvent.
We can't even run a fork lift back there without risking a bad fire. Everything

in that area has to be especially designed to be spark-proof. Furthermore, putting up a fireproof partition would run over $100,000 and I don't even see why we'd do that—there is plenty of unoccupied space in this factory now.

There is, however, one alternative that I thought of only yesterday that might be worth exploring. Since we're on the subject, I may as well see how it strikes the group. Since Tony's memo came out, I've been thinking about ways that we could achieve the benefits of higher temperature and speed by using release paper on the west line. A few years ago I experimented using a similar concept on the west line. As I recall, there were only a few minor technical problems that should be pretty easy to overcome. Since the bulk of what you call the real savings come from more accurate application of adhesive, however, I'd have to make one major modification to the adhesive spreader on the west line. All in all, I think that $40,000 in capital expenditure would let us run finger-bandage vinyl the new way and electricians' tape the old way, both on the west line. What do you think?

**DUNCAN**

That sounds like we can have our cake and eat it, too! Great idea!

**WHYTE**

Terrific, Brent. How soon can you get this into operation?

**MULLEN**

Within 2 or 3 months after a proposal is approved. There's some design work and, of course, several weeks fabrication and installation time.

**CATHCART**

Well, Brent, our capital budget is stretched a bit thin this year, but for a project with less than a 1-year payback I'm sure we can get an extension from the corporate office pretty quickly. Tell you what. Get your proposal to me in the next week or so. Bill, you and Tony give Brent all the support he needs. Let's get this one off the ground!

**EXHIBIT 1**

Summary of Savings (Costs) from Applying Adhesive
to Finger-Bandage Vinyl on East Solvent Spread Line[a]

|  | East Line (Proposed) | West Line (Present) | Savings |
|---|---|---|---|
| Speed (ft/min) | 30 | 10 | — |
| Temperature (°F) | 270 | 155 | — |
| Adhesive Applied (lb/sq yd) | .563 | .630 | — |
| Annual Adhesive Cost (at $1.07/lb) | $267,737 | $299,600 | $31,863 |
| Machine Hours/Year | 667 | 2,000 | 1,333 |
| Labor ($12.75/hr/crew) | $ 8,504 | $ 25,500 | $16,996 |
| Fixed Overhead Rate ($/hr) | $ 25 | $ 27 | — |
| Total Overhead | $ 16,675 | $ 54,000 | $37,325 |
| Release Paper @ .04/Linear Yard | | | |
|    −133,333 linear yards | | | |
|    (Reuse Twice) | ($ 5,333) | | ($ 5,333) |
| Net Savings | | | $80,851 |

[a]Assumption of 400,000 linear yards per year of 40-inch wide finger bandage vinyl (1976 yardage + 3.7%).

# Verdancy, Inc.

Verdancy, Inc., a small manufacturer, has just been unionized, and management faces their first labor negotiations. Up to this point, the hourly wage rate is approximately $3.85 (average) and the fringe-benefit package is about 30%, based on paid wages. Since negotiations began, the accounting department has supplied management with an enormous amount of information. Management seems to be unable to grasp the significance of these data. They have had difficulties with accounting information in the past and have been lax in the exercise of controls. Profit margins have continuously decreased and have now reached a dangerously low point. The negotiations could not have come at a worse time.

The union negotiator is satisified with the fringe-benefit package presently offered. He would, however, like the company to switch from an hourly pay system to a unit of production pay system, and is demanding a pay of $10.00 per unit. He claims that this increase wouldn't cost the company a penny. He substantiates this claim with the following information:

1   There is presently no incentive for an employee to produce efficiently. The piece rate will encourage higher efficiency and increased production.
2   The present day rate of $3.85 per hour is much too low. The work is hard, dirty, and hot. Many employees don't even stay on the job 3 weeks. During the first 6 months of the current year, the payroll department shows that 750 different production employees were paid. The normal production staff is 250 men.

Copyright © by Professor Felix P. Kollaritsch, The Ohio State University.

*3*  The $10.00 per unit requested represents only a 15% increase over the pre-
     sent actual cost per unit. This was demonstrated as follows:

|                              |             |
|------------------------------|-------------|
| 6 Months Total Labor Hours   | 243,750     |
| 6 Months Total Units Produced| ÷ 108,000   |
|                              | 2.25 hours  |
|                              |             |
| Suggested Pay per Unit       | $10.00      |
| Labor Hours per Unit         | 2.25        |
|                              | $ 4.44      |
|                              |             |
| Pay Increase ($4.44/$3.85)   | 15%         |

*4*  The incentive system and the increase in pay will virtually stop any turnover
     and thus save the company money in reducing the training expenses and in
     outfitting new employees. Eliminating the training expenses will save the
     company an estimated 10% of its payroll. It is claimed that the incentive
     system will reduce the current 2.25 labor hours per unit to 2.00 hours, a sav-
     ings of 12.5%. He points out that this amount is even below the current
     standard of the company of 2.1 hours per unit. The cut in "outfitting,"
     which is legally required, would save about 6% of the total payroll and is
     computed as follows:

|                                      |                  |
|--------------------------------------|------------------|
| Outfitting per Person                | $105             |
| Annualized Turnover (500 each ½ year)| X 1,000 workers  |
| Total Cost                           | $105,000         |
|                                      |                  |
| Yearly Pay (250 Employees X          |                  |
| 1,950 hours X $3.85)                 | $1,878,875       |
|                                      |                  |
| Savings ($105,000/$1,876,875)        | 6%               |

The management of Verdancy, Inc., sees the demands from an entirely different point of view.

*1*  The increase demanded represents a 25% increase in labor cost, determined as
     follows:

|                                      |                  |
|--------------------------------------|------------------|
| Standard Cost (Standard Hours 2.1    |                  |
|     X Standard Rate $3.85)           | $ 8.085 per unit |
| Union demand                         | 10.00            |
| Pay Increase ($10.00/$8.00)          | 25%              |

*2*  The savings estimated by the union are speculations without evidence. As a
     matter of fact, the evidence is to the contrary. Past history indicates that
     incentives have not worked.

*3*   The claimed turnover-rate decrease is wishful thinking. Admittedly, this company has a high turnover rate; however, the industry as a whole has a turnover rate of 25%. Therefore, the savings quoted by the unions due to outfitting are incorrect.

*4*   The company is already experiencing a profit squeeze. Any additional expenses would put it, as well as the union employees, out of business.

*5*   The company cannot afford the union demands financially, either. Although there is enough demand for the product, the company doesn't have sufficient working capital to expand production. Higher wages would mean reduced production because of the lack of working capital. The yearly production demand runs about 250,000 to 300,000 units, spread fairly evenly over the months of the year. Products can be stocked (stored) if necessary. The present backlog of orders is 150,000 units. Production varies between 200,000 to 220,000 units per year. Deliveries are running behind.

Your own investigation reveals that the company does need approximately 250 employees in production with the present efficiency. The production process is subject to a learning curve of 80%.[1] The first unit is expected to take 8 yours, and it takes about 64 units of production per man to reach maximum efficiency. During the first 6 months, 243,750 production hours were clocked and 108,000 product units produced. Although at the standard, 116,000 units should have been produced (243,750/2.1 hours), management attributes the difference to the turnover.

## REQUIRED

You have been hired by management to evaluate the union claims and to instruct management on a course of action. Write a memorandum substantiating all claims and suggestions in your evaluation by the above quantitative information.

---

[1] This means that a fully experienced worker can produce a unit in 20% of the time it takes a new worker.

# Midwest Steel (B)

In June 1978, Mr. Watts Humphrey, president of Midwest Steel, a division of National Steel, was reviewing requests for capital funds from his operating departments. As he thumbed through the stack of proposals, he shook his head and commented:

*This stack of paper represents capital proposals that total over $20 million. Getting these approved at the corporate level is absolutely crucial to our ability to continue in the long run to be an effective competitor in the world steel market. But I'll tell you one thing—I don't believe that these proposals stand much of a chance of getting that approval. The people in Pittsburgh aren't looking at the plant or at sales figures or at how hard we work out here. They're looking at our results compared to the resources we use to make the results. Their concern is that we manage about $300 million in assets but we earn only a few million dollars each year. What they're looking at is Midwest Steel's return on assets (ROA) and, frankly, from their perspective, I don't think I'd put any more money into this operation until we've shown some solid improvement in that measure. We're just not that sound an investment.*

This case was prepared by Mr. Farhat Ali and Professor John K. Shank as the basis for class discussion rather than to illustrate either effective or ineffective handling of an administrative situation. All numbers in the case have been disguised to protect confidential data. However, relationships among the numbers which are relevant to the issues in the case have not been distorted. All names have also been changed except for that of Mr. Humphrey, president of the firm.

National Steel Corporation, one of the largest steel producers in the United States, was vertically integrated with holdings that included mines, shipping facilities, basic steel production, finishing mills, and distribution facilities. Midwest Steel was a finishing mill built in 1960 to balance National's excess steelmaking capacity with additional finishing-mill capacity. Essentially, Midwest converted sales of National's hot-rolled bands (large coils of steel commonly called "hot bands") into sales of more finished products at higher margins. In 1976, Midwest's sales amounted to 16.8% of National Steel's sales, but Midwest's net income was only 4.5% of National's net income. Exhibit 1 details some summary statistics for major American steel companies in the years 1975 and 1976.

Midwest was located at the southern tip of Lake Michigan in Indiana. Shipments, profit margins, and contribution margins by product lines were as follows in 1977:

|  | Tons | Gross Profit Margin per Ton | Average Contribution Margin per Ton |
|---|---|---|---|
| Cold-Roll | 419,000 | $15.00 | $35.00 |
| Galvanized | 350,000 | 65.00 | 90.00 |
| Tin Mill | 470,000 | 20.00 | 45.00 |
| Total | 1,239,000 | | |

## WEEKLY MANAGEMENT MEETING

On July 1, 1978, the regular weekly meeting of Midwest Steel department heads was held. Attending besides Mr. Humphrey were: Tom Lee, Michigan's controller; Bill Mowery, manager of financial planning; Dan Sullivan, production superintendent; David Shortridge, head of plant engineering; Geof Bittner, quality control supervisor; and Hugh Crumay, sales and distribution manager.

Mr. Humphrey called the meeting to order and, after a few preliminary comments, announced that the subject of that week's meeting would be the division's return-on-assets (ROA) performance. He distributed copies of Midwest's summary financial statements (Exhibits 2 and 3) to each participant and said: "In this meeting I'd like to investigate ways to improve our return on assets. In my mind, such improvement is the key to getting the necessary capital to reinvest in our plant."

Each of the department heads began to silently scrutinize the financial statements except for Tom Lee. With a firm set to his jaw, he began to speak.

### TOM LEE:   Controller

Watts, it is clear that one way to improve our return on assets is simply to decrease our inventory level. Since inventories constitute about 30% of our total assets, any decrease in inventory will improve return on assets. I've felt for a long time that with better planning we should be able to reduce our inventory without affecting production. In the past few years, our inventory level has fluctuated widely and the fluctuations bear no relationship to production. Look at these graphs. (Mr. Lee began to circulate a piece of paper; see Exhibit 4.) Fluctuations of inventory levels, production, and sales seem to bear no relationship to each other. I think that this shows a general lack of proper inventory control.

HUGH CRUMAY:    Sales

I hate to disagree with you, Tom, but I think our real problem is sales volume. If we increase sales, profits will increase since the fixed costs of production will be distributed over the larger volume. On the other hand, I fail to see how profitability can be increased by reducing inventories. Funds tied up in inventories are simply a sunk cost, and everyone knows that it is foolish to worry about sunk costs. Any measure like ROA, which is the ratio of income to capitalized sunk costs, is a questionable measure of profitability in my view. My personal feeling is that we should only be concerned with the amount shown on the bottom line—profits.

BILL MOWERY:    Financial Planning

Hugh, inventory is not a sunk cost. We can reduce inventory, and if we do, we generate funds. That money can then be used for our capital investments to improve our operating efficiency. That, in turn, will improve our ROA, perhaps to the point that National will view further investments as worthwhile. We have several capital projects with returns of 20% or more on an after-tax basis. So you see, the opportunity cost of funds invested in inventory is pretty high.

HUGH CRUMAY:    Sales

Okay, Bill, but exactly what do you mean by "opportunity cost"?

BILL MOWERY:    Financial Planning

Opportunity cost is simply another name for the profit which could be generated if the money were invested in some other way than in inventory. Also, the corporation's estimate of the cost of capital is 12%. This means that their investors demand a 12% return on their investment and, therefore, it theoretically costs the corporation 12% a year to use the funds investors put at its disposal.

DON SULLIVAN:    Production

Bill, the real world is quite different from the theoretical costs you are talking about. If the cost of money to the corporation is 12%, and we make only a 4% return on it, we should not be in the steel business! But, in fact, we are in the steel business and we're going to stay in it. I agree with Hugh that the way to increase profitability is with volume, but our problem is that even now, when we are operating at close to capacity, we can't make a decent profit. The best way to increase profitability is producing efficiently. There are two ways of achieving this. First, sales should not take small orders or special orders. Small orders decrease productivity because they increase setup time, and special orders decrease productivity since they involve non-standard material flows. Second, we should increase our inventory from the present low level, which hurts operating efficiency. For example, the optimal inventory level ahead of the 52-inch tandem mill is 6,000 tons, but we have only had about 2,000 tons there recently. Dave, tell them about that study you did for me.

### DAVID SHORTRIDGE:    Plant Engineering

We looked at the record of production efficiency on the tandem mills and correlated that to the level of inventory held in front of the mill. We found that efficiency suffered both when there was too little inventory ahead of the mills and when there was too much. It seems that with too little inventory ahead of the mill, the foreman sometimes had to wait for delivery of the appropriate pickled hot band. With too much, he had to spend a lot of time searching around for the right material to run next. After defining the maximum achievable production efficiency as 100%, we were able to establish a definite relationship between inventory levels and efficiency (see Exhibit 5). As you can see, the best inventory level is the lowest level required for 100% efficiency. Also, my industrial engineers have estimated that improving efficiency by 1% on the tandem mill saves us $100,000 a year in the cost of operating that mill. In other words, a 1% increase in efficiency would reduce the number of hours the mill runs by 1%. In 1977, the mill ran for 6,250 hours. If the production efficiency had been 1% higher, it would have saved 62.5 hours of operation. Since it costs $1,650 per hour[1] to operate the mill, this translates into over $100,000 ($1,650 x 62.5 hours).

### GEOFFREY BITTNER:    Quality Control

The savings might even be greater than that. It seems to me that if you run fewer hours, you'll produce less scrap. There may be other effects as well.

### BILL MOWERY:    Financial Planning

Dave, you may save $100,000 a year in operating cost by increasing inventory, but you can't forget the costs associated with carrying a higher inventory. For example, a higher level of inventory requires more labor, more warehousing space, and more material-handling equipment, all of which affect profitability. I still believe that lowering inventory improves ROA by increasing net income as well as reducing the asset base. Besides, our inventories as a corporation are already 27% higher than the industry average for the amount of sales we generate (see Exhibit 1).

### HUGH CRUMAY:    Sales

I disagree, Bill. I think that lowering inventory might actually reduce net income. A lower inventory would increase delivery lead time. I guarantee that

[1]This is the full cost per hour. Variable cost per hour is about $1,000.

longer lead time will adversely affect sales. Since only sales generates revenues, lower sales will eventually translate into lower net income. And what will that do to your ROA?

**DAN SULLIVAN:**   Production

Now, Hugh, that's not necessarily so. Since we produce mostly to confirmed orders, a lower inventory might actually shorten lead times. Lowering work-in-process inventory would reduce backlogs at the producing units. A smaller backlog at a unit shortens the time an order has to wait before it is processed by the unit.

**DAVID SHORTRIDGE:**   Plant Engineer

Aren't you contradicting your own position, Dan? My analysis has shown that we should have a larger inventory because it increases production efficiency. Bill has been mentioning expenses related to carrying inventory. I'd like to see some figures on the expenses he has been talking about. And how much of that is real money, anyway? As far as I'm concerned, this cost-of-capital stuff is hogwash. Real money is cash. As long as all of our inventory is eventually sold, who cares how much steel we have around, anyway? I'd bet the effect on our cash flows is trivial.

**WATTS HUMPHREY:**   President

I think we've raised several interesting issues. Bill, why don't you collect some background information on inventory carrying costs? Accounting should be able to provide you with the data for some of the costs you have mentioned. We'll continue this discussion at next Monday's meeting. By that time, Bill should have some hard numbers on the costs associated with inventory. It will also give us some time to think over some of the issues raised today.

Mr. Mowery spent a considerable amount of time during the next week with Jim Blake, general supervisor of the accounting department. They were able to piece together information on Midwest Steel's cost of capital and inventory carrying costs (Exhibit 6). Mr. Mowery's assistant in the planning department was assigned the task of investigating inventory levels at the end of 1977 and classifying them according to type and function. His report is summarized in Exhibit 7.

As he prepared to analyze these data, Mr. Mowery was bothered by a few unanswered questions. First, he wondered what figure should be used for the cost of capital to estimate inventory carrying costs. The 20% marginal cost of capital made sense since this was what Midwest Steel could have earned by investing the funds in certain capital projects. On the other hand, 12% was clearly the corporation's official estimate of the cost of capital. A figure of 8% (the corporate average return on equity over the past 5 years) or 4% (the average return on assets for the last 5 years) seemed like plausible choices, too. Also, he was not sure how to deal with warehousing costs. Should he include only variable warehousing costs, or should he also consider the fixed costs? Finally, he was uncertain of the relevance of his assistant's classification of inventory functions. That seemed to confuse the issues more than it clarified them. Should he ignore that work? If not, how could it be used?

The more he thought about these questions, the more he felt himself thinking in circles. "To hell with it," he said to himself. "I've got to do something, so I may as well get started. Perhaps the process of working through the numbers will help clarify my thinking."

## CASE QUESTIONS

1   What was Midwest Steel's net income percent return on sales (net income/net sales), percent return on net investment, and percent return on assets for 1977? Which of these is a good measure for evaluating profitability of a firm? Why? Can you think of a better measure?

2   Should Midwest increase inventory ahead of the 52-inch tandem mill from 2,000 tons to 6,000 tons as suggested by the production superintendent?

3   How high must the percent return on sales be to cover inventory carrying costs?

4   How do you believe the balance sheet and the income statement for 1977 would change assuming that the overall inventory level was reduced by 25%? What effect would the inventory reduction have had on the profitability measures given in question 1?

5   Why is National's performance on "sales dollars per inventory dollar" the lowest of the five companies shown? How would ROA change if sales per inventory dollar were equal to the average of the other four steel companies? How much cash could thereby be freed for alternative investment uses?

6   How would you evaluate the marketing trade-off resulting from higher inventory levels—longer average lead times for all orders versus shorter lead times for those specific orders for which material is in stock?

7   At what stage of production should "marketing" inventory be held? What are the trade-offs?

**EXHIBIT 1**

Statistics of Major American Steel Corporations (1975-1976)

(Millions of Dollars)

| | Sales | Net Income | Inventory Raw Material and Supplies | Inventory Finished and Semi-finished | Equity | Long-Term Debt | Return on Equity (%) | ROA[a] (%) | Sales per Dollar of Inventory |
|---|---|---|---|---|---|---|---|---|---|
| *1975* | | | | | | | | | |
| U.S. Steel | $8,167 | $560 | $551 | $609 | $4,850 | $1,543 | 11.5 | 6.9 | $7.0 |
| Bethlehem | 4,977 | 242 | 283 | 337 | 2,612 | 857 | 9.7 | 5.3 | 5.8 |
| National | 2,241 | 58 | 253 | 192 | 1,209 | 534 | 4.9 | 2.4 | 5.0 |
| Republic | 2,333 | 72 | 171 | 160 | 1,279 | 362 | 5.9 | 3.5 | 7.0 |
| Inland | 2,107 | 83 | 220 | 99 | 969 | 507 | 8.6 | 4.4 | 6.6 |
| *1976* | | | | | | | | | |
| U.S. Steel | $8,604 | $410 | $665 | $722 | $5,129 | $1,960 | 8.0 | 4.5 | $6.2 |
| Bethlehem | 5,248 | 168 | 399 | 435 | 2,693 | 1,025 | 6.4 | 3.4 | 6.3 |
| National | 2,841 | 86 | 356 | 259 | 1,263 | 744 | 7.1 | 3.1 | 4.6 |
| Republic | 2,546 | 66 | 268 | 203 | 1,318 | 372 | 5.2 | 2.8 | 5.6 |
| Inland | 2,388 | 104 | 217 | 119 | 1,102 | 480 | 10.0 | 5.0 | 7.1 |

aROA = net income/total assets.

## EXHIBIT 2
### Balance Sheets
### MIDWEST STEEL
December 31, 1973-December 31, 1977[a]
(Thousands of Dollars)

| | 1973 | 1974 | 1975 | 1976 | 1977 |
|---|---|---|---|---|---|
| | | | *Assets* | | |
| Cash | $ 5,254 | $ 1,956 | $ 1,020 | $ 5,486 | $ 1,824 |
| Accounts Receivable | 34,192 | 33,100 | 31,862 | 39,952 | 44,515 |
| Inventories[b] | 30,637 | 17,995 | 58,088 | 92,527 | 61,221 |
| Current Assets | 70,084 | 53,051 | 90,970 | 137,965 | 107,560 |
| Property and Equipment | 212,994 | 212,418 | 212,079 | 217,594 | 217,812 |
| Less Depreciation | 104,534 | 112,607 | 121,238 | 129,974 | 138,933 |
| Net Property and Equipment | 108,460 | 99,811 | 91,841 | 87,620 | 78,879 |
| Other Assets | 880 | 2,082 | 318 | 904 | 1,262 |
| | $179,424 | $154,944 | $183,129 | $226,489 | $187,701 |
| | | | *Liabilities and Investment* | | |
| Accounts Payable | $ 8,590 | $ 10,821 | $ 11,955 | $ 8,688 | $ 8,847 |
| Accrued Expenses | 7,309 | 7,928 | 8,387 | 9,559 | 10,075 |
| Current Liabilities | 15,899 | 18,749 | 20,333 | 18,247 | 18,922 |
| Investment | 163,525 | 136,195 | 162,796 | 208,242 | 168,779 |
| | $179,424 | $154,944 | $183,129 | $226,489 | $187,701 |

[a]All numbers disguised.
[b]Inventory breakdown was as follows:

| | 1973 | 1974 | 1975 | 1976 | 1975 |
|---|---|---|---|---|---|
| Raw Material | $ 16,635 | $ 10,367 | $ 35,768 | $ 66,578 | $ 39,393 |
| Work in Process | 9,050 | 14,048 | 16,396 | 18,905 | 26,910 |
| Finished Goods | 15,339 | 9,557 | 22,020 | 22,591 | 30,538 |
| Supplies | 3,266 | 3,220 | 3,241 | 4,488 | 4,340 |
| | 44,290 | 37,192 | 77,425 | 112,502 | 101,181 |
| LIFO Reserve | 13,653 | 19,197 | 19,337 | 19,975 | 39,961 |
| Inventory (Book) | $ 30,637 | $ 17,995 | $ 58,088 | $ 92,527 | $ 61,221 |

**EXHIBIT 3**
Income Statement
MIDWEST STEEL
For the Years Ended December 31, 1973-December 31, 1977[a]
(Thousands of Dollars)

|  | 1973 | 1974 | 1975 | 1976 | 1977 |
|---|---|---|---|---|---|
| Gross Sales | $335,962 | $426,477 | $351,294 | $478,126 | $522,337 |
| Discounts and Allowances | 7,491 | 4,016 | 2,324 | 5,180 | 6,179 |
| Net Sales | 328,471 | 422,461 | 348,970 | 472,946 | 516,158 |
| Cost of Sales | 312,190 | 361,989 | 331,367 | 451,282 | 498,063 |
| Gross Profit | 16,281 | 60,472 | 17,603 | 21,664 | 18,095 |
| Selling, General, and Administrative | 5,564 | 5,572 | 5,202 | 5,931 | 6,328 |
| Operating Profit | 10,717 | 54,900 | 12,401 | 15,733 | 11,767 |
| Other Income | 203 | 241 | 393 | 192 | 526 |
| Income before Taxes and Depreciation | 10,920 | 55,141 | 12,794 | 15,925 | 12,293 |
| Depreciation | 8,808 | 9,309 | 8,889 | 8,955 | 8,954 |
| Income before Taxes | 2,112 | 45,832 | 3,905 | 6,970 | 3,339 |
| Taxes | 800 | 22,752 | 1,849 | 3,113 | 1,730 |
| Net Income | $ 1,312 | $ 23,080 | $ 2,056 | $ 3,857 | $ 1,609 |
| Total Assets | $179,424 | $154,944 | $183,129 | $226,489 | $187,701 |
| ROA (Average = 3.86%) | .73% | 14.90% | 1.12% | 1.70% | .86% |
| Invested Funds | $163,525 | $136,195 | $162,796 | $208,242 | $168,779 |
| ROI (Average = 4.38%) | .96% | 16.90% | 1.26% | 1.85% | .95% |

[a]All numbers disguised.

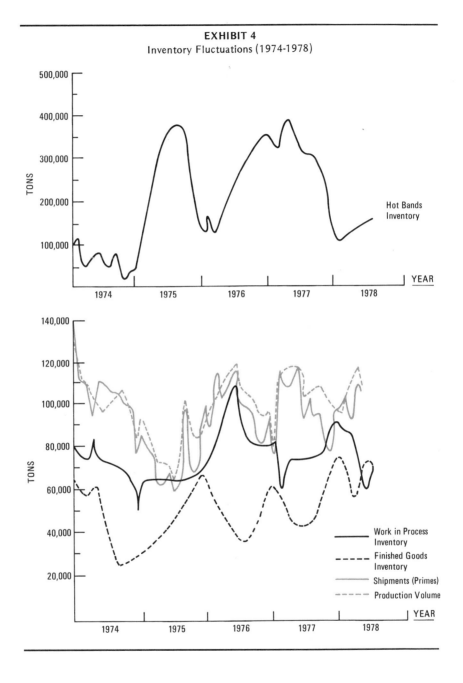

**EXHIBIT 4**
Inventory Fluctuations (1974-1978)

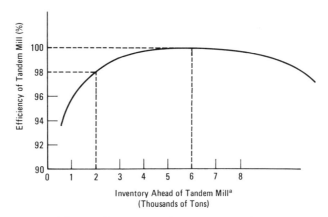

**EXHIBIT 5**
Effect of Inventory Level on Production Efficiency
At the 80-Inch Tandem Mill

Inventory Ahead of Tandem Mill[a]
(Thousands of Tons)

[a] The value of inventory ahead of the tandem mill was $300 per ton.

**EXHIBIT 6**
INVENTORY CARRYING COSTS
MIDWEST STEEL 1977

| | | Annual Cost (Behavior) | | |
|---|---|---|---|---|
| | | Fixed | plus | Variable[a] |
| 1. Inventory (Average) | $100,000,000 | | | $100,000,000 × $K$[b] |
|    Property Taxes | | | | 1% of inventory value/yr |
|    Loss and Spoilage | | | | 1% of inventory value/yr |
| 2. Warehouse Facilities | 22,000,000 | $22,000,000 × $K$[b] | | |
|    Repair and Maintenance | | 400,000 | | |
|    Real and Property Taxes | | 500,000 | | |
| 3. Materials Handling Equipment | 2,000,000 | 2,000,000 × $K$[b] | | |
|    Repair and Maintenance | | 150,000 | | 1/20 of 1% of inventory value/yr |
| 4. Utilities | | 1,000,000 | | 1/2 of 1% of inventory value/yr |
| 5. Labor | | 750,000 | | 1/2 of 1% of inventory value/yr |
| 6. Insurance | | 50,000 | | |

[a]The variable costs vary with inventory level.
[b]$K$ = cost of capital:

| | |
|---|---|
| 1. National Steel's Estimate. | 12.0% |
| 2. National Steel's Return on Equity | 8.0% (last 5-year average) |
| 3. Midwest Steel's Marginal Return on New Investments | 20.0% |
| 4. Midwest Steel's Return on Assets | 3.9% (last 5-year average) |

EXHIBIT 7
Type of Inventory Held by Function[a]
MIDWEST STEEL
(Millions of Dollars)

| Inventory Function[b] | Type of Inventory | | |
| --- | --- | --- | --- |
| | Finished Goods | Work in Process | Raw Material |
| Pipeline | $ 3 | $26[c] | $10 |
| Cycle | — | — | — |
| Buffer | $ 4 | — | $13 |
| Decoupling | — | c | $ 3 |
| Marketing | $21 | — | $ 7 |
| Miscellaneous[d] | $ 3 | $ 1 | $ 6 |
| Total | $31 | $27 | $39 |

[a]All numbers disguised.

[b]Inventory functions are as follows:

*Pipeline inventory:* This is equal to volume per day multiplied by the minimum lag in days associated with the production process (volume per day × lag in days). Pipeline inventory is the inventory needed to fill the production process pipeline. Each unit or work station needs to have some inventory to work on. A large portion of work-in-process inventory at Midwest Steel falls in this category. Most of the time lag is due to scheduling delays.

*Cycle inventory:* Some inventory is required because orders to suppliers cannot be placed in very small quantity. Also, customer order sizes vary and their orders don't come in evenly. At Midwest Steel very little inventory falls in this category because Midwest has a large customer base and order sizes are small compared to production volume.

*Buffer inventory:* To buffer against seasonal or temporary market fluctuations, firms generally carry some inventory. At Midwest Steel, about one-third of raw material inventory falls in this category. The inventory is a buffer against poor delivery performance by raw material suppliers. Lead time for raw material supply is 2 to 4 weeks.

*Decoupling inventory:* When an order has to pass through many units, it is advisable to have some inventory ahead of each unit to separate the effect of one unit on another. A unit might break down, product may be rejected for quality purposes, and production rates may be higher or lower than expected. A part of work-in-process inventory at Midwest Steel falls in this category.

*Marketing inventory:* Some inventory may be required to increase sales. For example, a customer may ask the firm to hold inventory until they request shipment. Also, inventories of some raw materials may be kept on hand to shorten average delivery times. At Midwest Steel, most of the finished goods and some raw material inventory are held for marketing purposes.

[c]Pipeline inventory also serves decoupling purposes.

[d]Includes goods produced ahead of delivery date, excess production, quality control holds, and canceled orders.

# Midwest Steel (C)

On August 2, 1978, Mr. Dan Sullivan, vice president for production at Midwest Steel Co., was discussing a recent meeting of department heads with Mr. Brian Carroll, his assistant.

> *Brian, at the meeting yesterday I found that the cost of holding $100 of inventory for 1 year is $26 before tax. This figure was estimated by considering Midwest's cost of capital, our out-of-pocket warehousing and material handling costs as well as real estate and property taxes. As you know, we've always assumed that inventory carrying cost is insignificant. Thus, we have never hesitated to increase inventory to improve production efficiency. There was some talk at the meeting that this increase in production efficiency may not compensate for the increase in inventory carrying cost. I was charged with doing some analysis to help decide whether or not to reduce our work-in-process inventory. As a first step, I think we should evaluate the inventory ahead of the tandem mills. How much does it cost us? Is it worth carrying that much? I want you to make a detailed study of the inventory ahead of the tandem mills and try to get some answers. Find out how much we can reduce our inventory there and what it will cost us in efficiency.*

This case was prepared by Mr. Farhat Ali and Professor John K. Shank as the basis for class discussion rather than to illustrate either effective or ineffective handling of an administrative situation. All numbers in the case have been disguised to protect confidential data. However, relationships among the numbers which are relevant to the issues in the case have not been distorted. All names have also been changed except for that of Mr. Humphrey, president of the firm.

National Steel Corporation, one of the largest steel producers in the United States, is vertically integrated with holdings that include mines, shipping facilities, basic steel production, finishing mills, and distribution facilities. Midwest Steel is a finishing mill built in 1960 to balance National's excess steelmaking capacity with additional finishing-mill capacity. Midwest converts National's hot-rolled bands (large coils of steel commonly called "hot bands") into sales of other finished products. In 1976, Midwest's sales amounted to 16.8 percent of National Steel's sales but Midwest's net income was only 4.5 percent of National's net income.

Midwest is located at the southern tip of Lake Michigan in Indiana. Shipments, profit margins, and contribution margins by product lines were as follows in 1977:

|  | Tons | Gross Profit Margin per Ton | Average Contribution Margin per Ton |
|---|---|---|---|
| Cold-Rolled | 419,000 | $15.00 | $35.00 |
| Galvanized | 350,000 | 65.00 | 90.00 |
| Tin Mill | 470,000 | 20.00 | 45.00 |
|  | 1,239,000 |  |  |

## PRODUCTION OPERATIONS

The Midwest Steel plant is divided into cost centers for control purposes. The cold reduction department, consisting primarily of the tandem mill operation, is one such cost center. Under this system, each producing unit operates with a flexible budget based on the number of tons of steel processed by the unit. Comparison of budgeted costs with actual costs allows judgments to be made regarding the relative effectiveness of the various departments. Management at Midwest Steel feels that the flexible budget system has considerable built-in motivational value for department foremen that encourages efficient operations. In fact, the primary criterion of success for production management is consistent generation of favorable or "black" variances between actual and budgeted costs.

Since Midwest's standard cost system treats some semifixed costs as if they were variable, variances in volume from standard change the budget by more than the marginal costs directly related to the change. Therefore, production foremen can significantly enhance the apparent performance of their cost center by increasing productivity in terms of tons processed per unit of time.

Most processing units at steel finishing plants have one or more sets of two rolls through which bands of steel are passed. Between units the coils are wound on themselves and stored. As a coil of steel is processed, the edges of the steel make imprints on the rolls. Coils of steel are scheduled to be run in order of diminishing width to avoid transferring these marks to subsequent coils. A schedule to run a sequence of coils by width is termed a *comedown*. After the narrowest width in a comedown is run, all the sets of rolls on that production unit are replaced with fresh sets of rolls and the worn sets are sent to the roll maintenance shop for grinding and eventual reuse. Changing rolls so that wider widths can be run is called a *wideout*. Individual sets of rolls are also changed when damaged or "worn out." Exhibit 1 details the expenses charged to operations when a set of rolls is replaced.

## Cold Reduction

The cold-reduction department consists of two giant machines, tandem mills, which apply tremendous pulling pressure to pickled hot bands, reducing their thickness in a process known as "cold reduction." Each of the tandem mills has five sets of rolls that apply pressure to the hot bands. The 80-inch tandem mill handles three kinds of comedowns: heavy-, medium-, and light-gauge product. The 52-inch mill handles steel earmarked for light-gauge galvanized and tin mill product. Comedowns on the narrow mill are scheduled according to whether the steel has been manufactured by a continuous casting or ingot process. Current operating practice is to schedule one comedown of each type per week. Thus, the 80-inch mill typically runs three comedowns per week and the 52-inch mill runs two. Production rates for the tandem mill comedowns are shown in Exhibit 2.

Although some products can be produced on either mill, technical factors dictate the majority of product-machine assignments. Technical reasons also prohibit intermixing different kinds of steel (heavy and light gauge, ingot and continuous cast) in the same comedown. Wideouts take one hour on the 52-inch mill and 30 minutes on the 80-inch mill.

In 1978 the 80-inch mill was usually scheduled to run about 15 shifts a week and the 52-inch mill 20 shifts. Both mills must be shut down one shift per week for repair and maintenance. The 52-inch mill is scheduled as close to capacity as possible because it costs about $8 per ton less to operate than the 80-inch mill.

## INTERVIEW WITH SUPERINTENDENT OF PRODUCTION CONTROL

Inventory between the pickle line and the tandem mills costs about $300 per ton. Although inventory levels vary considerably, there is an average of 9,000 tons ahead of the 80-inch mill and 5,000 tons awaiting processing ahead of the 52-inch mill. As a first step in his investigation, Brian Carroll asked Bob Wright, superintendent of production control, to discuss these inventory levels. After a brief explanation of his role in analyzing work-in-process inventory for their boss, Mr. Sullivan, the following conversation ensued:

### BRIAN CARROLL

Bob, why do we need 14,000 tons of inventory ahead of the tandem mills, especially since both mills can only produce about 1,800 tons per shift? This seems like enough for more than seven shifts.

**BOB WRIGHT**

Well, Brian, I know that seems like a lot, but there are three main reasons why we need all that inventory. First, the pickle line alternatively feeds both tandem mills. When the pickle line is running a tin comedown for the 52-inch mill, we need to have cold-rolled and galvanized inventory on hand so the 80-inch mill keeps running. O.K.?

Second, the schedulers only work the day shift. Before they leave at 4 P.M., they need to have schedules ready for the *three* following shifts. They need to know what the pickle line has produced in the last 24 hours before they schedule the next three shifts. Also, because production rates on the tandem mills can vary by as much as 30% from the standards, the schedulers actually make a schedule which, on average, would cover four shifts.

Third, some inventory simply can't be scheduled in the next three or four shifts. For example, when we run a continuous cast comedown on the 52-inch mill, the ingot cast inventory can't be scheduled. It has to wait its turn.

**BRIAN CARROLL**

How can this inventory be reduced?

**BOB WRIGHT**

Any substantial reduction in inventory would involve round-the-clock scheduling. I think if schedulers worked 24 hours a day we could just about cut the inventory ahead of the tandem mills in half if we simultaneously doubled the number of comedowns.

**BRIAN CARROLL**

Well, let's see now. How many more schedulers do you think would be needed for round-the-clock scheduling of the pickle line and the tandem mills?

**BOB WRIGHT**

Two more, one for each additional shift. Of course, that would increase our scheduling cost about $50,000 per year. However, the major cost of reducing inventory would be in the production area. If we increase the number of comedowns, roll costs would go way up. And don't forget, we'd likely lose a lot of production while we're changing those rolls.

**BRIAN CARROLL**

Would there really be that substantial an increase in roll costs? Don't you usually have to change some of those rolls for wear before the comedown is complete?

**BOB WRIGHT**

Well, yes, we do change rolls for wear, but we don't have predetermined times to make roll changes. Operators have rolls changed whenever quality deteriorates. A set of rolls on the tandem mills might last anywhere from zero to 1,500 tons. The average life is about 1,000 tons. A roll can get marked by bad steel the minute it's installed. Other times, rolls are remarkably durable. To answer your question, though, I believe that every extra wideout roll change on the tandem mills (that is, putting in five fresh sets of rolls) should eliminate one unscheduled roll change in which, on average, two sets of rolls would have to be changed.

**BRIAN CARROLL**

Do you foresee any other effects of doubling the number of comedowns?

**BOB WRIGHT**

Yes, definitely. If we increase the number of comedowns, we'll certainly show an increase in the number of pass-up[1] hot bands.

**BRIAN CARROLL**

That's something that has always puzzled me. Why do we have pass-ups anyway?

**BOB WRIGHT**

Simple. The most common kind of pass-up occurs when the operator sees that a set of rolls is worn out when there's only one or two coils of steel left to process in a comedown. Since replacing any one set of rolls takes about half as long as a complete wideout it makes sense to pass up those remaining coils, do the complete wideout and start a new comedown. Another kind of pass-up might occur when the operator can tell a coil will give him trouble. If he's behind schedule or if he's already running a red variance, he'll often pass that coil up and leave it for some future comedown. Then, when its turn finally comes, it may show up on a different shift which may not be his problem.

**BRIAN CARROLL**

Then what you're saying is that by doubling the number of comedowns we'll about double the number of pass-ups. But, since we'll run a particular comedown twice as often, the pass-ups will only sit around half as long. The way I see it, that's no change. Right?

**BOB WRIGHT**

Perhaps. That sounds okay in theory, but I'm not sure that that is the way the world works. It is true that we'll eventually run all the pass-up coils, but a lot of times they don't get run until someone screams about them. Frankly, I don't see anything that will change that. We'll just have more pass-ups and more screaming. But look, Brian, you don't really have to worry about pass-ups. Even though there may be a substantial number of hot bands, there isn't much tonnage because pass-ups are almost always the narrowest widths.

---

[1] "Pass-up" coils were coils that had been scheduled for processing in a comedown but which were not run.

**BRIAN CARROLL**

You're right, Bob. Well, I think I've got everything I came for. Thanks a lot.

Late that night, as he reviewed his notes from his meeting with Mr. Wright, Brian Carroll was still uncertain whether or not he had enough information on the cost tradeoffs involved to make a coherent report to Dan Sullivan. Should he include the cost of lost output due to roll-change delay as a cost of wideout? What cost should be associated with the increased probability of stockouts that he suspected might result from operating at a lower inventory?

In addition to these purely technical concerns, Mr. Carroll began to think about the implications of his analysis on the people who would have to work with the results. Would he have difficulty implementing the results of his analysis? He realized that even if he were able to figure out the system of monetary tradeoffs which he should make to arrive at a better inventory level, there was little hope that the general foreman responsible for operating the tandem mills would be motivated to follow the form of his analysis. This was a result of Midwest Steel's cost center control system. It is advantageous for a foreman to work with larger inventories because they allow longer comedowns, which lower roll-change costs. Further, since the foreman is judged on his department's performance against budget, he wants to maximize production volume (tons), since his department's budget is more liberal with higher volume. Additional wideouts would cause delays, reducing daily output. Unless Midwest's cost center system were somehow modified, the tandem mill foreman would have no motivation to reduce inventory. Larger-than-needed inventory levels have no penalty associated with them, since the cost centers are not charged for inventory investment. For the schedulers, moreover, low inventories increase the probability of stockouts, which are considered to be scheduling errors. Also, a lower inventory level would make the scheduler's task more difficult because of decreased scheduling flexibility. Any plan to reduce work-in-process inventory ahead of the tandem mills would have to somehow cope with the motivations of the tandem mill foreman and the schedulers. Part of the solution to these problems seemed to lie with changes in the cost system used to judge the tandem mill forman's performance. But changes in that system would undoubtedly meet with considerable resistance because they would have to somehow be made equitably throughout the entire organization. As the enormity of this implied task became clear, Brian put aside his notes and started home for a cold supper. Maybe tomorrow, he thought to himself, it'll seem clearer whether to start with the chicken or the egg.

## QUESTIONS

1   Evaluate the cost implications of the proposal to double the number of comedowns on the tandem mills:

    *a*   What is the cost of a wideout on the 52-inch tandem mill? On the 80-inch mill?

b   What is the net cost of the wideout after considering saved unscheduled
     roll changes?
c   What is the financial impact of the time involved in the roll changes?
d   What other factors should be considered in the cost analysis?
2   Who controls inventory levels ahead of the tandem mills?
3   Does the cost control system at Midwest motivate managers to make the
     appropriate trade-offs regarding inventory levels? Should the system be
     modified? If so, how?

---

**EXHIBIT 1**
**MIDWEST STEEL**
Cost Associated with Changing and Grinding One Set of Rolls[a]

|                         | Fixed Cost[b] | Variable Cost[c] |
|-------------------------|---------------|------------------|
| Roll Stock Loss         | –             | $148.00          |
| Labor                   | $ 9.00        | 42.50            |
| Repair and Maintenance  | 6.25          | 9.75             |
| Grinding Wheels         | –             | 10.00            |
| Utilities               | 1.50          | 1.00             |
| Miscellaneous Supplies  | .25           | 1.75             |
| Depreciation            | 20.00         | –                |
| Total Cost              | $37.00        | $213.00          |

[a]At the end of a comedown, rolls are removed from the mill and sent to
the roll shop for grinding before reuse. In 1977, the roll shop operated near
capacity and ground 24,000 sets of rolls. It was estimated that increasing roll
shop capacity by 10% requires a capital investment of $1 million.
  [b]Fully absorbed per set of rolls at 1977 volume.
   [c]Per set of rolls.

---

**EXHIBIT 2**
**MIDWEST STEEL**
PRODUCTION RATE ON THE TANDEM MILL[a]

| Comedowns          | Production Shift | Percent of Total Shipments |
|--------------------|------------------|----------------------------|
| **80-Inch Mill**   |                  |                            |
| Heavy              | 1,450            | 25                         |
| Medium             | 1,150            | 16                         |
| Light              | 800              | 19                         |
| Average            | 1,164            | 60                         |
| **52-Inch Mill**   |                  |                            |
| Ingot              | 600              | 20                         |
| Continuous Cast    | 650              | 20                         |
| Average            | 625              | 40                         |

[a]The variable cost per running hour on each tandem mill was $1,080. This in-
cluded direct labor, utilities, and other expenses incurred as the mill was running.

# Midwest Steel (D)

In March of 1979, Midwest Steel was evaluating a proposed capital expenditure to expand the capacity of the batch anneal department by 5%. This project was regarded as a "round-out" expenditure, an expenditure that removed a bottleneck from Midwest's steelmaking process. Round-out expenditures were thought to be highly profitable since they usually showed very high returns on an incremental basis.

## THE COMPANY

Midwest Steel is a division of National Steel Corporation, a large, fully integrated steel manufacturer. Midwest Steel is a finishing mill which is supplied with basic steel by her sister divisions. Because of its relatively new plant (1960), Midwest is the low-cost producer for these finished products. For this reason, National Steel tries to allocate as much production to Midwest as possible.

In early 1979, the batch anneal process was the bottleneck for the mill. Some products normally needing batch annealing had been transferred to the continuous-anneal line. Installing new batch-anneal capacity was expected to move the bottleneck to the cold-reduction mills, which were among the most expensive units in the plant, with replacement value of about $100 million in 1978.

This case was prepared by Mr. James MacDonald, under the supervision of Professor John K. Shank, with the cooperation of a major steel company. All information in the case is disguised.

## CAPITAL EXPENDITURES

Capital expenditure requests developed by each division are sent to the parent company for approval. Corporation management then allocates available funds among the divisions. Since the divisions operate on a decentralized profit center basis, all expenditures are expected to earn a sufficient return on the divisional level. National Steel expects projects to earn a minimum of 20% before taxes.

Within Midwest Steel, a proposal for capital expenditure could be originated by an operating department, by engineering, or by top management. Each proposed project is evaluated for capital costs by the engineering department and for potential savings by the cost and methods department. Finally, the financial planning department analyzes the data and presents a summary financial analysis to top management. If approved, the proposal is then sent on to corporate headquarters.

## THE PROJECT

The proposal to increase batch-anneal capacity involves purchasing one new furnace and the corresponding number of bases, thus adding 694 furnace hours of capacity (at the expected 95% utilization rate). Steel coils are placed on the bases and the furnace is lowered over the coils to perform the annealing. At any point in time, some coils are being heated and some are cooling. This allows one furnace to be used on more than one set of bases.

Engineering estimated that purchasing and installing the new batch capacity would cost $714,000. Of this amount, $550,000 would have to be capitalized (the IRS specified a 12-year life on this type of asset) and depreciated. The remaining $164,000 could be expensed in the first year of operation. The additional capacity could be ready for 1980 production. For tax purposes, Midwest Steel used the fastest allowable depreciation method (a combination of "double declining balance" and "sum-of-the-years' digits" methods) as calculated in Exhibit 1. In 1979, the government allowed a 10% investment tax credit on capital expenditures (10% of the asset cost could be deducted immediately from income taxes due).

Space in the mill is limited. To find room for the new batch capacity, eight "open-coil" anneal bases (one-half of the current "open-coil" capacity) would have to be removed. The "open-coil" method was an old form of batch annealing. Therefore, "open-coil" annealing is no longer being used for normal production. Twelve of the "open-coil" facilities were purchased with the original plant and were fully depreciated in 1979. The other four were purchased in 1970 and were carried at $62,500 on the company's books. Since the "open-coil" facilities were not being used anyway, Midwest decided to remove the four newer bases and four of the fully depreciated bases. It was estimated that these could be sold for $10,000 total, net of removal costs.

The cost and methods staff saw two potential gains from the additional batch-annealing capacity. First, independent of market expansion, production costs could be decreased by transferring two cold-rolled products, CRCQ and

116

NACOR, currently processed by continuous anneal, back to batch anneal. This would absorb over half (398 hours) of the proposed expansion capacity. The additional 296 hours of batch capacity could be used to increase output. The demand for extra production could come from increasing sales or from transferring production from one of Midwest's higher-cost sister divisions. As noted earlier, there was already excess continuous-anneal capacity.

The costs associated with the batch- and continuous-anneal processes are given in Exhibit 2. The continuous-anneal line was having problems producing at the standard hours per ton for CRCQ and NACOR; an average 6-month actual rate was .0253 hr/ton. The 1979 market plan expected sales of CRCQ and NACOR to be 1,100 tons/month and 1,610 tons/month, respectively. Sales were expected to remain near these levels in the foreseeable future. Exhibit 2 also shows the difference in scrapped material for each process, which is not included in the "cost above"[1] numbers.

Exhibit 3 shows how the remaining 296 furnace hours could be utilized, assuming the same product mix as was experienced in early 1979. Gaining additional capacity assumes that no other bottlenecks would develop before the batch capacity fills up. Historically, the mill had operated at full capacity only about 25% of the time. Exhibit 4(A) shows the gross profit and contribution figures for Midwest's product groups in March 1979. March profitability figures were low because a price increase for cold-rolled and tin products was overdue. Over recent years, Midwest had experienced average profitability shown in Exhibit 4(B). Another consideration was that Midwest expected to have $55 worth of inventory and $45 worth of accounts receivable supporting each ton of new sales.

The corporation financed many large expenditures partially with debt which was presently obtainable at an 11% rate, before taxes.

## THE DECISION

Mr. G.W. Humphrey, Jr., president of Midwest Steel, was interested in the results of the cash flow analysis for the batch-anneal expansion, but he was also concerned about whether an incremental analysis was valid in this situation. He knew that incremental analysis of a "roundout" decision would allocate all additional gains from the additional capacity to the bottleneck unit. He was not sure this was valid, considering that another unit would then become the bottleneck. Then, capacity expansions at other units (especially the proposed galvanizing line expansion) would require additional cold-mill capacity as part of that expansion project or else purchasing more expensive processed steel at market prices (making these other projects look less appealing). In fact, on the market, full-finished cold roll (annealed and tempered) currently cost the same amount as full-hard cold roll (only cold-reduced). Thus, it might seem that additional batch-anneal capacity might actually cost Midwest money compared with purchasing full-finished cold roll.

[1] "Cost above" refers to manufacturing costs over and above the raw material cost.

Mr. Humphrey was also concerned that a marketing-mix change might move the plant's bottleneck unit away from batch anneal. For example, since the galvanized line had its own annealing section, a marketing-mix change toward more galvanized tonnage might leave excess batch-anneal capacity because the cold-mill capacity would be filled up with galvanized products. These considerations made Mr. Humphrey wonder if any numerical analysis would be sufficient to judge the desirability of this project.

## QUESTIONS

*1*   Develop the cash flow analysis for the batch-anneal expansion project following the format of Exhibit 5.

*2*   Evaluate whether or not this is a worthwhile project using payback, internal rate of return, net present value, and the profitability index. Which method is the most useful?

*3*   Do a sensitivity analysis on the net present value calculation by assuming a pessimistic cost of capital of 30%, before taxes.

*4*   How would your cash flow numbers be affected if Midwest expected to have enough orders to use the capacity only 2 out of every 3 years?

*5*   Is a "roundout" analysis valid for this project?

*6*   Would you recommend investment in the additional batch-anneal capacity?

---

**EXHIBIT 1**
MIDWEST STEEL
Depreciation Schedule for Tax Purposes
(Thousands of Dollars)

| Year | |
|------|------|
| 1 | $ 92 |
| 2 | 76 |
| 3 | 69 |
| 4 | 62 |
| 5 | 55 |
| 6 | 49 |
| 7 | 42 |
| 8 | 35 |
| 9 | 28 |
| 10 | 21 |
| 11 | 14 |
| 12 | 7 |
| | $550 |

## EXHIBIT 2
### MIDWEST STEEL
Comparative Costs: Batch vs. Continuous Anneal

|  | Batch Anneal | Continuous Anneal |
|---|---|---|
| Standard Hours/Ton |  |  |
| CRCQ (1,100 tons/month) | .1706 hr/ton | .0176 hr/ton[a] |
| NACOR (1,610 tons/month) | .1309 | .0176[a] |
| Standard Cost/Hour |  |  |
| Labor | $ 2.60[b] | $ 87 |
| Natural Gas | 10.60 | 90 |
| Electricity | 3.50 | 68 |
| Inert Gas | 2.70 | 31 |
| Steam | -0- | 60 |
| Replaceable hardware | 1.80 | 30 |
| Repairs and Maintenance | 5.50 | 130 |
| Supervision | 6.10 | 158 |
| Total Cost Above | $32.80/hr | $654/hr |
| Standard Material Loss (Tons/Finished Ton) |  |  |
|  | .0005 ton | .0194 ton |
| Cost of Loss | $.14 | $5.55 |

[a]Recent 6-month average for NACOR and CRCQ showed an actual performance of .0253 hr/ton.

[b]Labor for batch anneal was provided if any furnace was in operation. It was not dependent on the level of activity.

## EXHIBIT 3
### MIDWEST STEEL
Allocation of Additional Furnace Hours

|  | Furnace Hours/Ton | Tons/Month | Hours |
|---|---|---|---|
| Cold-Rolled | .167 | 1190 | 199 |
| Tin Mill | .190 | 512 | 97 |
|  |  |  | 296 hr/month |

**EXHIBIT 4**
MIDWEST STEEL
Product Profitability

| | Gross Profit per ton[a] | Contribution per ton |
|---|---|---|
| A. Product Profitability, March 1979 | | |
| Cold-Rolled | $10 | $30 |
| Tin Mill | $13 | $38 |
| Galvanized | $65 | $90 |
| B. Average Product Profitability | | |
| Cold-Rolled | $15 | $35 |
| Tin Mill | $20 | $45 |
| Galvanized | $65 | $90 |

[a]Gross profit is profit before mill overhead, S.G.&A., and depreciation.

**EXHIBIT 5**
**MIDWEST STEEL**
Cash Flow Analysis

| Year | Investment | | Marginal Profit Increase | Depreciation | Profit before Taxes | Taxes (48%) | Investment Tax Credit | Profit after Taxes | Noncash Items | Other | Cash Flow |
|------|---------|---------|---|---|---|---|---|---|---|---|---|
| | Capital | Expense | | | | | | | | | |
| 0 | | | | | | | | | | | |
| 1 | | | | | | | | | | | |
| 2 | | | | | | | | | | | |
| 3 | | | | | | | | | | | |
| 4 | | | | | | | | | | | |
| 5 | | | | | | | | | | | |
| 6 | | | | | | | | | | | |
| 7 | | | | | | | | | | | |
| 8 | | | | | | | | | | | |
| 9 | | | | | | | | | | | |
| 10 | | | | | | | | | | | |
| 11 | | | | | | | | | | | |
| 12 | | | | | | | | | | | |
| 13 | | | | | | | | | | | |
| 14 | | | | | | | | | | | |
| 15 | | | | | | | | | | | |
| 16 | | | | | | | | | | | |
| 17 | | | | | | | | | | | |
| 18 | | | | | | | | | | | |

# Mavis Machine Shop

Early in 1980, the management of Mavis Machine Shop was considering a project to modernize its plant facilities. The company operated out of a large converted warehouse in Salem, West Virginia, and produced assorted machined metal parts for the oil and gas drilling and production industry in the surrounding area. One of Mavis's major customers was Buckeye Drilling, Inc., which purchased specialized drill bits and replacement parts for its operations. Mavis had negotiated an annual contract with Buckeye to supply its drill bit requirements and related spare parts in each of the past 8 years. In the past the requirements had been about 8,400 bits per year.

The present arrangement of the machine shop included four large manual lathes currently devoted to the Buckeye business. Each lathe was operated by a skilled worker, and each bit required machining at all four lathes. The management was considering replacing these manual lathes with an automatic machine, capable of performing all four machining operations necessary for a drill bit. This machine would produce drill bits at the same rate as the four existing lathes, and would only require one skilled operator.

The four existing manual lathes were 3 years old, could each produce 2,100 drill bits on a two-shift, 5-day/week basis, and had cost a total of $590,000. The useful life of these lathes, calculated on a two-shift/day, 5-day/week basis, was estimated to be 15 years. The salvage value at the end of their useful life was estimated to be $5,000 each. Depreciation of $114,000 had been accumulated on the four lathes. Cash for the purchase of these lathes had been partially sup-

This case is based on a similar exercise prepared by Professor Robert Anthony of the Harvard Business School. The case was written by Thomas Graham under the supervision of Professor John K. Shank.

plied by a 10-year, unsecured, 10% bank loan, of which $180,000 was still out-standing. The best estimate of the current selling price of the four lathes in their present condition was $240,000, after dismantling and removing costs. The loss from the sale would be deductible for tax purposes, resulting in a tax savings of 46% of the loss.

The automatic machine being considered needed only one highly skilled operator to feed in raw castings, observe its functioning, and make necessary adjustments. It would have an output of 8,400 drill bits annually. Because it would be specially built by a machine tool manufacturer, there was no catalog price. The cost was estimated to be $680,000, delivered and installed. The useful life would be 15 years. No reliable estimate of its scrap value could be made. An educated guess was that the value would equal the removal costs.

The automatic lathe had been a fairly new idea in 1975 and at that time the cost was $750,000. It was expected that as the manufacturing techniques became more generally familiar, the price would continue to drop somewhat over the next few years.

As a result of a study prepared by the cost accountant for use in deciding what action to take, the following information was compiled. The direct labor rate for lathe operations was $10 per hour. The new machine would use less floor space, which would save $1,600 annually on the allocated charges for square footage of space used, although the layout of the plant was such that the freed space would be difficult to utilize and no other use was planned. Miscellaneous cash expenses for supplies and power would be $20,000 less per year if the auto-matic machine were used.

If purchased, the new lathe would be financed with a secured bank loan at 14%. Some additional financial data for the company are given in Exhibit 1. This information is considered to be typical of the company's financial condition, with no major changes expected in the foreseeable future.

**REQUIRED**

*1*   Summarize the net cash flows for the proposed project.

*2*   For the project, calculate the internal rate of return, the accounting rate of return, the payback period, the net present value (at 20%, after taxes) and the profitability index.

*3*   What qualitative factors should be considered in evaluating this project?

*4*   What decision would you recommend?

## EXHIBIT 1
### MAVIS MACHINE SHOP
#### Selected Financial Information

Condensed Income Statement, 1979

| | | |
|---|---|---|
| Net Sales | | $5,364,213 |
| Expenses | | 4,138,647 |
| Profit before Taxes | | $1,225,566 |
| Income Taxes | | 602,851 |
| | Net Income | $ 622,715 |

Condensed Balance Sheet, 12/31/79

| | | | |
|---|---|---|---|
| Current Assets | $3,051,349 | Current Liabilities | $ 930,327 |
| Property Assets | 4,239,210 | 10% Bonds Outstanding | 500,000 |
| Other Assets | 151,491 | Common Stock | 1,000,000 |
| | $7,442,050 | Retained Earnings | 5,011,723 |
| | | | $7,442,050 |

# Ajax Petroleum

Bill MacGregor was still puzzled as he thought about the financial report lying on his desk (see Exhibit 1). The report summarized the key financial statistics for a capital expenditure project which one of MacGregor's subordinates was recommending. MacGregor was the general manager for Ajax Petroleum's Middletown, Ohio, refinery. Although he was a chemical engineer by training, his policy was to rely on the people reporting to him for recommendations about the technical side of the business. He strongly objected to second-guessing his managers on things for which they were responsible.

John Patterson, general superintendent for the catalytic cracking unit ("cat cracker") was pushing strongly for MacGregor's approval of a proposal to install a solvent-decarbonizing unit (SDU) in the refinery at a cost of roughly $30,000,000. The function of an SDU is to clean and purify residual fuel oil so that it can serve as raw material ("feedstock") for the cat cracker. The cat cracker would then convert this feedstock into gasoline. Residual or No. 6 oil is one of the outputs when crude oil is refined. However, it represents, literally, what is left after the desirable end products are extracted from the barrel of crude. As the dregs, "resid" is dirty, smelly, and so viscous that it will not even flow at room temperature. It was considered in Ajax to be more a nuisance than anything else. However, there is an established nationwide market for resid, at a low enough price, with uses ranging from heating apartment buildings to generating electricity to powering other equipment designed to run on low-grade fuels. John Patterson was convinced that

This case was prepared by Professor John K. Shank with the cooperation of a major oil company. It is designed for classroom discussion use and is not intended to reflect either effective or ineffective management action. All data in the case are generally realistic as of April, 1980, but proprietary information has been disguised.

converting resid into more gasoline was a great idea, particularly since gasoline prices at the refinery were stable at $39.00/bbl. while resid prices were very volatile, having been as low as $18/bbl. in recent weeks. There was sufficient excess capacity at the cat cracker to process the extra feedstock, and no alternative external source of additional feedstock was available.

MacGregor had been intrigued by Patterson's idea because he was no great fan of No. 6 oil either. Because of wide seasonal swings in demand and supply and a relatively thin market, residual prices were notoriously volatile and unpredictable. MacGregor knew that the current price was about $25/bbl., but it had been as low as $18/bbl. and as high as $35/bbl. in recent months. Patterson had also told MacGregor that many of Ajax' competitors already had SDUs in their refineries and that there was always a waiting list for installation of an SDU, so they must be a good investment. MacGregor wasn't particularly impressed by these arguments, however, because he knew that the major oil companies often differed on strategic issues. Just because Ashland and Marathon were deemphasizing heavy oil (No. 6) to yield more light oil (gasoline) from the barrel of crude did not mean Ajax should automatically follow along. In fact, this might make the heavy-oil business a lot better for the remaining suppliers. MacGregor had heard that Exxon, for one, still considered heavy oil to be a viable item in the product line. Also, MacGregor knew that Ajax' marketing department might not agree with deempahsizing resid, since there were residual oil sales managers in each sales district and many long-standing customer relationships involved, including many electric utilities in the politically sensitive northeast. MacGregor did know, however, that the additional gasoline could easily be sold in the wholesale market. Long-run prospects for gasoline demand were less certain.

MacGregor had told Patterson that the key in selling the SDU idea would be return on investment. He told Patterson to work with the economic analysis department to pull together the numbers for the SDU proposal. If it was such a good idea the numbers would show it and MacGregor could then recommend the project to the corporate capital expenditures committee. The corporate "hurdle rate" for new investment proposals was currently 20%, after taxes. Patterson had eagerly accepted this idea, noting that an acquaintance of his at Ashland Oil had called the SDU in his refinery one of the more profitable investments he had seen in 20 years in the business. When MacGregor received the financial summary report, he was puzzled because the numbers for the SDU project just didn't look that good.

When MacGregor showed the report to Patterson, the latter accused the "bean counters" of trying to scuttle the project with "funny numbers." He took exception to two items in the report, the cost of $29.00/bbl. for fuel gas and the cost of $32.30/bbl. for residual oil. He said that fuel gas was really free because there wasn't anything else to do with it except use it as fuel. He argued that since the refinery gets it automatically when a barrel of crude is processed and it has no sales value, it should be considered as free. In fact, he said, fuel gas should show a negative cost since it costs money for equipment to flare it off if it isn't used. He should be encouraged to use it up, he said, to save this cost and to save the hassle with EPA about the air pollution when fuel gas is flared. He was even more unhappy with the reported cost of $32.30/bbl. for resid. He said it was absolutely crazy to show resid at a higher cost than crude itself when, in fact, resid is what's left after you take all the desired products out of the crude. Why should resid show a higher value than raw crude when it was dramatically less desirable to customers? Raw crude itself, although dangerous to handle because of static electricity buildup, is a substitute product for resid in nearly all applications. Patterson had said that he had never been much interested in cost calculations because he figured that the accountants were accurate, but if this report was an example of how they think, Ajax was in trouble. MacGregor had agreed that Patterson's points seemed to make sense.

MacGregor had subsequently called in Ben Anderson to discuss Patterson's objections to the cost calculations in Anderson's report. Anderson had assured MacGregor that he had no desire to scuttle Patterson's idea. In fact, he said, the analysis in the report was slanted in favor of the proposal and he had even felt guilty about leaning over backward to make the project look good. The problem with the report, he said, was that fuel gas should be costed at $32.30/bbl. rather than $29.00. It is true, he continued, that fuel gas shows an actual cost of $29.00 per equivalent barrel under Ajax' cost accounting system and that this is the cost approved by DOE for determining gasoline "ceiling" prices. However, he said, actual historical cost was not relevant for the proposed new capital investment. Anderson noted that about one-half of the refinery's current fuel needs were being met by fuel gas and the other half by residual oil. The SDU project would not increase the amount of fuel gas generated at the crude still, but it would consume as fuel some of the fuel gas already being generated. The net result for the refinery as a whole would be to increase the consumption of resid used as fuel by an amount equal to the fuel needs of the SDU. Since resid costs $32.30/bbl., fuel cost for the SDU project should be $32.30. Anderson called this the "opportunity-cost" concept, as opposed to actual historical cost.

Regarding the question of what No. 6 costs, Anderson said he sympathized with Patterson but that the $32.30 was a factual number. In fact, he said, the refinery *does* produce a set of products at the crude still, *including* residual oil, and these products *must each* carry a share of the costs incurred in producing them. A barrel of residual oil thus costs whatever a barrel of crude oil costs, plus some share of the operating costs at the crude still. These crude-still operating costs, he said, could be allocated based on value of products produced, volume of products produced, total energy value (BTUs) of products produced, or some other basis. But under any allocation scheme, outputs from the crude still will cost more than crude oil. Anderson concluded by saying that with fuel gas and resid at $32.30, the SDU actually would be even less profitable than as shown in Exhibit 1 and that the project just couldn't be justified on economic grounds. But, since most companies use historical costs rather than opportunity costs in their accounting systems, he

(Anderson) could "bend" as far as the analysis in the report, as an accommodation to Patterson. The meeting had ended with MacGregor agreeing that Anderson's points seemed to make sense.

MacGregor's background included very little training in cost accounting. He had always considered this area as a technical specialty for which general managers could hire the expertise they needed. He was, however, feeling very frustrated about which cost numbers to believe for the solvent decarbonizing project. He also felt a little foolish for agreeing with both Patterson and Anderson when they talked to him.

He asked his plant controller, Fred Morton, to have lunch with him one day to look at Ben Anderson's report and comment on John Patterson's objections to it. Morton said the basic issue was what cost to show for No. 6 oil in the calculations. He said that Anderson was correctly using the cost numbers generated by Ajax' cost accounting system. Resid was considered to be one of the joint set of products produced in the refinery and, accordingly, was assigned a cost of $32.30/bbl. (as compared to middle distillate at $32.90 and gasoline at $34.80). He agreed that the *particular* allocation scheme (weight, volume, heat value, etc.) was essentially arbitrary, but he emphasized that charging a share of refining cost to resid makes it more costly.

He said that one way to show significantly lower cost on resid would be to consider it a "by-product" rather than a "joint product." A by-product has the following characteristics:

1   It is not a desired output from the production process; it just happens to be created in the process of making the desired products.
2   It is low in sales value relative to the main products.
3   It is produced in relatively small quantities.

A clear example of the distinction between a by-product and a joint product is pigs feet versus bacon to a hog butcher. Morton went on to say that normal cost accounting procedure shows a zero cost for by-products. They are just sold for whatever the market will bring, and the sales revenue is netted back against the costs which must be assigned to the desired products. For the refinery, this would mean allocating the sum of crude cost plus crude-still operating costs minus resid sales revenue to gasoline and middle distillate (jet fuel, diesel fuel, and home heating oil), with resid showing a zero cost for accounting purposes. He noted that several of the major oil companies follow this approach, although several others use the same approach as Ajax.

Under the by-product approach, resid would be valued in the capital expenditure analysis at whatever you could sell it for if you didn't convert it to cracking stock or use it as refinery fuel. With gasoline selling for $39/bbl., he thought resid would average around $20 over its price cycles. However, he added that the long-run average price of resid would certainly be heavily influenced by regulatory pressures to stop utilities from burning resid and by trends in gasoline consumption.

The average price by 1985 could be as low as $17/bbl. or as high as $25/bbl., even if crude prices didn't change. Morton said this is what Anderson termed the opportunity-cost approach, as opposed to the historical-cost approach. He concluded by saying that this same idea applies to the fuel gas item—the reported cost incurred is $29.00/bbl. and the opportunity cost will average around $20/bbl. (the revenue forgone by not selling a barrel of resid).

MacGregor went back to Anderson the next day and asked him to refigure the SDU project showing both the joint product costing and by-product costing approaches for resid and both recorded cost and opportunity cost approaches for fuel gas. Anderson said that would be no problem and agreed to get the information to MacGregor by the next day. MacGregor wondered how much impact these accounting questions would have on the profitability of the SDU project. He couldn't imagine that bookkeeping issues would be that important to the overall analysis. He was anxious to see Anderson's revised report.

## QUESTIONS

1    Using the same format as in Exhibit 1, recalculate the economic return for the project, using both joint product costing ($32.30) and by-product costing ($20.00) for resid and using DOE costing ($29.00) and opportunity costing for fuel gas ($20.00 or $32.30, depending on the assumed cost of resid). All the basic data will be the same as in Exhibit 1 except for the cost of fuel gas and resid.

2    What do you believe is the best accounting method for fuel gas and residual oil? Why? Which set of accounting numbers produces the most meaningful economic return calculations?

3    Is the proposed solvent decarbonizing unit profitable enough to justify the investment?

4    As MacGregor, would you recommend the SDU project to headquarters? What economic analysis would you present to support your recommendation? What qualitative (versus quantitative) factors influence your decision?

EXHIBIT 1
Memorandum

March 17, 1980

TO:    W. MacGregor
FROM:  B. Anderson, Economic Analyst
RE:    The Solvent Decarbonizing Unit Proposal

Here is the information you requested concerning the economics of the SDU project. I have the backup file if you want to dig deeper.

1) Investment cost                       $30,000,000 (delivered and installed)
      Less Investment Tax Credit       3,000,000 (10% of cost)
                *Net Investment*   $27,000,000

2) Annual Operating Costs (three-shift basis)   $ 3,300,000 (Labor, maintenance,
                                                      insurance, property taxes,
                                                      supplies)

*Per barrel of Cracking Stock Produced*

3) Fuel                              $     2.90 bbl. (See Note 1 below)
4) Feedstock Cost                 $    32.30/bbl. (See Note 2 below)
5) Value of Cracking Stock Produced   $    37.50/bbl. (See Note 3 below)
6) Thruput is 9,000 bbls. per day (assuming an average of 90% utilization of theoretical capacity on a 365-day/year basis). One bbl. of resid will produce one bbl. of cracking stock.
7) Economic life is 20 years. (This is also the depreciable life for tax purposes. The current tax rate is 46%.) Use straight-line depreciation for simplicity and to be conservative.
8) Inflation in costs and prices is ignored. This would tend to offset for a project like this one.

*Project Profitability*
Payback = 9.10 years
Net Present Value (at 20% after taxes) = negative $12.6 million
Economic Rate of Return = 9%
Profitability Index = .72
Return on Capital Employed = 19.8%

*Note 1*    The SDU runs on fuel gas,[a] to which Ajax currently assigns a cost of $29.00 per equivalent bbl. It takes .10 bbl. of fuel gas to produce a barrel of thruput at the SDU. Thus, fuel gas costs $2.90 per barrel of thruput.

*Note 2*    Feedstock for the SDU is No. 6 oil. The cost of No. 6 is computed by assigning crued oil cost and crude-still operating costs to the set of outputs at the crude still, based on reiltive production volumes for each product. With crude running $29.00 average for the refinery, this equates currently to about $32.30/bbl. for resid.

*Note 3*    Gasoline is currently selling for about $39/bbl. at the refinery. The cost is about $1.50/bbl. at the cat cracker to convert feedstock into gasoline. Thus, the net realizable value of thruput at the SDU which feeds the cat cracker is $37.50/bbl. ($39 minus $1.50).

---

[a]"Fuel gas" is generated at the crude still in a gaseous state as one of the products when a barrel of crude is "cracked." It is not feasible to convert the fuel gas into a salable end product, but it can be used as fuel to power the various production units in the refinery. The DOE-approved guidelines for measuring the allowable cost of gasoline for price control purposes, charge fuel gas for a proportionate share of the average cost of crude oil but not for any portion of the operating costs of the crude still. Currently, about 5% of the equivalent volumetric production at the crude still is fuel gas. With crude cost at $30.45 for the incremental barrel and $29.00 on average, Ajax followed the DOE-approved approach and costed fuel gas at $29.00 per equivalent barrel.

# part 2

# COST ANALYSIS FOR PERFORMANCE EVALUATION

# Randhart Foam Co.

Anton Leone, president of Randhart Foam, was reviewing summary departmental cost reports early in January, 1980 when the data for the automotive department caught his eye.

|  | *Automotive Department Summary* | | |
|---|---|---|---|
|  | *1978* | *1979* | *Variance* |
| Raw Materials | $425,000 | $522,000 | $ 97,000 U |
| Direct Labor | 65,000 | 87,000 | 22,000 U |
| Department Overhead |  |  |  |
| ✓ Indirect Labor | 39,500 | 10,500 | (29,000)F |
| ⨍ Supervision | 10,000 | 10,000 | — |
| ✓ Factory Overhead | 32,720 | 36,295 | 3,575 U |
| ⨍ Depreciation | 25,000 | 50,000 | 25,000 U |
| ⨍ General Burden | 73,700 | 84,500 | 10,800 U |
| Total | $670,920 | $800,295 | $129,375 U |

Mr. Leone was surprised and a bit disappointed at the cost increases shown. The only area which seemed to have improved was indirect labor. He immediately requested an in-depth investigation. This investigation produced the following information.

The automotive department produces only two types of padding for car seats. The two types, bucket seats and bench seats, require different amounts of

This case was suggested by a similar exercise written by Professor Robert Jaedicke of the Stanford Business School. The case was written by Thomas Graham under the supervision of Professor John K. Shank.

foam padding. A bench seat requires more material since it is much larger (three persons versus one for a bucket seat). The bucket seat, however, requires significantly more direct labor, because it must be cut and shaped. The supervisor explained that all the foam required for both seat types is produced in huge "buns." These buns are then cut into smaller units of foam to be further processed into the car seat padding. He further explained that bench seats use two units of foam whereas bucket seats use only one, when the department operated at normal efficiency. Any investigation of the records indicated that 85,000 units of foam had been cut for use in the automotive department in 1978, and 87,000 units in 1979.

The amount of direct labor required to produce a bucket seat is twice as much as that required for a bench seat. The foreman allowed that, under normal conditions, the department could produce five bucket seats per labor hour. Since the skill level required to produce bucket and bench seats is the same, the work force was regularly rotated between two tasks, reducing boredom and promoting better labor relations. Union pressure has resulted in steadily rising wage rates. In 1978, the hourly rate was $8.00; in 1979 it rose 25%. Poor work scheduling and the unpredictable nature of the automobile industry in the last few years sometimes required the use of a night shift, which received a 10% premium. It is the company's policy to avoid night-shift work whenever possible. A payroll investigation showed that 8,000 hours were paid in 1978, and 8,500 were paid in 1979. The actual direct labor rate varied from the union rate because of some night-shift work. The price of foam has gone up due to the use of petroleum by-products in its manufacture. In 1978, one unit of foam used in the seats cost about $5.00 to produce; the cost in 1979 was $6.00.

General burden (overhead) is an allocated cost. The costs for accounting, personnel, and other administrative departments are allocated to the production departments on the basis of total labor dollars, both direct and indirect. Total general overhead for the company was $670,000 in 1978 and $650,000 in 1979. The total labor cost for all production departments was $950,000 in 1978 and $750,000 in 1979.

During 1979, Randhart purchased a new conveyor system to move the buns from department to department. The new systems helped expedite the cutting process. This resulted in eliminating two material handlers who were included in indirect labor expense. The decision to install the new material-handling system was made using a capital budgeting analysis which assigned a 10-year life to the equipment. A full year's depreciation was taken for 1979.

Factory overhead, which includes the utility costs of heating and lighting, is also an allocated cost. Since the amount of overhead incurred is largely a function of the level of capacity utilization in the factory, the amount of overhead is allocated to production departments based on direct labor hours. The rate in 1979 was $4.27/hr. while in 1978 it was $4.09/hr. The increase in 1979 was due to increased utility costs for the factory resulting primarily from a severe shortage of natural gas during the winter of 1978-1979.

A check of the production records showed the following:

|                | 1978   | 1979   |
|----------------|--------|--------|
| Bucket Seats   | 20,000 | 25,000 |
| Bench Seats    | 30,000 | 30,000 |

## REQUIRED

1   Prepare the analysis of cost variations between 1978 and 1979 requested by Mr. Leone.
2   Should the department manager be commended or criticized for cost center performance.

# Barrett Box Company, Inc.

In November, 1975, Mr. Wilton Burrell, a Boston management consultant, paid a visit to Fall River, Massachusetts, to meet with Mr. William Barrett, president of the Barrett Box Company, Inc. Mr. Barrett had asked Mr. Burrell to come out to help him to "take a look at where my company is right now, and help me evaluate the way we do things."

As Mr. Barrett explained the situation to Mr. Burrell: "The company is making satisfactory profits, and I expect it to continue to do so. I'm not really concerned about current profitability, but I do want to be sure that nothing has been overlooked in making the business as efficient as is feasible." He went on to suggest that Mr. Burrell might start his review by taking a look at the company's accounting and control system, simply because this particular aspect had not been studied by an outsider for some time. He reiterated that he was not particularly dissatisfied with the present setup. Major elements in the current system, according to Mr. Barrett, were a complete annual budget, a standard cost system for all elements of manufacturing costs, and a regular reporting procedure that produced monthly financial statements by the middle of the following month.

The box factory had 10 principal cost centers, each consisting of a single press or a group of similar presses and associated equipment. Each cost center was headed by a foreman. Minor operations such as ink manufacture, quality control, and the storage warehouse were also treated as separate cost centers.

The annual budget was drawn up each fall[1] under the direction of Ms. Janis Clark, the treasurer. The budget was synthesized from estimates of sales prepared

Copyright © 1976 by the President and Fellows of Harvard College. Reproduced by permission. This case was adapted by Professor John K. Shank and Professor Joseph San Miguel from an older case. It is designed for discussion purposes and is not intended to illustrate either effective or ineffective handling of an administrative situation.

[1] The budget for 1975 was prepared in the fall of 1974.

by the sales staff and from corresponding activity rates and cost expectations developed by manufacturing personnel. The latter would participate in the discussions of the relevant portions of the budget. Ms. Clark used her experience with past budgets to combine the separate elements into a meaningful whole. The budget was stated in terms of a specified dollar amount per month for each major item in each of the manufacturing cost centers. The budget amount for a given month was based on the anticipated level of activity in that month, as estimated when the budget was prepared. The level of production activity was measured in machine hours.

Mr. Burrell obtained from Mr. Barrett a copy of a typical monthly spending report for one of the cost centers. This report is reproduced as Exhibit 1.

## QUESTIONS

1   Evaluate the cost performance of Cost Center No. 014 for the month of October.

2   What suggestions would you make to Mr. Barrett regarding the content and format of this cost report?

3   What is the nature of the item which Barrett Box Company calls "overhead variance"? What information is reflected in this item?

## EXHIBIT 1
## BARRETT BOX COMPANY, INC.

Spending Report

Cost Center No. 014—Two-Color Miehle Printing Presses
Ocotber 1975

|  | Budget | Actual | Variance Favorable (Unfavorable) |
|---|---|---|---|
| Allocated Fixed Charges (1) | $ 3,350 | $ 3,450 | $ (100) |
| General Press—Fixed Overhead (2) | 2,432 | 2,432 | — |
| General Press—Variable Overhead (3) | 8,755 | 8,721 | 34 |
| Press Supplies | 215 | 373 | (158) |
| Repairs | 808 | 1,472 | (664) |
| Power | 728 | 484 | 244 |
| Indirect Labor—Pressmen | 8,025 | 5,315 | 2,710 |
| Indirect Labor—Helpers | 2,950 | 2,074 | 876 |
| Payroll Taxes | 817 | 580 | 237 |
| Totals | $28,080 | $24,901 | $ 3,179 |
| Overhead Absorbed |  |  | $19,386 |
| Gain (Loss) on Budget |  |  | 3,179 |
| Overhead Variance |  |  | (8,694) |
| Over (Under) Absorbed Overhead |  |  | $(5,515) |
| Number of Machine Hours—Make Ready |  | 389 |  |
| Number of Machine Hours—Running Time |  | 1,047 |  |
| Total Machine Hours | 2,080 | 1,436 |  |
| Indirect Labor Hours—Pressmen | 1,664 | 1,181 |  |
| Fixed Cost/Machine Hour[a] | $ 2.78 | $ 4.10 |  |
| Variable Cost/Machine Hour | 10.72 | 13.24 |  |
| Total Cost/Machine Hour | $13.50 | $17.34 |  |

[a]Includes allocated fixed charges and general press—fixed overhead.

*Explanatory Comments (These Comments Are Not Part of the Spending Report)*

1   This is the share of general corporate overhead expense charged to Cost Center No. 014. The charge is based on allocation formulas set once a year. Actual corporate overhead expense each month is allocated to the cost centers based on the set percentages.

2   This is the charge for fixed overhead items which are directly assignable to this cost center. It includes such items as supervision and depreciation, among others.

3   This item represents miscellaneous variable overhead charges directly assignable to cost center No. 014.

# Able Company

The Able Company, manufacturers of two well-known products, used a standard cost system. Standard costs represented the company's best estimate of what costs would be during the year. The company also used a variable overhead budget determined annually; the budgeted allowance consisted of a nonvariable element and a variable (straight-line) element. The following is a list and brief explanation of the variance accounts that were a part of the system:

1   *Raw material price variance:* This was the difference between the price actually paid for material and the standard price at which it was taken up in raw material inventory.

2   *Raw material quantity variance:* Work in process was debited for the standard quantity of material in products worked on during the month, whereas raw material inventory was credited for the actual quantity of material withdrawn from inventory. Both quantities were valued at standard material prices. The difference between this debit and credit appeared in the raw material quantity variance.

3   *Labor variance:* Work in process was debited with the standard direct labor cost of operations performed during the month. The labor variance was the difference between this debit and actual direct labor expense incurred.

4   *Factory overhead variance:* Work in process was debited for the overhead expenses absorbed into production by means of a factory-wide, annually determined rate. The factory overhead variance was the difference between this debit and actual overhead expenses incurred in the month.

The balances in each variance account were closed monthly to loss and gain (i.e., profit and loss).

This very old and very difficult problem is in the public domain.

The income statements for September, 1980 and October, 1980 were as shown below. No changes in standard unit costs or selling prices were made during these two months. Assume that no errors were made in collecting and recording data during the two months.

|  | September 1980 | | October 1980 | |
|---|---:|---:|---:|---:|
| Net Sales |  | $600,000 |  | $450,000 |
| Cost of these Sales at Standard: |  |  |  |  |
| Material | $160,000 |  | $120,000 |  |
| Direct Labor | 150,000 |  | 100,000 |  |
| Overhead | 120,000 |  | 80,000 |  |
| Total Standard Cost of Sales |  | 430,000 |  | 300,000 |
| Gross Profit (as standard) |  | $170,000 |  | $150,000 |
| Less Manufacturing Variances: |  |  |  |  |
| Raw Material Price Variance | $ 2,000 |  | $ 6,000 |  |
| Raw Material Quantity Variance | 1,000 |  | 3,000 |  |
| Labor Variance | 1,000 |  | 4,000 |  |
| Factory Overhead Variance | 45,000 | 49,000 | 15,000 | 28,000 |
|  |  | $121,000 |  | $122,000 |
| Selling, General, and Administrative Expense |  | 90,000 |  | 90,000 |
| Operating Profit |  | $ 31,000 |  | $ 32,000 |

## QUESTIONS

For each of the following questions, give your answer. *Give explanations only where they are requested and limit them to a few words. (For most questions, 10 words should be adequate.)* Notice that in certain questions new facts are introduced. These additional facts are not needed for any questions that precede the point where they are introduced, but they may be necessary for subsequent questions. [A summary of the additional information introduced in these questions is given in Exhibit 1.]

*1* In both September and October, was it costing more to manufacture Able Company products than had been expected would be true on the average?

Yes _____    No _____    Can't tell _____

*2* Total actual factory overhead was practically the same in the two months. What probably accounted for the decrease in factory overhead variance for October?

*3* Actual factory overhead expense for September was at the budgeted level anticipated for standard volume. Was September production above or below standard?

*4* The figures in the income statement for September and October suggest which of the following?

*a* Factory output rose in October above normal levels. _____

*b* Factory output fell in October to below normal levels. _____

*c* Factory output rose in October but was still below normal. _____

*d* Factory output fell in October but was still above
normal.                                                                  _____

5 The percentage decrease in gross profit from September to October was less
than the percentage decrease in net sales for the same period. What probable
explanation could there be for this?

6 In October, there was a decrease in the purchase price of one of the company's raw materials. In view of this, what possible explanations could there
be for the increase in the raw material price variance?

7 Some of the raw material purchased at the lower price was put into production in October. What items in the October income statement, if any, were
affected by this fact?

8 Some of the raw material purchased at the lower price was included in
products that were sold during October. What effect did this have on gross
profit as shown on the income statement?

9 Standard factory overhead was absorbed on the basis of either total direct
labor dollars or total material dollars. Which basis was used, and what was the
rate? Explain.

10 Product A of the Able Company's two products, A and B, had a total standard cost of $37 per unit including standard material cost of $10 per unit.
What was the standard direct labor cost per unit of product A?

11 At standard volume of production, direct labor totaled $100,000 per month.
Standard material cost absorbed into production of product A was $28,500
in September and $25,500 in October. Standard material cost absorbed into
production of product B was $1,500 in September and $64,500 in October.
Could performance with respect to raw material usage actually have improved
from September to October? Explain.

12 Was the combined dollar balance in the finished goods and work-in-process
inventory accounts at the end of October higher or lower than the combined
balance at the end of September? Explain.

13 Did the proportion of product A sold increase from September to October?
Explain.

14 Standard direct labor costs were $110,000 in August. Budgeted factory over-
head expense for August was $83,000. What was the spending variance for
factory overhead in October?

15 What was the factory overhead volume variance in September?

16 What was the factory overhead spending variance in September?

17 What was the factory overhead volume variance in October?

18 What can you reasonably conclude about the method of compensation of
salespersons?

19 On the basis of the information given, which of the following seems to describe best the basis on which the raw material inventories would be valued
for monthly balance sheet purposes?
*a* Market
*b* Invoice cost
*c* Standard cost
*d* Average cost
*e* Lower of cost or market

20 Compute the percent of product of B in the product mix sold in September
and in October.

## EXHIBIT 1
### ABLE COMPANY
Recapitulation of Additional Information Given
in the Questions

| | August | September | October | Standard Volume |
|---|---|---|---|---|
| Material | | | | |
| Product A[a] | | Standard: $28,500 | Standard: $25,500 | |
| Product B | | Standard: 1,500 | Standard: 64,500 | |
| Direct Labor | Standard: $110,000 | | | Standard: $100,000 |
| Factory Overhead | Budgeted: $83,000 | Actual: same as October actual | Actual: same as September actual | Budgeted: same as September actual |

| aMaterial Standard | $10 |
|---|---|
| Total Standard Cost | $37 |

# Buchanan Steel

In July of 1979, Buchanan Steel president Phil Palmintere called a meeting of his executive staff to discuss the current status of the theoretical minimum weight billing program. In attendance were production control manager Brad Schmidt, chief metallurgist Al Falenski, financial planning manager David Houston, product sales manager Max Heilburg, controller Andy Birrel, and cost and methods analysis manager Ed Lorachusky.

Until 1970, virtually all steel in the United States was sold by weight. Steel companies established prices per ton which, when multiplied by the actual shipped weight of a particular order, would give the total selling price.

In 1970, a theoretical minimum weight (TMW) billing program was initiated by one of Buchanan's competitors as a marketing ploy in response to customer complaints regarding the industry-wide practice of rolling orders heavier than the gauge specified by the customer. Due to this additional thickness, a customer specifying a given footage had to accept more weight and thus higher cost than he ordered.

The TMW program was immediately matched by the other steel companies. It effectively changed the marketing practices of the industry for the products affected from selling by the actual tonnage shipped to selling by surface area times desired gauge. Under the program, the customer orders a minimum gauge. The amount billed on the order is the theoretical weight of the coil, calculated as follows:

$$\text{Ordered minimum gauge x actual length x ordered width x}$$
$$\text{standard steel density factor}$$

This case was prepared by Mr. David Templin under the supervision of Professor John K. Shank, with the cooperation of a major steel company. All information in the case has been disguised.

For example, for a .0280-gauge 48-inch-wide order and a coil 98,010 feet long, as measured coming off the finishing unit, the theoretical weight of that order is

$$(.0280 \text{ in.}) \times (980,010 \text{ ft.}) \times (12 \text{ in./ft.}) \times (48 \text{ in.}) \times (.2833 \text{ lb./cu. in.}) \div$$
$$(2,000 \text{ lb./ton}) = 224 \text{ tons}$$

This figure multiplied by the price per ton gives the selling price of the coil.

Under the TMW system, the customer pays only the amount that the surface area shipped would weigh if it were rolled at exactly the ordered gauge. The customer doesn't pay for the additional weight resulting from the steel being rolled heavier than the ordered gauge.

In recent years, the TMW program had been causing progressively larger losses for Buchanan. Accordingly, Mr. Palmintere felt that a review of the program and some discussion regarding its continuation were in order.

MR. PALMINTERE:   President

Gentlemen, I think you all know why we're here. In the last few months we've been taking a bath on our TMW billing program. According to these figures from Dave, we've lost approximately $6.9 million so far this year due to TMW (see Exhibit 1). Furthermore, as Exhibit 2 shows, our "percent giveaway" has been increasing steadily over the last 3 years. Couple this with rising prices for finished steel and you get the current state of our giveaway losses.

MR. HEILBURG:   Sales

Dave, just how are you computing the dollar loss due to TMW?

MR. HOUSTON:   Financial

For any particular product, we simply multiply the difference between the actual tons shipped and theoretical tons billed by the corresponding revenue-per-ton figure. The reason is that under normal billing practice we'd charge for the actual tons shipped, while under TMW we're only charging for the theoretical tons shipped. The cost of what we ship is the same either way.

MR. BIRRELL:   Controller

I don't think that's the appropriate way to figure the TMW loss, Dave. TMW essentially changed our billing practices from selling by the ton to selling by the foot. The customer stamps parts, say for fender panels, out of the coil. In order to produce the desired number of parts, he wants a certain number of feet at a particular gauge. When we roll heavier than the ordered minimum gauge, we're giving the customer something that he isn't particularly interested in having and doesn't want to pay for. The revenue will be the same whether we roll right on the ordered gauge or heavier than the ordered gauge, since the selling price of the coil is calculated using the actual footage and the ordered gauge rather than the actual gauge. What we're losing is the manufacturing cost of the giveaway weight. The overall loss is more like $6.7 million than $6.9 million for the first 6 months of 1979.

MR. LORACHUSKY:   Cost and Methods

Really, Andy, the fixed portion of the cost is irrelevant since it won't actually change. I agree that we should look at cost instead of revenue to measure our loss, but we should only consider the variable costs.

MR. BIRRELL:   Controller

Ignoring the fixed costs makes sense in short-run analyses, Ed, but TMW isn't a short-run problem. We've been in the program for 9 years already, and over that long a time frame nearly all of our costs are variable. I still think that full cost of the giveaway tonnage is the best measure of what we're losing.

MR. LORACHUSKY:   Cost and Methods

The question, Andy, is how much are we losing this year? The fixed costs are there regardless of our billing practices. What we're losing this year is only the variable cost of the steel.

MR. SCHMIDT:   Production Control

Whether we take a long- or short-run view of variable production costs may not make any difference anyway since most of our production costs vary more as a function of lineal footage than tonnage. Under TMW, the lineal footage is given. Therefore, nearly all the production costs are given. The problem is extra thickness, and that additional thickness doesn't cost us anything extra to produce aside from the additional material cost. Accordingly, we should be multiplying the difference between actual and theoretical tons by our hot-band costs (raw material) to get our relevant loss, in which case it goes down to about $4.9 million for the first half of 1979.

MR. FALENSKI:   Metallurgy

I agree with you except for one small point, Brad. You're ignoring our yields. For cold-roll and galvanized, the yield is 88%, while it's 87% for Unikote. In other words, we have to buy 1.136 tons of hot band in order to give away 1 ton of cold-roll or galvanized, and we have to buy 1.149 tons of full-finished cold-roll in order to give away 1 ton of Unikote. Taking this into consideration would raise our TMW dollar loss to $5.6 million for the period in question.

MR. HOUSTON:   Financial

What you're suggesting, Al, totally undercuts our basic accounting system. The entire steel industry, Buchanan included, measures costs on a per ton rather than a per foot basis. Standard costs per ton are designed to reflect run speed, gauge, and width variations. In other words, all of these other variables are taken into accounting in computing standard cost per ton for a given product. What we lose from the TMW giveaway therefore includes processing costs as well as material costs.

MR. SCHMIDT:    Production Control

Well, Dave, over the 2 to 5% deviations that we're talking about here, I just can't see that the processing costs will change. I still think it's only material cost that changes over this range.

MR. FALENSKI:    Metallurgy

You know, Brad, the more I think about it, the more I think that we may have been too hasty in dismissing Dave's argument about sales revenue as the relevant measure of our loss. The lineal feet aren't really fixed at all on a given TMW order. Let me give you an example. Suppose a customer orders 5,000 tons of .028-inch minimum gauge steel with a particular width and quality. That order is based on the customer's calculation of the weight needed to yield the desired lineal footage. In order to yield the desired number of lineal feet of the specified width and quality, we schedule, say, 5,500 tons of, say, .029 gauge. However, we end up running .030 gauge. We then bill the customer according to the theoretical weight of the actual footage shipped which, as Andy pointed out, is calculated using the ordered gauge. However, if we had "squeezed" that coil tighter to .028 thickness and converted that extra gauge into additional footage, the coil would have a higher selling price. The cost of the coil is whatever it is. The loss is due to producing the coil thicker instead of longer. Lost revenue per ton is thus the proper measure of the profit impact.

MR. BIRRELL:    Controller

Wait a minute, Al. That customer is only going to buy a given number of lineal feet from us over time because he only needs to stamp out a given number of parts. If we ship him longer coils now, he'll just cut back on future orders. Over time, we're already collecting all the revenue we're going to get. The problem is the extra weight of the footage that we're selling. Our loss is thus the cost of that extra weight.

MR. HEILBURG:    Sales

Andy, I think you're being too technical about the amount of footage the customer will take. Generally, he takes whatever footage is in the coil he ordered. Hell, a lot of the customers don't even have footage counters on their equipment.

MR. BIRRELL:    Controller

What we're talking about, Max, is a difference of opinion about the scrap control practices of our customers. I think their controls are pretty tight in the long run and you don't.

MR. PALMINTERE:    President

Well, any way you slice it, because of TMW our profits are less than they could be and should be. As I see it, we're giving away an average of 4.53% of our actual tonnage of these products according to the June figures (Exhibit 1). Al, can you give me some kind of a breakdown of that figure?

MR. FALENSKI:    Metallurgy

As a matter of fact, Phil, I just happen to have such a report with me [see Exhibit 3]. I used the percent giveaway figures for last March since they were a bit high, although not too far above the year-to-date average. Please bear in mind, however, that these numbers are pretty soft. As the table shows, the four main categories that our TMW loss falls into are incoming raw material, providing practices, operating practices, and reapplications of dispositioned material.

MR. HEILBURG:    Sales

Excuse me, Al, but I'm a little vague on some of the terms you're using. Can you fill me in on the meanings of 'providing' and 'operating' practices?

MR. FALENSKI:    Metallurgy

Sure thing, Max. First, when we're rolling steel, we aim for a particular gauge. However, the gauge that we finally produce varies around that target gauge. Sometimes it comes out heavier than aimed for, and sometimes lighter. Graphically, we get something like this:

If we aimed for the customer's ordered minimum gauge, some of the steel would come out too thin to be acceptable to the customer. This would lead to an increase in our 'light gauge claims,' which would really hurt our reputation in the market. To avoid this, we aim for a gauge that's sufficiently thicker than the ordered gauge; therefore, the actual gauge is almost always heavier than the ordered gauge, like this:

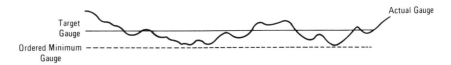

This is the purpose of our providing practices. They tell the amount by which we must aim above the ordered minimum gauge to ensure that almost none of the steel comes out lighter than that gauge.

Our providing practices can be broken down into the part pertaining to the steel and the part pertaining to the zinc-coating process. You see, just as we try to ensure that the steel satisfies minimum thickness requirements, we also want to avoid coating the galvanized products too lightly.

It may interest you to know that the deviation from the ordered minimum gauge that we aim for through our providing practices is significantly smaller than that considered to be acceptable by the American Iron and Steel Institute.

I've compiled some examples of the standard AISI tolerances, the associated percent deviations for various gauges, and the percent anticipated deviations resulting from our providing practices. Please take a minute to look these over.

| Gauge (in.) | Std. ½ AISI Tolerance | AISI Acceptable Deviation (%) | Buchanan's Providing Practice (%) Deviation |
|---|---|---|---|
| | | Cold-Roll | |
| .0168 | + .002 | 11.90 | 4 |
| .0304 | + .003 | 9.87 | 3 |
| .0494 | + .004 | 8.11 | 3 |
| .0786 | + .005 | 6.37 | 3 |
| | | Galvanized (Including Unikote) | |
| .0181 | + .003 | 16.57 | 4 |
| .035 | + .004 | 11.43 | 3 |
| .054 | + .005 | 9.26 | 4 |
| .069 | + .006 | 8.70 | 4 |
| .0876 | + .008 | 9.14 | 4 |

Given the percent deviation that's acceptable according to industry standards, it's perhaps less surprising that we're having so much trouble adhering to our strict divisional standards.

The operating practices category is composed of the cold mill, the sheet-temper mill, and zinc coating. To a large extent, the operating practices detail the difference between what we aim for and what we actually produce. As I mentioned before, to ensure that our steel is no thinner than a specified minimum gauge we aim, via our providing practices, for a slightly heavier gauge. However, as the last illustration shows, the actual gauge we produce varies around our aimed-for gauge. It's this variation that the 'operating practices' illustrate.

The portion of our giveaway coming from incoming raw material exists because whenever we order a hot band from one of our sister divisions, they roll the steel a bit heavier than the specified gauge, much as we do for our TMW customers. However, they bill us for the *actual* weight shipped rather than the theoretical weight. This category also captures the portion of our giveaway that's due to the 'crown' that's imparted to the hot band when our sister divisions produce it.

MR. HEILBURG:    Sales

Excuse me, Al, but that's another term that I've been meaning to ask you about. Could you briefly explain 'crown' to me?

MR. FALENSKI:  Metallurgy

Gladly, Max. Steel producers and steel users would like the finished product to have a 'flat' profile (see diagram A below):

A.

However, because of technical factors in the production process, the strip always comes out with a 'rounded' profile (see diagram B below):

B.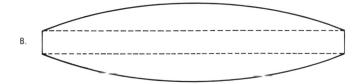

The area outside the desired rectangular shape is called 'crown.'

As I was saying, even for cold-roll and galvanized, where we're doing our own cold reduction, the crown that's imparted to the hot band stays on the steel throughout the finishing process. The greater the crown that our sister divisions send us, the more steel we end up giving away in the form of additional gauge to ensure that it satisfies the minimum-gauge requirements at the edges as well as at the center of the strip.

The cold mill is used to achieve the main portion of the reduction in gauge between the incoming hot band and the desired customer coil. Our percent loss increases whenever the cold mill takes less of a reduction than is being aimed for.

Among other things, the sheet-temper mill is designed to further reduce the gauge of the steel by 1%. However, it often takes as little as a .75% reduction, which explains the sheet-temper portion of our giveaway loss.

Finally, we come to the zinc-coating portion of our giveaway. Zinc coating increases our percent giveaway whenever we put a thicker coating on the steel than we're aiming for via our providing practices. This can be particularly important since zinc costs us about $750 per ton as compared to $310 per ton for hot bands. We can't really do much better here without spending the money to get better zinc measuring and monitoring equipment.

Now, are there any more questions on this information?

MR. HEILBURG:  Sales

Yes, Al, I've got a few. First of all, why isn't Unikote affected by our operating practices on the cold mills?

MR. SCHMIDT:    Production Control

I think I can answer that one, Max. We're buying full-finished cold roll from our sister divisions in order to make Unikote. Even though our giveaway percent is affected by that steel having passed through both hot and cold mills, it's been through both mills by the time that we get it. Accordingly, we don't know how much is accounted for by each mill. This component of our giveaway instead gets combined as part of incoming raw material.

MR. HEILBURG:    Sales

I see. Well, is there a reason for the relative importance of reapplications?

MR. FALENSKI:    Metallurgy

Due to the current AISI tolerances and customer concern with length more than gauge, we can wind up with deviations as high as 21% on reapplications of dispositioned material. Let me give you an example from a reapplication that I recently approved. A coil of galvanized with an ordered gauge of .0278 and an actual gauge of .0292 was 'dispositioned' (returned by the customer as unsatisfactory quality). The best 'reapplication' (reuse of the coil on an order requiring lower quality) that we were able to make within a reasonable amount of time was to a .0260-minimum-gauge order. In doing so, we immediately went from a poor 5.04% giveaway to an awful giveaway of 12.3%. Even though only about 10% of our total tonnage becomes re-applications, it all adds up to a pretty big dollar figure. A computer model is probably required to do much better on reapplications.

MR. HEILBURG:    Sales

All right, one more question. You've already explained the concept of crown. However, you mention crown compensation along with the providing practices. What's that?

MR. FALENSKI:    Metallurgy

Recall the illustration of our steel with its rounded contour. In order to be sure that the steel satisfies the minimum-gauge requirement at the edges as well as at the center of the strip, orders for which gauge is critical are rolled a bit heavier than our normal providing practices dictate. And as always seems to be the case, whenever we aim for extra gauge it comes out thicker still.

MR. PALMINTERE:    President

What I really want to know, Al, is, what's the profit-improvement potential from these factors?

MR. FALENSKI:    Metallurgy

Well, Mr. Palmintere, each of the percent giveaway figures multiplied by the appropriate total actual tons gives the tonnage effect of that factor. The tonnage effect multiplied by *some* dollar amount gives us that factor's profit impact. However, *which* dollar figure to use brings us back to where we were earlier in the meeting. What's the most appropriate—sales price, full cost, variable cost, raw material cost, or who knows what?

**MR. PALMINTERE:**   President

All right then, Dave, prepare a schedule for me showing the profit improvement potential for each of the factors in Exhibit 3 for the month of March. I'll be expecting it within the week. Good day, gentlemen.

## QUESTIONS

1   What, in your opinion, was the profit impact of TMW for the first 6 months of 1979? Be prepared to support your computation. (See Exhibits 2, 4, and 5 for necessary information.)
2   Prepare the schedule requested by Mr. Palmintere at the end of the meeting.
3   Consider the components of Buchanan's percent giveaway. In what order would you try to attack them, and why?
4   Can you think of a different breakdown of the percent giveaway figure that would provide more useful information?

| EXHIBIT 1 | | | | |
|---|---|---|---|---|
| | *Actual Tons* | *Theoretical Tons* | *Difference* | *Percent of Actual* | *Dollar Giveaway* |
| Unikote | | | | | |
| June | 7,881 | 7,442 | 439 | 5.57 | $   235,409 |
| Year-to-Date | 31,211 | 29,728 | 1,483 | 4.75 | 795,210 |
| Galvanized | | | | | |
| June | 22,746 | 22,043 | 703 | 3.09 | 358,249 |
| Year-to-Date | 153,919 | 148,996 | 4,923 | 3.20 | 2,537,228 |
| Cold-Rolled | | | | | |
| June | 28,377 | 26,846 | 1,531 | 5.40 | 616,427 |
| Year-to-Date | 198,728 | 189,710 | 9,018 | 4.54 | 3,643,760 |
| Total Composite | | | | | |
| June | 59,004 | 56,331 | 2,673 | 4.53 | 1,210,085 |
| Year-to-Date | 383,858 | 368,434 | 15,424 | 4.02 | 6,976,198 |

EXHIBIT 2

| Year | Unikote Actual Tons | Unikote Percent Giveaway | Galvanized Actual Tons | Galvanized Percent Giveaway | Cold-Roll Actual Tons | Cold-Roll Percent Giveaway |
|------|------|------|------|------|------|------|
| 1976 | 11,292 | 2.86 | 315,937 | 3.17 | 227,119 | 3.22 |
| 1977 | 57,907 | 3.10 | 244,089 | 3.31 | 247,960 | 3.50 |
| 1978 | 58,722 | 3.83 | 270,297 | 3.17 | 279,847 | 3.68 |
| 1/79 | 4,294 | 2.17 | 23,773 | 2.68 | 29,759 | 3.39 |
| 2/79 | 3,128 | 4.73 | 18,050 | 2.92 | 31,174 | 3.71 |
| 3/79 | 4,681 | 4.98 | 32,473 | 3.38 | 40,942 | 4.68 |
| 4/79 | 4,143 | 5.24 | 30,292 | 3.47 | 30,999 | 5.14 |
| 5/79 | 7,084 | 4.98 | 26,585 | 3.41 | 37,477 | 4.84 |
| 6/79 | 7,881 | 5.57 | 22,746 | 3.09 | 28,377 | 5.40 |
| 1979 Year-to-Date | 31,211 | 4.75 | 153,919 | 3.20 | 198,728 | 4.54 |

**EXHIBIT 3**
Rough Breakdown of TMW Percentage Giveaway by Products
March 1979

| | Unikote | Galvanized | Cold-Roll |
|------|------|------|------|
| Providing Practices | | | |
| Pickling, Cold Reduction, and Annealing (Including Crown Compensation) | 3.05 | 3.42 | 3.51 |
| Zinc Coating | .15 | .30 | — |
| Incoming Raw Material | 1.13 | .03 | .03 |
| Operating Practices | | | |
| Cold Mill | — | (1.27) | .65 |
| Sheet-Temper Mill | .20 | — | .10 |
| Zinc Coating | .25 | .40 | — |
| Reapplications of Distressed Material | .20 | .50 | .39 |
| Total | 4.98 | 3.38 | 4.68 |

EXHIBIT 4
Cost-Per-Ton Figures
March 1979

|  | Unikote | Galvanized | Cold-Roll |
|---|---|---|---|
| Raw Material Cost per Finished Ton | $471.00 | $358.00 | $352.00 |
| + Variable Cost Above per Ton | 35.40 | 40.75 | 25.75 |
| + Average Fixed Cost per Ton | 23.60 | 27.16 | 17.17 |
| = Mill Cost per Ton | 530.00 | 425.91 | 394.92 |
| + Average Allocated Depreciation per Ton | 7.00 | 4.97 | 4.06 |
| + Average Allocated Mill Overhead per Ton | 9.64 | 6.84 | 5.59 |
| + Average Allocated Selling, General, and Administrative Expenses per Ton | 8.67 | 6.15 | 5.03 |
| = Total Cost per Ton | $555.31 | $443.87 | $409.60 |
| Selling Price per Ton | $527.46 | $514.75 | $394.49 |
| Profit | ($27.85) | $70.88 | ($15.11) |

|  | Unikote | Galvanized | Cold-Roll |
|---|---|---|---|
| **6/79** | | | |
| Average Selling Price/Ton | $534 | $521 | $400 |
| Fully Absorbed Cost/Ton | 558 | 441 | 412 |
| Variable Cost/Ton | 508 | 397 | 379 |
| Material Cost/Ton | 471 | 358 | 352 |
| **5/79** | | | |
| Average Selling Price/Ton | 541 | 522 | 397 |
| Fully Absorbed Cost/Ton | 560 | 441 | 410 |
| Variable Cost/Ton | 509 | 397 | 378 |
| Material Cost/Ton | 471 | 358 | 352 |
| **4/79** | | | |
| Average Selling Price/Ton | 532 | 513 | 396 |
| Fully Absorbed Cost/Ton | 556 | 439 | 411 |
| Variable Cost/Ton | 506 | 396 | 378 |
| Material Cost/Ton | 471 | 358 | 352 |
| **3/79** | | | |
| Average Selling Price/Ton | 527 | 515 | 395 |
| Fully Absorbed Cost/Ton | 555 | 444 | 410 |
| Variable Cost/Ton | 506 | 399 | 378 |
| Material Cost/Ton | 471 | 358 | 352 |
| **2/79** | | | |
| Average Selling Price/Ton | 527 | 517 | 399 |
| Fully Absorbed Cost/Ton | 549 | 440 | 411 |
| Variable Cost/Ton | 503 | 396 | 378 |
| Material Cost/Ton | 471 | 358 | 352 |
| **1/79** | | | |
| Average Selling Price/Ton | 528 | 484 | 394 |
| Fully Absorbed Cost/Ton | 556 | 437 | 410 |
| Variable Cost/Ton | 506 | 394 | 378 |
| Material Cost/Ton | 471 | 358 | 352 |
| **1979 Year-to-Date** | | | |
| Average Selling Price/Ton | 533 | 512 | 397 |
| Fully Absorbed Cost/Ton | 557 | 441 | 411 |
| Variable Cost/Ton | 507 | 397 | 378 |
| Material Cost/Ton | 471 | 358 | 352 |

EXHIBIT 5

# Quality Pies, Inc.

In preparing its profit plan for 1980, the management of the Quality Pies Company ignored monthly seasonal variations because they were not significant. For the year as a whole, the profit before taxes was expected to total $480,000:

|  | 1980 Budget Amount |
|---|---|
| Sales | $4,800,000 |
| Standard Cost of Goods Sold |  |
| Material and Labor | 1,920,000 |
| Factory Overhead | 1,680,000 |
| Total Standard Cost | $3,600,000 |
| Gross Profit | $1,200,000 |
| Selling, General, and Administrative Expenses | 720,000 |
| Profit before Taxes | $ 480,000 |

Labor and materials were strictly variable with the quantity of production in the factory. That is, these costs are fixed at the unit level. The overhead in the factory included both fixed and variable elements; management's estimate was that, within a sales volume range of plus or minus $2,000,000 per year, variable factory overhead would be equal to 25% of material and labor cost. All of the selling and administrative cost was budgeted at a fixed amount except for sales commissions at 4% of sales.

This case is adapted from a similar exercise prepared by Professor Richard Vancil of the Harvard Business School. The case was written by Thomas Graham under the supervision of Professor John K. Shank.

Mr. Nicholas, the president of the company, approved the budget, stating that: "A profit of $40,000 a month isn't bad for a little company trying to compete against the food industry giants." During January, however, sales suffered an unexpected dip and production in the factory was also cut back to avoid an inordinate inventory accumulation. The results, which came as some surprise to the president, was that January showed a loss of $14,000.

Operating Statement
January 1980

| | | |
|---|---|---|
| Sales | | $280,000 |
| Standard Cost of Goods Sold | | 210,000 |
| Standard Gross Profit | | $ 70,000 |
| Manufacturing Variances | Favorable (unfavorable) | |
| Prime Cost Variance | $ (7,000) | |
| Factory Overhead | | |
| Spending Variance | 2,000 | |
| Volume Variance | (25,000) | (30,000) |
| Actual Gross Profit | | $ 40,000 |
| Selling and General Overhead | | 54,000 |
| Loss before Taxes | | $(14,000) |

## ASSIGNMENT

Although it is not necessary to do so, you may assume for calculation convenience that planned and actual selling price was $1 per unit.

1   Explain, as best you can with the data available, why the January profit was $54,000 less than the average monthly profit expected by the president.
2   What was the January production level?
3   How much did finished-goods inventory change in January?
4   What is the company's monthly breakeven volume?
5   Recalculate the planned profit and actual profit for January using direct costing.
6   Analyze the profit variance for January under direct costing.
7   Explain the difference between actual January profit as shown in the table and actual January profit under direct costing.

# Midwest Ice Cream Company

Frank Roberts, marketing vice-president of Midwest Ice Cream Company, was pleased when he saw the final earnings statement for the company for 1973 (see Exhibit 1). He knew that it had been a good year for Midwest, but he hadn't expected the results to be quite this good.

Only the year before the company had installed a new financial planning and control system. This was then the first year that figures comparing budgeted and actual results were available. Jim Peterson, president of Midwest, had asked Frank to make a short presentation at the next board of directors meeting commenting on the major reasons for the favorable operating income variance of $71,700. He asked him to draft his presentation in the next few days so that the two of them could go over it before the board meeting. Mr. Peterson wanted to illustrate to the board how an analysis of the profit variance could highlight those areas needing management attention as well as those deserving of a pat on the back.

## THE FINANCIAL PLANNING AND CONTROL SYSTEM AT MIDWEST ICE CREAM

The following description of the financial planning and control system which was installed at Midwest in 1972 is taken from an internal company operating manual.

Copyright © 1974 by the President and Fellows of Harvard College. Reproduced by permission. This case was prepared by Associate Professor John K. Shank and William J. Rauwerdink, Research Assistant, as the basis for class discussion rather than to illustrate either effective or ineffective handling of an administrative situation. Distributed by the Intercollegiate Case Clearing House, Soldiers Field, Boston, Mass. 02163. All rights reserved to the contributors. Printed in the U.S.A.

*The beginning point in making a profit plan is separating cost into fixed and variable categories. Some costs are pure variable and as such will require an additional amount with each increase in volume levels. The manager has little control over this type of cost other than to avoid waste. The accountant can easily determine the variable manufacturing cost per unit for any given product or package by using current prices and yield records. Variable marketing cost per unit is based on the allowable rate, for example, $.06 per gallon for advertising. Costs that are not pure variable are classified as fixed, but they, too, will vary if significant changes in volume occur. There will be varying degrees of sensitivity to volume changes among these costs, ranging from a point just short of pure variable to an extremely fixed type of expense which has no relationship to volume. The reason for differentiating between fixed and variable so emphatically is because a variable type cost requires no decision as to when to add or take off a unit; it is dictated by volume. Fixed costs, on the other hand, require a management judgment and decision to increase or decrease the cost. Sugar is an example of a pure variable cost. Each change in volume will automatically bring a change in the sugar cost; only the yield can be controlled. Route salesmen's salaries would be an example of a fixed cost that is fairly sensitive to volume, but not pure variable. As volume changes, pressure will be felt to increase or decrease this expense, but management must make the decision; the change in cost level is not automatic. Depreciation charges for plant would be an example of a relatively extreme fixed cost, in that large increases in volume can usually be realized before this type of cost is pressured to change. In both cases, the fixed cost requires a decision from management to increase or decrease the cost. It is this dilemma that management is constantly facing: to withstand the pressure to increase or be ready to decrease when the situation demands it. It would be a mistake to set a standard variable cost for items like route salesmen's salaries or depreciation based on past performance, because they must constantly be evaluated for better and more efficient methods of doing the task.*

*The first step in planning, then, is to develop a unit standard cost for each element of variable cost by product and package size. Examples of four different products and/or packages are shown in Step 1. As already pointed out, the accountant can do this by using current prices and yield records for material costs and current allowance rates for marketing costs. Advertising is the only cost element not fitting the explanation of a variable cost given in the preceding paragraph. Advertising costs are set by management decision rather than being an "automatic" cost item like sugar or packaging. In this sense, advertising is just route salesmen's expense. For our company, however, management has decided that the* allowance for advertising expense is equal to $.06 per gallon for the actual number of gallons sold. This management decision, therefore, has transformed advertising into an expense which is treated as variable for profit planning. After the total unit variable cost has been developed, this amount is subtracted from the selling price to arrive at a marginal contribution per unit, by product and package type. At any level of volume, it is easy to determine the contribution that should be generated to cover the fixed costs and provide profits. This will be illustrated in Step 4.

Step 2 is perhaps the most critical of all the phases in making a profit plan, because all plans are built around the anticipated level of sales activity. Much thought should be given in forecasting a realistic sales level and product mix. Consideration should be given to the number of days in a given period, as well as to the number of Fridays and Mondays, as these are two of the heaviest days and will make a difference in the sales forecast.

Other factors that should be considered are:

1   General economic condition of the marketing area
2   Weather
3   Anticipated promotions
4   Competition

Step 3 involves the setting of fixed-cost budgets based on management's judgment as to the need in light of the sales forecast. It is here that good planning makes for a profitable operation. The number of routes needed for both winter and summer volume are planned. The level of manufacturing payroll is set.[1] Insurance and taxes are budgeted, and so on. After Step 4 has been performed, it may be necessary to return to Step 3 and make adjustments to some of the costs that are discretionary in nature.

Step 4 is the profit plan itself. By combining our marginal contribution developed in Step 1 with our sales forecast, we arrive at a total marginal contribution by month. Subtracting the fixed cost budgeted in Step 3, we have an operating profit by months. As mentioned above, if this profit figure is not sufficient, then a new evaluation should be made of the fixed costs developed in Step 3.

The following four tables illustrate each of the four planning steps for a hypothetical ice cream plant.

---

[1] Because this system is based on a 1-year time frame, manufacturing labor is considered to be a fixed cost. The level of the manufacturing work force is not really variable until a time frame longer than 1 year is adopted.

Establish Standards for Selling Price, Variable Expenses,
and Marginal Contribution per Gallon of Vanilla Ice Cream

| | Regular | | | Premium |
|---|---|---|---|---|
| Item | 1-Gallon Paper Container | 1-Gallon Plastic Container | 2-Gallon Paper Container | 1-Gallon Plastic Container |
| Dairy Ingredients | $ .53 | $ .53 | $ .53 | $ .79 |
| Sugar | .15 | .15 | .15 | .15 |
| Flavor | .10 | .10 | .105 | .12 |
| Production | .10 | .16 | .125 | .16 |
| Warehouse | .06 | .08 | .07 | .08 |
| Transportation | .02 | .025 | .02 | .025 |
| Total Manufacturing | .96 | 1.045 | 1.00 | 1.325 |
| Advertising | .06 | .06 | .06 | .06 |
| Delivery | .04 | .04 | .04 | .04 |
| Total Marketing | .10 | .10 | .10 | .10 |
| Total | 1.06 | 1.145 | 1.10 | 1.425 |
| Selling Price | 1.50 | 1.70 | 1.45 | 2.40 |
| Marginal Contribution before Packaging | .44 | .555 | .35 | .975 |
| Packaging | .10 | .25 | .085 | .25 |
| Marginal Contribution per Gallon | .34 | .305 | .265 | .725 |

STEP 2
Vanilla Ice Cream Sales Forecast in Gallons

| | January | February | December | Total |
|---|---|---|---|---|
| 1 Gallon, Paper | 100,000 | 100,000 · · · | 100,000 | 1,200,000 |
| 1 Gallon, Plastic | 50,000 | 50,000 · · · | 50,000 | 600,000 |
| 2 Gallons, Paper | 225,000 | 225,000 · · · | 225,000 | 2,700,000 |
| 1 Gallon, Premium | 120,000 | 120,000 · · · | 120,000 | 1,440,000 |
| Total | 495,000 | 495,000 · · · | 495,000 | 5,940,000 |

Budget for Fixed Expenses

| | January | February | $\cdots\cdots$ December | Total |
|---|---|---|---|---|
| **Manufacturing Expense** | | | | |
| Labor | $ 7,280 | $ 7,280 | $\cdots\cdots$ $ 7,920 | $ 88,000 |
| Equipment repair | 3,332 | 3,332 | $\cdots\cdots$ 3,348 | 40,000 |
| Depreciation | 6,668 | 6,668 | $\cdots\cdots$ 6,652 | 80,000 |
| Taxes | 3,332 | 3,332 | $\cdots\cdots$ 3,348 | 40,000 |
| Total | $20,612 | $20,612 | $\cdots\cdots$ $21,268 | $248,000 |
| **Delivery Expense** | | | | |
| Salaries—General | $10,000 | $10,000 | $\cdots\cdots$ $10,000 | $120,000 |
| Salaries—Drivers | 10,668 | 10,668 | $\cdots\cdots$ 10,652 | 128,000 |
| Helpers | 10,668 | 10,668 | $\cdots\cdots$ 10,652 | 128,000 |
| Supplies | 668 | 668 | $\cdots\cdots$ 652 | 8,000 |
| Total | $32,004 | $32,004 | $\cdots\cdots$ $31,956 | $384,000 |
| **Administrative Expense** | | | | |
| Salaries | $ 5,167 | $ 5,167 | $\cdots\cdots$ $ 5,163 | $ 62,000 |
| Insurance | 1,667 | 1,667 | $\cdots\cdots$ 1,663 | 20,000 |
| Taxes | 1,667 | 1,667 | $\cdots\cdots$ 1,663 | 20,000 |
| Depreciation | 833 | 833 | $\cdots\cdots$ 837 | 10,000 |
| Total | $ 9,334 | $ 9,334 | $\cdots\cdots$ $ 9,326 | $112,000 |
| **Selling Expense** | | | | |
| Repairs | $ 2,667 | $ 2,667 | $\cdots\cdots$ $ 2,663 | $ 32,000 |
| Gasoline | 5,000 | 5,000 | $\cdots\cdots$ 5,000 | 60,000 |
| Salaries | 5,000 | 5,000 | $\cdots\cdots$ 5,000 | 60,000 |
| Total | $12,667 | $12,667 | $\cdots\cdots$ $12,663 | $152,000 |

STEP 4
The Profit Plan

| | Marginal Contribution (See Step 1) | Gallons Sold | January | February · · · December | Total |
|---|---|---|---|---|---|
| 1 Gallon, Paper | .34 | 100,000 | $ 34,000 | $ 34,000 · · · · $ 34,000 | $ 408,000 |
| 1 Gallon, Plastic | .305 | 50,000 | 15,250 | 15,250 · · · · 15,250 | 183,000 |
| 2 Gallons, Paper | .265 | 225,000 | 59,625 | 59,625 · · · · 59,625 | 715,500 |
| 1 Gallon, Premium | .725 | 120,000 | 87,000 | 87,000 · · · · 87,000 | 1,044,000 |
| Total Marginal Contribution | | | $195,875 | $195,875 · · · $195,875 | $2,350,500 |
| *Fixed Cost* (see Step 3) | | | | | |
| Manufacturing Expense | | | $ 20,612 | $ 20,612 · · · · $ 21,268 | $ 248,000 |
| Delivery Expense | | | 32,004 | 32,004 · · · · 31,956 | 384,000 |
| Administrative Expense | | | 9,334 | 9,334 · · · · 9,326 | 112,000 |
| Selling Expense | | | 12,667 | 12,667 · · · · 12,663 | 152,000 |
| Total Fixed | | | $ 74,617 | $ 74,617 · · · $ 75,213 | $ 896,000 |
| Operating Profit | | | $121,258 | $121,258 · · · $120,662 | $1,454,500 |
| Income Tax | | | 60,629 | 60,629 · · · · 60,331 | 727,250 |
| Net Profit | | | $ 60,629 | $ 60,629 · · · $ 60,331 | $ 727,250 |

To illustrate the control system, we will take the month of January and assume the level of sales activity for the month to be 520,000 gallons, as shown in Exhibit A. Looking back to our sales forecast (Step 2) we see that 495,000 gallons had been forecasted. When we apply our marginal contribution per unit for each product and package, we find that the 520,000 gallons have produced $6,125 less standard contribution than the 495,000 gallons would have produced at the forecasted mix. So even though there has been a nice increase in sales volume, the mix has been unfavorable. The $6,125 represents the difference between standard profit contribution at forecasted volume and standard profit contribution at actual volume. It is thus due to differences in volume and to differences in average mix. The impact of each of these two factors is shown on the bottom of Exhibit A.

Exhibit B shows a typical departmental budget sheet comparing actual costs with budget. A sheet is issued for each department, so the person responsible for a particular area of the business can see the items that are in line and those that need attention. In our example, there is an unfavorable operating variance of $22,750. You should note that the budget for variable cost items has been adjusted to reflect actual volume, thereby eliminating wide cost variances due strictly to the difference between planned and actual volume.

Since the level of fixed costs is independent of volume anyway, it is not necessary to adjust the budget for these items for volume differences. The original budget for fixed-cost items is still appropriate. The totals for each department are carried forward to an earnings statement, Exhibit C. We have assumed all other departments' actual and budget are in line, so the only operating variance is the one for manufacturing. This variance, added to the sales volume and mix variance of $6,125, results in an overall variance from the original plan of $28,875, as shown at the bottom of Exhibit C.

The illustration here has been on a monthly basis, but there is no need to wait until the end of the month to see what is happening. Each week, sales can be multiplied by the contribution factor to see how much standard contribution has been generated. This can be compared to one-fourth of the monthly forecasted contribution to see if volume and mix are in line with forecast. Neither is it necessary to wait until the end of the month to see if expenses are in line. Weekly reports of such items as production or sugar can be made, comparing budgeted with actual costs. By combining the variances as shown on weekly reports and adjusting the forecasted profit figure, an approximate profit figure can be had long before the books are closed and monthly statements issued. More important, action can be taken to correct an undesirable situation much sooner.

Following the four-step approach outlined above, the management group of Mid-west Ice Cream prepared a profit plan for 1973. The timetable they followed was as follows:

|  |  | *October 1972: Week* | | | | *November 1972: Week* | | | |
|---|---|---|---|---|---|---|---|---|---|
|  |  | *1* | *2* | *3* | *4* | *1* | *2* | *3* | *4* |
| I | Variable Cost Standards |  | X |  |  |  |  |  |  |
| II-A | Sales Forecast |  | X |  |  |  |  |  |  |
| II-B | Approval of Sales Forecast |  |  | X |  |  |  |  |  |
| III-A | Preliminary Payroll Budget |  |  | X |  |  |  |  |  |
| III-B | Preliminary Budget for Other Operating Expenses |  |  | X |  |  |  |  |  |
| III-C | Approval of Payroll Budget and Other Expenses Budget |  |  |  | X |  |  |  |  |
| IV-A | Preliminary Profit Plan |  |  |  |  | X |  |  |  |
| IV-B | Approval of Profit Plan |  |  |  |  |  | X |  |  |
| IV-C | Board of Directors Meeting |  |  |  |  |  |  | X |  |

Based on an anticipated overall ice cream market of about 11,440,000 gallons in their marketing area and a market share of 50%, Midwest forecasted overall gallon sales of 5,720,329 for 1973. Actually, this forecast was the same as the latest estimate of 1972 actual gallon sales.[2] Rather than trying to get too sophisticated on the first attempt at budgeting, Mr. Peterson had decided just to go with 1972's volume as 1973's goal or forecast. He felt that there was plenty of time in later years to refine the system by bringing in more formal sales-forecasting techniques and concepts.

This same general approach was also followed for variable product standard costs and for fixed costs. Budgeted costs for 1973 were just expected 1972 results, adjusted for a few items which were clearly out of line in 1972.

## *ACTUAL RESULTS FOR 1973*

By the spring of 1973 it had become clear that sales volume for 1973 was going to be higher than forecast. In fact, Midwest's actual sales for the year totaled over 5,968,000 gallons, an increase of about 248,000 gallons over budget. Market research data indicated that the total ice cream market in Midwest's marketing area was 12,180,000 gallons for the year as opposed to the budgeted figure of about 11,440,000 gallons.

---

[2] Since the 1973 budget was being done in October of 1972, final figures for 1972 were not yet available. The latest revised estimate of actual gallon volume for 1972 was thus used.

A summary of the profit for 1973 follows.

Profit Plan for 1973

|  | Standard Contribution Margin/Gallon | Forecasted Gallon Sales | Forecasted Contribution Margin |
|---|---|---|---|
| Vanilla | $.4329 | 2,409,854 | $1,043,200 |
| Chocolate | .4535 | 2,009,061 | 911,100 |
| Walnut | .5713 | 48,883 | 28,000 |
| Buttercrunch | .4771 | 262,185 | 125,000 |
| Cherry Swirl | .5153 | 204,774 | 105,500 |
| Strawberry | .4683 | 628,560 | 294,400 |
| Pecan Chip | .5359 | 157,012 | 84,100 |
| Total | $.4530 | 5,720,329 | $2,591,300 |

Breakdown of Budgeted Total Expenses

|  | Variable Costs | Fixed Costs | Total |
|---|---|---|---|
| Manufacturing | $5,888,100 | $ 612,800 | $6,500,900 |
| Delivery | 187,300 | 516,300 | 703,600 |
| Advertising | 553,200 | — | 553,200 |
| Selling | — | 368,800 | 368,800 |
| Administrative | — | 448,000 | 448,000 |
| Total | $6,628,600 | $1,945,900 | $8,574,500 |

Recap

| Sales | $9,219,900 |
|---|---|
| Variable Cost of Sales | 6,628,600 |
| Contribution Margin | 2,591,300 |
| Fixed Costs | 1,945,900 |
| Income from Operations | $ 645,400 |

The revised profit plan for the year at the actual volume level is shown on page 166.

The fixed costs in the revised profit plan are the same as before, $1,945,900. The variable costs, however, have been adjusted to reflect a volume level of 5,968,000 gallons instead of 5,720,000 gallons, thereby eliminating wide cost variances due strictly to the difference between planned volume and actual volume. Assume, for example, that cartons are budgeted at $.04 per gallon. If we forecast volume of 10,000 gallons, the budget allowance for cartons is $400. If we actually sell only 8,000 gallons but use $350 worth of cartons, it is misleading to say that there is a favorable variance of $50. The variance is clearly unfavorable by $30. This only shows up if we adjust the budget to the actual volume level.

Revised Profit Plan for 1973
(Budgeted Profit at Actual Volume)

| | Standard Contribution Margin/Gallon | Actual Gallon Sales | Standard Contribution Margin |
|---|---|---|---|
| Vanilla | $.4329 | 2,458,212 | $1,064,200 |
| Chocolate | .4535 | 2,018,525 | 915,400 |
| Walnut | .5713 | 50,124 | 28,600 |
| Buttercrunch | .4771 | 268,839 | 128,300 |
| Cherry Swirl | .5153 | 261,240 | 134,600 |
| Strawberry | .4683 | 747,049 | 349,800 |
| Pecan Chip | .5359 | 164,377 | 88,100 |
| Total | $.4539 | 5,968,366 | $2,709,000 |

Breakdown of Budgeted Total Expenses

| | Variable Costs | Fixed Costs | Total |
|---|---|---|---|
| Manufacturing | $6,113,100 | $ 612,800 | $6,725,900 |
| Delivery | 244,500 | 516,300 | 760,800 |
| Advertising | 578,700 | – | 578,700 |
| Selling | – | 368,800 | 368,800 |
| Administrative | – | 448,000 | 448,000 |
| Total | $6,936,300 | $1,945,900 | $8,882,200 |

Recap

| | |
|---|---|
| Sales | $9,645,300 |
| Variable Costs of Sales | 6,936,300 |
| Contribution Margin | 2,709,000 |
| Fixed Costs | 1,945,900 |
| Income from Operations | $ 763,100 |

| | | |
|---|---|---|
| Carton Allowance | = | $.04 per gallon |
| Forecast Volume | = | 10,000 gallons |
| Carton Budget | = | $400 |
| Actual Volume | = | 8,000 gallons |
| Actual Carton Expense | = | $350 |

Variance (Based on Forecast Volume) = $400 − $350 = $50F
Variance (Based on Actual Volume) = $320 − $350 = $30U

For costs which are highly volume dependent, variances should be based on a budget which reflects the volume of operation actually attained. Since the level of fixed costs is independent of volume anyway, it is not necessary to adjust the budget for these items for volume differences. The original budget for fixed-cost items is still appropriate.

Exhibit 1 referred to earlier is the earnings statement for the year. The figures for the month of December have been excluded for purposes of this case. Exhibit 2· is the detailed expense breakdown for the manufacturing department. The detailed expense breakdowns for the other departments have been excluded for purposes of this case.

## ANALYSIS OF THE 1973 PROFIT VARIANCE

Three days after Jim Peterson asked Frank Roberts to pull together a presentation for the board of directors analyzing the profit variance for 1973, Frank came into Jim's office to review his first draft. He showed Jim the following schedule:

| | | |
|---|---|---|
| Favorable Variance Due to Sales: | | |
| Volume | $117,700F | |
| Price[a] | 12,000F | $129,700F |
| Unfavorable Variance Due to Operations: | | |
| Manufacturing | $ 99,000U | |
| Delivery | 54,000F | |
| Advertising | 29,000U | |
| Selling | 6,000F | |
| Administration | 10,000F | 58,000U |
| Net Variance—Favorable | | $ 71,700F |

[a]This price variance is the difference between the standard sales value of the gallons actually sold and the actual sales value ($9,657,300 − $9,645,300).

Frank said that he planned to give each member of the board of directors a copy of this schedule and then to comment briefly on each of the items. Jim Peterson said he thought the schedule was okay as far as it went, but that it just didn't highlight things in a manner which indicated what corrective actions should be taken in 1974 or indicated the real causes for the favorable overall variance. He suggested that Frank try to break down the sales volume variance into the part attributable to sales mix, the part attributable to market share shifts, and the part actually attributable to volume changes. He also suggested breaking down the manufacturing variance to indicate what main corrective actions are called for in 1974 to erase the unfavorable variance: how much of the total was due to price diffeences versus quantity differences, for example. Finally, he suggested that Frank call on John Vance, the company controller, if he needed some help in the mechanics of breaking out these different variances.

As Frank Roberts returned to his office, he considered Jim Peterson's suggestion of getting John Vance involved in revising the schedule to be presented to the board. Frank did not want to consult John Vance unless it was absolutely necessary because Vance always went overboard on the technical aspects of any accounting problem. Frank couldn't imagine a quicker way to put the board members to sleep than to throw one of Vance's number-filled six-page memos at them. Jim Peterson specifically wants a nontechnical presentation for the board, Frank thought to himself, and that rules out John Vance. Besides, he thought, you don't have to be a CPA to focus on the key variance areas from a general management viewpoint.

A telephone call to John Vance asking about any written materials dealing with mix variances and volume variances produced, in the following day's mail, the two-page excerpt from the company accounting manual, which is reproduced as Appendix A. Armed with this excerpt and his common sense, Frank Roberts dug in again to the task of preparing a nontechnical breakdown of the profit variance for the year.

## QUESTIONS

1   What changes, if any, would you make in the variance analysis schedule proposed by Frank Roberts?

2   Can the suggestions offered by Jim Peterson be incorporated without making the schedule "too technical" for the board of directors?

3   Indicate the corrective actions you would take for 1974, based on this profit variance analysis, if you were Jim Peterson. Also indicate those areas which deserve commendation for 1973 performance.

## EXHIBIT A
### January

|  | Actual Gallon Sales | Standard Contribution per Gallon | Total Standard Contribution |
|---|---|---|---|
| 1 Gallon, Paper | $ 90,000 | $.34 | $ 30,600 |
| 1 Gallon, Plastic | 95,000 | .305 | 28,975 |
| 2 Gallons, Paper | 245,000 | .265 | 64,925 |
| 1 Gallon, Premium | 90,000 | .725 | 65,250 |
| Total | $520,000 |  | $189,750 |
| Forecast (Step 2) |  |  |  |

495,000 gallons

| Forecasted Marginal Contribution (at 495,000 Gallons) | 195,875 |
|---|---|
| Over (Under) Forecast | (6,125) |

|  | Planned | Actual |
|---|---|---|
| Gallons | 495,000 | 520,000 |
| Contribution | $195,875 | $189,750 |
| Average per Gallon | $.3957 | $.3649 |
| Difference | $.0308 |  |

Variance Due to Volume
25,000 gallons X $.3957 =   $  9,892F

Variance Due to Mix
$.0308 X 520,000 gallons =   16,017U
Total variance = $  6,125U

aF, favorable; U, unfavorable.

## EXHIBIT B
### Manufacturing Cost of Goods Sold
### January

| Month | | | Year-to-Date | |
|---|---|---|---|---|
| Actual | Budget | | Actual | Budget |
| $312,744 | $299,000 | Dairy Ingredients | | |
| 82,304 | 78,000 | Sugar | | |
| 56,290 | 55,025 | Flavorings | | |
| 38,770 | 37,350 | Warehouse | | |
| 70,300 | 69,225 | Production | | |
| 11,514 | 11,325 | Transportation | | |
| $571,922 | $549,925 | Subtotal—Variable | | |
| 7,300 | 7,280 | Labor | | |
| 4,065 | 3,332 | Equipment Repair | | |
| 6,668 | 6,668 | Depreciation | | |
| 3,332 | 3,332 | Taxes | | |
| $ 21,365 | $ 20,612 | Subtotal—Fixed | | |
| $593,287 | $570,537 | Total | | |

## EXHIBIT C
### Earnings Statement
### January

| Month | | | Year-to-Date | |
|---|---|---|---|---|
| *Actual* | *Budget* | | *Actual* | *Budget* |
| $867,750 | $867,750 | Total Ice Cream Sales | | |
| $593,287 | $570,537 | Manufacturing Cost of Goods Sold | | |
| 52,804 | 52,804 | Delivery Expense | | |
| 31,200 | 31,200 | Advertising Expense | | |
| 76,075 | 76,075 | Packaging Expense | | |
| 12,667 | 12,667 | Selling Expense | | |
| 9,334 | 9,334 | Administrative Expense | | |
| $775,367 | $752,617 | Total Expense | | |
| 92,383 | $115,133 | Profit or Loss | | |
| 46,192 | — | Provision for Income Taxes | | |
| $ 46,191 | — | Net Profit or (Loss) | | |

| | | |
|---|---|---|
| Actual Profit before Taxes | 92,383 | (1) |
| Original Profit Forecast (Step 4) | 121,258 | (2) |
| Revised Profit Forecast Based on Actual Volume | 115,133 | (3) |

Variance Due to Volume and Mix
(Unfavorable)
$$= \underset{(2)}{121,258} - \underset{(3)}{115,133} = 6,125\text{U}$$

Variance Due to Operations
(Unfavorable)
$$= \underset{(3)}{115,133} - \underset{(1)}{92,383} = 22,750\text{U}$$

Total Variance
$$= (\underset{(2)}{121,258} - \underset{(1)}{92,383}) = 28,875\text{U}$$

**EXHIBIT 1**
MIDWEST ICE CREAM COMPANY
Earnings Statement
December 31, 1973

| Month | | | Year-to-Date | |
| Actual | Budget | | *Actual* | *Budget* |
|---|---|---|---|---|
| | | Sales–Net | $9,657,300 | $9,645,300 |
| | | Manufacturing Cost of Goods Sold | | |
| | | Schedule A-2a | 6,824,900 | 6,725,900 |
| | | Delivery Schedule A-3 | 706,800 | 760,800 |
| | | Advertising–Schedule A-4 | 607,700 | 578,700 |
| | | Selling–Schedule A-5 | 362,800 | 368,800 |
| | | Administrative–Schedule A-7 | 438,000 | 448,000 |
| | | Total Expenses | $8,940,200 | $8,882,200 |
| | | | | |
| | | Income from Operations | $ 717,100 | $ 763,100 |
| | | Other Income Schedule A-8 | 12,500 | 12,500 |
| | | Other Expense Schedule A-9 | 6,000 | 6,000 |
| | | Income before Taxes | 723,600 | $ 769,600 |
| | | Provision for Income Taxes | 361,800 | |
| | | Net Earnings | $ 361,800 | |

Analysis of Variance from Forecasted Operating Income

| Month | | | Year-to-Date | |
| Actual | Budget | | *Actual* | *Budget* |
|---|---|---|---|---|
| | | (1) Actual Income from Operations | $ 717,100 | |
| | | (2) Budgeted Profit at Forecasted Volume | 645,400 | |
| | | (3) Budgeted Profit at Actual Volume | 763,100 | |
| | | Variance Due to Sales Volume [(3) minus (2)] | 117,700F | |
| | | Variance Due to Operations [(1) minus (3)] | 46,000U | |
| | | Total Variance [(1) minus (2)] | $ 71,700U | |

aSchedules A-3 through A-9 have not been included in this case. Schedule A-2 is reproduced as Exhibit 2.

## EXHIBIT 2
### MIDWEST ICE CREAM COMPANY
Schedule A-2
Manufacturing Cost of Goods Sold
December 31, 1973

| Month | | | Year-to-Date | |
|---|---|---|---|---|
| Actual | Budget | | Actual | Budget |
| | | Variable Costs | | |
| | | Dairy Ingredients | $3,679,900 | $3,648,500 |
| | | Milk Price Variance | 57,300 | — |
| | | Sugar | 599,900 | 596,800 |
| | | Sugar Price Variance | 23,400 | — |
| | | Flavoring (Including Fruits and Nuts) | 946,800 | 982,100 |
| | | Cartons | 567,200 | 566,900 |
| | | Plastic Wrap | 28,700 | 29,800 |
| | | Additives | 235,000 | 251,000 |
| | | Supplies | 31,000 | 35,000 |
| | | Miscellaneous | 3,000 | 3,000 |
| | | Subtotal | $6,172,200 | $6,113,100 |
| | | | | |
| | | Fixed Costs | | |
| | | Labor—Cartonizing and Freezing | $ 425,200 | $ 390,800 |
| | | Labor—Other | 41,800 | 46,000 |
| | | Repairs | 32,200 | 25,000 |
| | | Depreciation | 81,000 | 81,000 |
| | | Electricity and Water | 41,500 | 40,000 |
| | | Miscellaneous | 1,500 ⎫ | 30,000 |
| | | Spoilage | 29,500 ⎭ | — |
| | | Subtotal | $ 652,700 | $ 612,800 |
| | | Total | $6,824,900 | $6,725,900 |

## APPENDIX A
### Step 1: Compute Planned Profit Contribution

| Product | Planned Sales (Units) | Standard Profit Contribution per Unit | Planned Profit Contribution |
|---|---|---|---|
| A | 16,000 | $1.0152 | $16,243 |
| B | 8,000 | .9514 | 7,611 |
| C | 20,000 | .8529 | 17,058 |
| D | 20,000 | .7921 | 15,842 |
| E | 8,000 | .7504 | 6,003 |
| F | 8,000 | .9365 | 7,492 |
| Total | 80,000 | Standard Profit Contribution at Planned Volume | $70,249 |

APPENDIX A (continued)

Step 2: Compute Standard Profit Contribution at Actual Volume

| Product | Actual Sales (Units) | Standard Profit Contribution per Unit | Standard Profit Contribution |
|---|---|---|---|
| A | 5,000 | $1.0152 | $ 5,076 |
| B | 5,000 | .9514 | 4,757 |
| C | 5,000 | .8529 | 4,265 |
| D | 36,000 | .7921 | 28,516 |
| E | 28,000 | .7504 | 21,011 |
| F | 5,000 | .9365 | 4,683 |
| Total | 84,000 | | |

Standard Profit Contribution at Actual Volume $68,308

Step 3: Compare Planned Standard Contribution with Actual Standard Contribution

From Step 1 $70,249
From Step 2 68,308
Difference $ 1,941U

| | Planned | Actual |
|---|---|---|
| Units | 80,000 | 84,000 |
| Standard Contribution | $70,249 | $68,308 |
| Average per Unit | $ .879 | $ .814 |
| Difference | $ .065 Unfavorable | |

Step 4: Compute the Volume and Mix Variances

Variance Due to Volume:
4,000 units × $.879 = 3,512F

Variance Due to Mix:
$.065 × 84,000 units = 5,453U
1,941U

Total Variance = 1,941U = Mix Variance + Volume Variance

173

# Kinkead Equipment, Ltd.

Andrew MacGregor, managing director of Kinkead Equipment, Ltd., glanced at the summary profit and loss statement for 1978 which he was holding (Exhibit 1), then tossed it to Douglas McCosh and looked out the window of his office overlooking the industrial center of Glasgow.

*As you can see Douglas, we beat our turnover goal for the year, improved our trading margin a bit, and earned more profit than we had planned. Although our selling costs did seem to grow faster than our turnover, all things considered, I would say 1978 was a good year for the firm.*

Douglas McCosh, a recent graduate of a well-known European business school, was serving a training period as executive assistant to Mr. MacGregor. He looked over the figures and nodded his agreement.

*"Douglas, I'd like you to prepare a short report for the managing committee meeting next week summarizing the key factors which account for the favorable overall profit variance of 24,000 pounds. That might not be much for a firm like ours, but it would still pay your salary for quite a while, wouldn't it," he laughed. "I think you're about ready to make a presentation to the committee if you can pull together a good report."*

*Check with the financial director's staff for any additional data you may need or want. Just remember to keep it on a commonsense level—*

This case was prepared by Professor John Shank based on materials originally collected by Professor Frank Aguilar. It is designed for class discussion rather than to reflect either effective or ineffective handling of an administrative situation. All rights reserved.

*no high-powered financial double-talk. How about giving me a draft to look at in a day or so?*

Douglas McCosh smiled somewhat meekly as he rose to return to his office. "I'll give it a try, sir," he said. His first step was to gather the additional information shown in Exhibit 2.

## REQUIRED

Prepare the report which you feel Douglas McCosh should present to Mr. MacGregor.

**EXHIBIT 1**
**KINKEAD EQUIPMENT, LTD.**
Preliminary Operating Results
January 15, 1979
(Thousands of Pounds)

|  |  | *Budget 1978* | *Percent of Turnover* | *Actual 1978* | *Percent of Turnover* |
|---|---|---|---|---|---|
| Turnover |  | £6,215 | (100) | £6,319 | (100) |
| Trading Margin |  | 2,590 | (41.7) | 2,660 | (42.1) |
| Less Other Expenses |  |  |  |  |  |
| Selling | £706 |  | (11.4) | £740 | (11.7) |
| Administrative | 320 |  | (5.1) | 325 | (5.1) |
| Research | 318 | 1,344 | (5.1) | 325 | 1,390 | (5.1) |
| Profit before Taxes |  | £1,246 | (20.05) |  | £1,270 | (20.10) |

Summary for 1978

|  | *Budget* | *Actual* | *Variance* |
|---|---|---|---|
| Turnover | £6,215 | £6.319 | 104F |
| Expenses | 4,969 | 5,049 | 80U |
| Profit before Taxes | £1,246 | £1,270 | 24F |

EXHIBIT 2
Additional Information[a]

| | Electric Meters | Electronic Instruments |
|---|---|---|
| Selling Prices per Unit | | |
| Average Standard Price | £30.00 | £150.00 |
| Average Actual Prices, 1978 | 29.00 | 153.00 |
| Product Costs per Unit | | |
| Average Standard Manufacturing Cost | 15.00 | 40.00 |
| Average Actual Manufacturing Cost | 16.00 | 42.00 |
| Average Standard Selling Commission | 1.00 | 15.00 |
| Average Actual Selling Commission | .98 | 14.90 |
| Volume Information | | |
| Units produced and sold—actual | 65,369 | 28,910 |
| Units produced and sold—planned | 82,867 | 24,860 |
| Total Industry Turnover, 1978 | £24,860,000 | £37,290,000 |
| Kinkead's Share of the Market—Planned | 10% | 10% |
| Kinkead's Share of the Market—Actual | 10% | 8% |

Firm-wide Expenses
(Thousands of Pounds)

| | Planned | Actual |
|---|---|---|
| Fixed Manufacturing Expenses | £1,388 | £1,399 |
| Fixed Selling Expenses | 250 | 245 |
| Fixed Administrative Expenses | 320 | 325 |
| Fixed Research Expenses | 318 | 325 |

[a]Kinkead's products are grouped into two main lines of business for internal reporting purposes. Each line includes many separate products, which are averaged together for purposes of this case.

# Martin Products, Inc.

Fred Martin, President of Martin Products, Inc., called Irene Hall into his office one morning during early November of 1974. Irene was a recent business school graduate who was working as an assistant to Fred Martin. "Irene," he said, "look at this item I clipped out of the latest issue of the *Financial Executive.*"

## SEC Requires Explanation of Material Changes

*In a significant move into a new area, the SEC now requires a company filing with it to explain any material changes in annual revenues and expenses. In the past, the SEC has, for the most part, allowed financial state-ments to speak for themselves. Now a company must comment on them under a separate cap-tion, Management's Discussion and Analysis of the Summary of Operations.*

He went on: "The SEC is currently considering a ruling that would require firms to include in their annual reports an analysis of why reported profits in the current year differ from profits reported last year. Their idea sounds like a good one to me and I'd like to implement it in our upcoming annual report, regardless of

Copyright © 1975 by the President and Fellows of Harvard College. Reproduced by permission. This case was prepared by Associate Professor John K. Shank, as the basis for class discussion rather than to illustrate effective or ineffective handling of an administrative situation. Distributed by the Intercollegiate Case Clearing House, Soldiers Field, Boston, Mass. 02163. All rights reserved to the contributors. Printed in the U.S.A.

how they decide. I'd like you to take the figures from last year and this year and prepare an analysis of the variation. You must have had some training in that in business school. I don't want to get our accounting department involved unless we have to because I want to keep the analysis on a commonsense level."

Fred Martin handed Irene the data shown in Exhibit 1. "I'd like to have a draft to look at by lunchtime," he said.

## REQUIRED

Prepare an analysis of why the income before taxes declined $10,500 between fiscal 1973 and fiscal 1974. You may assume the inventory to be valued at $.75 per unit in both years.

### EXHIBIT 1
#### For the Year Ended October 31

|                                      | 1973 | 1974 |
|--------------------------------------|------|------|
| Sales                                | $250,000[a] | $262,500[a] |
| Cost of Goods Sold                   | 150,000[b] | 174,500[b] |
| Gross Margin                         | $100,000 | $ 88,000 |
| Selling, General, and Administrative | 64,000[c] | 62,500[c] |
| Income before Taxes                  | $ 36,000 | $ 25,000 |

| 1973 | 1974 |
|------|------|
| [a]200,000 units at $1.25. | [a]210,000 units @ $1.25. |
| [b]200,000 units at $.75. | [b]Including all factory cost variances. |
| [c]$.06 per unit sold + $52,000. | [c]$.06 per unit + $49,900. |
| Production equaled sales in 1973. | Production was 160,000 units in 1974. |

Production costs per unit were as follows:

| Material Cost | $.30 | (.5 lb × $.60/lb) | 85,000 lb of material was consumed at a price of $.70/lb. |
|---|---|---|---|
| Labor Cost | .15 | ($6/hr ÷ 40 units/hr) | 3,600 labor hours were used at a rate of $6.25/hr. |
| Variable Overhead | .05 | (.05/unit) | Variable overhead incurred was $9,000 |
| Fixed Overhead | .25* | | |
| | .75 | | |

*The fixed overhead per unit is based on $50,000 of cost and normal production volume of 200,000 units.

# Ramada Inns-Europe (A)

The following financial data and comments are excerpted from the response by
Ramada Inns, Inc., to the request by the Financial Accounting Standard Board
for public comment on its exposure draft on foreign currency accounting.

*Ramada translates its foreign currency statements into U.S. dollars using
the current-noncurrent method and any resulting translation gains or losses
are included in current net income. As of Feburary 28, 1975, Ramada
Europe's Consolidated balance sheet and its balance sheet exposure (stated
in equivalent U.S. dollars and based on the current-noncurrent translation
method) were as follows:*

|  | Balance Sheet (at 2/28/75) | Exposure Unexposed | Exposure Exposed |
|---|---|---|---|
| Assets |  |  |  |
| Cash, Receivables | $ 2,777 |  | $2,777 |
| Inventory, Prepaids | 317 |  | 317 |
| Net Fixed Assets | 35,434 | $35,434 |  |
| Deferred and Other | $ 1,490 | 1,490 |  |
|  | $40,018 | $36,924 | $3,094 |

Copyright © 1976 by the President and Fellows of Harvard College. Reproduced by permission. This case was prepared by Associate Professor John K. Shank as a basis for class discussion rather than to illustrate either effective to ineffective handling of an administrative
situation.

|  | Balance Sheet (at 2/28/75) | Exposure | |
|  |  | Unexposed | Exposed |
| --- | --- | --- | --- |
| Equities |  |  |  |
| Short-Term Payables | $ 3,091 |  | $3,091 |
| Long-Term Debt: |  |  |  |
| Swedish Kronor | 5,465 |  |  |
| German Marks | 16,090 |  |  |
| French Francs | 2,751 |  |  |
| Belgian Francs | 5,026 |  |  |
| Total | $29,332 | $29,332 |  |
| Equity and U.S. Dollar Debt | 7,595 | 7,595 |  |
|  | $40,018 | $36,927 | $3,091 |
| Net Exposure (Long) |  |  | $3 |

Several points are apparent from the balance sheet and exposure report:

1   Ramada Europe is very capital intensive. (Essentially all fixed assets represent the cost of hotels which are 100% owned by Ramada Europe.)
2   Ramada Europe has financed its hotels largely with foreign currency debt (most debt is 15 to 25-year mortgage debt).
3   Ramada's exposure to translation gains and losses under the current-non-current method is negligible.

*We feel that the monetary-nonmonetary translation method is not appropriate for Ramada and that this translation method violates the accounting principle of matching revenue and expenses when applied to Ramada.*

*In our opinion the proper translation method for a company such as Ramada is the current rate method. Our reasoning for this opinion can first be illustrated by reference to the flowchart [shown in Exhibit 1] which describes our approach in building, financing, and operating a foreign hotel.*

*From the flowchart it is apparent to us that only our equity and U.S. dollar loans are exposed. These are exposed because foreign currency earnings and cash flow are used to pay dividends and repay U.S. dollar loans. Following this reasoning, the current rate method is the appropriate method for Ramada since under this method our translation gains and losses would be equal to our total dollar loans and equity, times the percentage by which the U.S. dollar changes in value, relative to the local currency in each country of operation. . . .*

*We have not adopted the current rate method because it is not permissible under present accounting rules. We therefore have adopted the current-*

*noncurrent method, which is permitted and which provides much more realistic results for Ramada than the monetary-nonmonetary method. . . .*

*The monetary-nonmonetary method as proposed in the draft would essentially force us to finance all future foreign hotels with U.S. dollars in order to minimize translation losses. This would be unfortunate because (a) it would be against the U.S. public interest, as it would cause an outflow of U.S. dollars; (b) it would hamper our expansion if the U.S. government should again impose controls such as the former OFDI regulations; and (c) financing in U.S. dollars runs counter to what we should do from an economic standpoint. . . .*

*In our opinion the monetary-nonmonetary translation method is not appropriate for Ramada or other capital-intensive companies which have similar operations. We believe that the current rate method is clearly the most appropriate for Ramada, and that the Board should permit the use of this method—at least for certain types of companies such as Ramada.*

## QUESTIONS

1   Calculate the "exposure" to the translation gains or losses for Ramada-Europe under the "monetary-nonmentary" (M/NM) translation method and the "all current rate" (CR) translation method.[1]

2   If the average of all foreign currencies in which Ramada-Europe has borrowed devalued 10% versus the dollar in 1975, what translation gain or loss would Ramada-Europe report in 1975 under the M/NM method? What gain or loss qould be reported under the CR translation method? What about an average 10% upward revaluation versus the dollar?

3   Should Ramada-Europe now finance European hotels with U.S. dollar loans rather than with local currency loans?

4   Which translation method should Ramada use, internally, to assess the performance of its foreign operations?

---

[1] Assume for question 1 that up to 1975 historic exchange rates for Ramada are about equal to current exchange rates, on average.

**EXHIBIT 1**
Building, Financing, and Operating a Ramada Inn Abroad

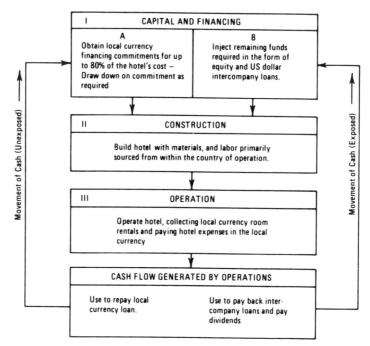

# Infant Care, Inc.

Seymor Phillipson, chairman of the board, attended the monthly meeting of the board of directors with much on his mind. "Gentlemen, now that we have foreign subsidiaries, our problems have multiplied. We must act now or we will lose control of the situation."

Infant Care, Inc., a major domestic producer of infant formula and related baby food products, had been experiencing problems in the world market. The company's products had experienced great popularity worldwide, especially in the underdeveloped Third World countries. The problems began when the cost of fuel increased dramatically and the Third World countries began asserting their independence. In the past, Infant Care had used its only plant, located in Savannah, Georgia, to manufacture all the products sold worldwide. Transportation costs had risen so dramatically that it no longer was feasible to supply the world markets from the American plant. In addition, the governments of many underdeveloped countries began to move in the direction of requiring that only companies with local production could sell in their country. These orders stemmed from a desire to increase the number of jobs for the local population and to help the foreign exchange problems by reducing dollar imports. The government of Brazil had recently proposed such an order applying to agricultural foostuffs, including Infant Care's products.

These two developments required the company to restructure the distribution system for its products. After much consideration, the management decided to expand its production facilities and to locate the new plants in foreign countries.

This case is adapted from a similar exercise written by Dr. Mary Wehle, formerly of the Harvard Business School. The case was written by Mr. Thomas Graham under the supervision of Professor John K. Shank.

One of those countries of course must be Brazil or Infant Care would lose that market for its products. The other country was Germany. Because of its central European location, the plant could serve the European and surrounding markets without the high transportation costs now required to ship the products from Georgia.

Infant Care searched for a local manufacturer in these countries whose facilities would be most compatible with its operations. Two manufacturers were finally located, Kinderstoffe in Nuremburg, and Bahia Products in Rio de Janeiro. Both were small operations with their own sales force. Kinderstoffe was a producer of milk products and Bahia packaged traditional baby foods.

Mr. Phillipson continued his discussion of the situation: "Now that we have acquired these companies, we must decide on the method of management. We haven't used a formal control system in the past because we had only one plant, which could be managed by our present team. We can't maintain as tight control over these new plants because they are so far away and are run by the locals. We can't replace the existing management—that would create bad feelings internally. Mr. Weisman, our controller, has suggested sending one of our people to each plant. He believes this will expedite the reporting process. We have been consistently receiving the financial data several weeks late since the acquisitions."

A decision that must be made is the type of management incentive program. One method would be to include the managers in our bonus plan. Right now our bonus plan is based on ROI [return on investment]. The objective is to achieve a 30% ROI before taxes. Is 30% ROI appropriate to use for the foreign manager? Should we get a separate standard for them? A related question is whether to set the ROI in local currency or U.S. dollars. The numbers in our financial statements reflect that the subs have earned for Infant Care in dollars, not marks or cruzeiros.

Mr. Weisman foresees accounting problems with measuring the managers' performance in dollars. We've always measured performance with ROI using the accounting figures. It seems that there is more than one way to calculate the dollar equivalent of the subsidiary investment. Mr. Weisman has put together a summary of the results of the subsidiary's operations using two methods of calculating the figures. Another complication is added when the dollar is not stable. Each exchange-rate change produces a different set of numbers. Mr. Weisman has calculated the figures using two different exchange rates. In front of you is the report Mr. Weisman produced [Exhibit 1]. What are your thoughts?

EXHIBIT 1
INFANT CARE, INC.
Memorandum

TO:     Board of Directors
FROM:   Arthur Weisman, Controller

The following summarizes the results of operations for Kinderstoffe and Bahia in local currency and in dollars. Accounting methods have been standardized so that the only difference is the exchange rate used.

### Bahia
### (in thousands)

| | Cruzeiros 12/31/80 | 1/1/80 Exchange Rate 45 = $1 12/31/79[a] | Current Exchange Rate 50 = $1 All Current | C/NC |
|---|---|---|---|---|
| Cash | 6,750 | $  150 | $  135 | 135 |
| Accounts Receivable | 11,250 | 250 | 225 | 225 |
| Inventory | 4,500 | 100 | 90 | 90 |
| Fixed Assets (Net) | 90,000 | 2,000 | 1,800 | 2,000 |
| | 112,500 | $2,500 | $2,250 | $2,450 |
| | | | | |
| Current Liabilities | 7,200 | $  160 | $  144 | $  144 |
| Long-Term Debt | 17,100 | 380 | 342 | 380 |
| Equity, 1/1/80 | 74,700 | 1,660 | 1,660 | 1,660 |
| Earnings, 1980 | 13,500 | 300 | 104 | 266 |
| | 112,500 | $2,500 | $2,250 | $2,450 |

### Kinderstoffe
### (in thousands)

| | DM 12/31/80 | 1/1/80 Exchange Rate 2.5 = $1 12/31/79[a] | Current Exchange Rate 2 = $1 All Current | C/NC |
|---|---|---|---|---|
| Cash | 135 | $  54 | $  67.5 | $  67.5 |
| Accounts Receivable | 225 | 90 | 112.5 | 112.5 |
| Inventory | 90 | 36 | 45 | 45 |
| Fixed Assets (Net) | 1,800 | 720 | 900 | 720 |
| | 2,250 | $900 | $1,125 | $945 |
| | | | | |
| Current Liabilities | 480 | $192 | $  240 | $240 |
| Long-Term Debt | 1,000 | 400 | 500 | 400 |
| Equity, 1/1/80 | 500 | 200 | 200 | 200 |
| Earnings, 1980 | 270 | 108 | 185 | 105 |
| | 2,250 | $900 | $1,125 | $945 |

[a]Assume, for simplicity, that the balance sheets for Kinderstoffe and Bahia were exactly the same at 12/31/79 and that both firms were acquired on 12/31/79.

# Forever Stores, Inc. (B)

Karl Stone, president and principal stockholder of Forever Stores, Inc., sat at his desk reflecting on the condition of his business in general, and on the 1973 results (see Exhibits 1 and 2) in particular. It hadn't been a great year, he mused, but it hadn't been a disaster either. At least he didn't have to worry about the energy crisis; his 94 jewelry stores were all located in high-pedestrian-traffic areas of major metropolitan areas, and he had recently been assured by his regional managers that there had been no noticeable slump in sales. Still, Stone felt mildly uncomfortable about another problem in the U.S. economy that didn't seem to want to go away: inflation. He felt that if he could only get some feel for the parameters of the situation as it affected Forever, he would be better able to deal with it. With this in mind, he called his assistants, two recent graduates of a well-known eastern business school, into his office.

"Ladies," he began, "I have the feeling that we're getting clobbered by rising prices, but these statements look as healthy as ever. Since it looks as though inflation is here to stay, at least for a while, I think that this might be a good time to review some of our financial policies: capital structure, dividend policy, credit policies, things of that sort. But I have to be able to *see* what I'm fighting first; I need *information*. Do you see what I'm driving at?

Carole Schultz shifted in her chair. "Yes, I believe I do," she replied. "What you're referring to are price-level adjusted financial statements; the techniques

This case was prepared by David Clark, MBA student, under the supervision of Associate Professor John K. Shank as a basis for class discussion rather than to illustrate either effective or ineffective handling of an administrative situation. Copyright © 1974 by the President and Fellows of Harvard College. Distributed by the Intercollegiate Case Clearing House, Soldiers Field, Boston, Mass., 02163. All rights reserved to the contributors. Printed in the U.S.A.

involved here have been part of GAAP for years, but have been largely ignored in practice. They relate a company's reported results to general price-level changes in the economy."

Stone leaned back, looking slightly relieved. "Excellent. What do you need to construct these statements?"

"First, I'll need a table of the Gross National Product Implicit Price Deflator (GNPI) going back to 1963, the year the company was formed," she responded, "but I can get that at the library (see Exhibit 3). Then, in addition to the basic financial statements, I'll need schedules that show the age of individual items in our 'nonmonetary' accounts: Plant and Equipment, Other Current Assets, Other Assets, Other Liabilities, and Common Stock and Surplus" (Exhibit 4).

Georgia Finkel was not entirely satisfied. "The techniques you are referring to may not reflect the results of our company accurately. You see, the index that you want to use is a national average. The GNPI shows the effect of all the goods and services in the United States. If we want to give a better picture of what inflation has done to the value of our company, more specific data are needed. What I propose we use to construct the statements is a combination of your GNPI and the industry figures published for our plant and inventory assets" (Exhibit 5).

Mr. Stone was quite perplexed. He had not expected different opinions on how to measure the effects of inflation. "It seems that we have a greater problem than I anticipated. Why don't you both work up some statements for me and I'll try to make some sense of all this."

"While you're at it, I'd like you to think about the implications of the figures you come up with. I'd like to know what kinds of decisions the price-level adjusted data will help us make, with regard to our internal operations, things like our cost structure, pricing policy, and ROI. I'd also like to get your ideas on some of the weaknesses or pitfalls that we should watch out for. I have a meeting with another director later today, so I'd like to go over your results with you before then. I'll see you at three."

Carole and Georgia got up and turned to leave. Before they reached the door, Stone called out, "Oh, and don't worry about lunch; I'll send one of the boys out for sandwiches."

EXHIBIT 1

FOREVER STORES, INC.
Comparative Balance Sheets
12/31/73 and 12/31/72
(Millions of Dollars)

| | December 31 | |
| --- | --- | --- |
| | 1973 | 1972 |
| **Assets** | | |
| Cash | $ 2.3 | $ 2.3 |
| Accounts Receivable | 56.3 | 53.7 |
| Inventories (FIFO) | 34.3 | 32.7 |
| Deposits | 0.6 | 0.6 |
| | 93.5 | 89.3 |
| Plant and Equipment | 10.6 | 10.6 |
| Less Accumulated Depreciation | 3.9 | 3.4 |
| | 6.7 | 7.2 |
| Investments (@ Cost) | 3.5 | 3.5 |
| | $103.7 | $100.0 |
| **Liabilities** | | |
| Accounts Payable | $ 31.5 | $ 29.9 |
| Accruals | 4.4 | 4.2 |
| Other Current Liabilities | 1.4 | 1.3 |
| | 37.3 | 35.4 |
| Long-Term Debt | 15.3 | 14.9 |
| Deferred Taxes | 10.5 | 10.1 |
| Capital Stock | 33.6 | 33.6 |
| Retained Earnings | 7.0 | 6.0 |
| | 40.6 | 39.6 |
| | $103.7 | $100.0 |

EXHIBIT 2
FOREVER STORES, INC.
Statement of Income
and Retained Earnings
for year ended December 31, 1973
(Millions of Dollars)

| | | |
| --- | --- | --- |
| Sales | | $100.00 |
| Cost of Goods Sold (FIFO) | | |
| Opening Inventory | $32.7 | |
| Purchases | 81.6 | |
| Closing Inventory | 34.3 | 80.0 |
| Gross Margin | | 20.0 |
| Depreciation | | 0.5 |
| Other Expenses | | 13.8 |
| Operating Profit | | 5.7 |
| Interest (@ 7.5%) | | 1.7 |
| Profit before Taxes | | 4.0 |
| Profit after Taxes | | $ 2.0 |
| Retained Earnings, 12/31/72 | | $ 6.0 |
| | | 8.0 |
| Less: Dividends paid, 1973 | | 1.0 |
| Retained Earnings, 12/31/73 | | $ 7.0 |

## EXHIBIT 3
### FOREVER STORES, INC.
Implicit Price Deflators for Gross National Product
for Years 1963-1973[a]
(1958 = 100)

| Year | GNPI | Relative to Index at 12/31/73 | Relative to Index at 12/31/72 |
|------|------|-------------------------------|-------------------------------|
| 1963 | 107.2 | 1.478 | 1.377 |
| 1964 | 108.8 | 1.456 | 1.357 |
| 1965 | 110.9 | 1.428 | 1.331 |
| 1966 | 113.94 | 1.390 | 1.296 |
| 1967 | 117.59 | 1.347 | 1.255 |
| 1968 | 122.30 | 1.294 | 1.207 |
| 1969 | 128.20 | 1.235 | 1.152 |
| 1970 | 135.24 | 1.171 | 1.092 |
| 1972 | 141.60 | 1.118 | 1.043 |
| 1972 | 146.10 | 1.084 | 1.010 |
| 1973 | 153.94 | 1.029 | — |

Quarterly Averages

| Quarter | 1972 | Relative to 12/31/73 | Relative to 12/31/72 |
|---------|------|----------------------|----------------------|
| I | 144.85 | 1.093 | 1.019 |
| II | 145.42 | 1.089 | 1.015 |
| III | 146.42 | 1.082 | 1.008 |
| IV | 147.63 | 1.073 | 1.000 |
| | *1973* | | |
| I | 149.81 | 1.057 | — |
| II | 152.46 | 1.039 | — |
| III | 155.06 | 1.021 | — |
| IV | 158.36 | 1.000 | — |

[a]From U.S. Department of Commerce, Bureau of Economic Analysis, *Survey of Current Business,* February 1974, for 1973 data; 1972 *Business Statistics* for all other data.

### EXHIBIT 4
### FOREVER STORES, INC.
Chronological Analysis of
Selected Accounts
(Millions of Dollars)

Plant and Equipment

| Year Acquired | Gross Investment | Accumulated Depreciation[a] 12/31/72 | Net Amount | |
|---|---|---|---|---|
| | | | 12/31/72 | 12/31/73 |
| 1963 | $ 3.6 | $1.8 | $1.8 | $1.6 |
| 1965 | 1.5 | 0.6 | 0.9 | 0.8 |
| 1968 | 2.4 | 0.6 | 1.8 | 1.7 |
| 1970 | 2.1 | 0.3 | 1.8 | 1.7 |
| 1971 | 1.0 | 0.1 | 0.9 | 0.8 |
| | $10.6 | $3.4 | $7.2 | $6.7 |

[a]All plant and equipment depreciated straight-line over 20 years.

Common Stock and Surplus

| Year Acquired | Amount |
|---|---|
| 1963 | $16.8 |
| 1966 | 8.4 |
| 1970 | 8.4 |
| | $33.6 |

Deposits,
Investments, and
Deferred Taxes

(For simplicity, assume that entire amounts appearing on the
1972 statements were acquired in 1968.)

## EXHIBIT 5
Industry Average Inflation Rate Index (IAIR)

### Plant Assets

| Year Acquired | IAIR | Relative to 1973 | Relative to 1972 |
|---|---|---|---|
| 1963 | 109.4 | 3.436 | 3.206 |
| 1964 | 115.6 | 3.251 | 3.034 |
| 1965 | 130.7 | 2.876 | 2.684 |
| 1966 | 145.8 | 2.578 | 2.406 |
| 1967 | 120.9 | 3.109 | 2.901 |
| 1968 | 140.8 | 2.669 | 2.491 |
| 1969 | 150.9 | 2.491 | 2.324 |
| 1970 | 200.6 | 1.873 | 1.748 |
| 1971 | 300.7 | 1.250 | 1.166 |
| 1972 | 350.8 | 1.071 | 1.000 |
| 1973 | 375.9 | 1.000 | |

### Inventory

| Year | IAIR | Relative to 12/31/72 | Relative to 12/31/73 |
|---|---|---|---|
| 1970 | 110.5 | 1.145 | 1.170 |
| 1971 | 115.6 | 1.094 | 1.119 |
| 1972 | 125.7 | 1.006 | 1.029 |
| 1973 | 130.3 | — | .992 |

### Quarterly Averages

| 1972 | | Relative to 12/31/72 | Relative to 12/31/73 |
|---|---|---|---|
| I | 124.8 | 1.014 | 1.036 |
| II | 125.2 | 1.010 | 1.032 |
| III | 126.3 | 1.002 | 1.024 |
| IV | 126.5 | 1.000 | 1.022 |
| 1973 | | | |
| I | 127.6 | | 1.013 |
| II | 132.5 | | .976 |
| III | 131.6 | | .983 |
| IV | 129.3 | | 1.000 |

# Sierra International Corporation

In early June of 1975, Mr. Glen Evans, president of Sierra International (SI), was facing one of his most difficult decisions since acceding to the presidency of the firm nearly 10 months ago. Mr. Evans had been with Sierra for 15 years, spending the last 3 years as vice-president in charge of international operations. Within the past month, two very large RFEs (Requests for Expenditure) had been submitted for corporate approval, one each from SI's two largest foreign subsidiaries. Three weeks ago, Evans had received a detailed proposal from the Brazilian Exploration Corporation (BEC) requesting $108 million for a capital investment program to develop additional oil exploration equipment and auxiliary facilities. Last week's mail had brought a similar request from SI's West German telephone subsidiary (WGT). They proposed expansion totaling $120 million in computer-controlled electronic switching systems (ESS) to further automate their call transmission facilities.

Individually, each RFEs represented one of the largest dollar investments in expansion of physical plant ever considered by SI. The detailed analyses presented indicated that the respective projects would each contribute significantly to corporate earnings growth. Furthermore, each would allow the sponsoring subsidiary to at least maintain the ROI[1] level achieved in the past.

Copyright © 1975 by the President and Fellows of Harvard College. Reproduced by permission. This case was prepared by William J. Rauwerdink, Research Assistant, under the supervision of John K. Shank, Associate Professor as the basis for class discussion rather than to illustrate either effective or ineffective handling of an administrative situation. Distributed by the Intercollegiate Case Clearing House, Soldiers Field, Boston, Mass., 02163. All rights reserved to the contributors. Printed in the U.S.A.

[1] The success of subsidiary management was monitored primarily on an ROI basis. ROI was designed to be net earnings for the subsidiary divided by net working capital plus net property, plant, and equipment.

SI, founded in 1946, was a large, diversified, multinational company headquartered in Los Angeles. Annual sales exceeded $1.1 billion. Currently, 11 subsidiaries, including 5 foreign-based firms, comprised SI's investment "portfolio." All 11 were 100% owned. Top management at SI had always been very concerned about maintaining investments only in growth-oriented industries. SI's board of directors strongly encouraged all 11 subsidiaries to concentrate on markets with significant potential for growth. The approved 5-year plans for both BEC and WGT were predicated on aggressive growth strategies requiring significant continued capital investment. Although 5-year plans calling for major capital outlays had already been approved for both divisions, actual investment proposals had to be approved again individually.

The Brazilian Exploration Corporation had been purchased in 1969. Not directly associated with any of the major international petroleum companies, BEC was nevertheless considered to be a major off-shore driller. After geologic testing, BEC would negotiate for rights to drill in selected offshore areas. If drilling proved successful, the crude oil would be sold on a "wellhead" basis (i.e., at the wellhead). Normally, complex long-term formulas would be set up under which BEC received royalty revenues on the crude oil pumped. With the recent dramatic rise in world petroleum prices, BEC was under substantial market pressure to expand its development activities.

West German Telephone had been acquired in 1967. At that time, WGT switching equipment was primarily of the "step-by-step" and "cross-bar" types. These types were late-generation versions of the original electromechanical switching equipment. The worldwide thrust in telecommunication in the 1970s was to install computer-based ESS. Numerous cost savings were possible in the areas of maintenance, operator salaries, and installation. With ESS, for example, changing the service for a client often involves only the alteration of a computer program, not a rerouting and rewiring of the actual circuits. One large telephone company using ESS had reported achieving a 34% increase in calls over a 4-year period with only a 4% increase in employees.

## THE PROBLEM

Glen Evans was satisfied that the two proposals represented important and worthwhile expansion projects for the respective subsidiaries and for Sierra as a whole. The requests were well documented and were consistent with overall corporate growth strategies. However, Evans realized that the two requests could not both be funded in the foreseeable future. During the current year, SI had already committed over $200 million in capital investment. Over the past 6 years, they had averaged about $300 million annually for all 11 subsidiaries combined and they had never spent $400 million in one year.

As shown in Exhibits 1 and 2, both BEC and WGT had consistently surpassed budgeted ROI figures over the last 5 years. Although SI's custom was to favor the more successful subsidiaries in the granting of expansion funds, requests did not normally involve mutually exclusive projects such as these. Evans was thus unaccustomed to selecting one project and one division over another to receive capital funds. Based on his current understanding, no other subsidiaries would be submitting additional major requests for funds within the current fiscal year. Other subsidiaries would, however, be submitting large RFEs next year. Sierra could thus not really bunch 2 years of capital spending now to approve both projects. Improvement in the equity markets or loosening in the bond markets might permit a major infusion of new capital next year, but one or the other of the two proposals now on his desk was going to have to be shelved for the present.

As Evans thought about his problem, he called in Chip Nedder, who was manager of the financial analysis department.

"Chip, you know quite a bit about how we operate around here. I'm sitting on RFEs from the Brazilian and West German subs and I can't submit them both to the board. These two groups have produced such excellent and nearly comparable results for the past few years that it's not obvious to me which one deserves the money more. I don't want to foreclose one or the other just because the ROIs are different at the sixth decimal place. The amount of money involved is too large for that kind of hairsplitting."

Evans continued, "I guess what I would really like to get a handle on is what all the cruzeiros and deutsche marks mean to me here in L.A. Since none of our foreign subs have ever repatriated any earnings, nor do I expect that they ever will in my lifetime, I don't really know how to view their financials. The controller's staff does all the currency translation for the monthly statements. I never have been very involved in the mechanics and I'm wondering whether an ROI in cruzeiros is as good as one in marks, or vice versa."

"Also, this whole inflation mess has been confusing me for months! I know that price-level-adjusted financial statements may be required in our annual report in the future, but I don't care about that. My concern is how inflation affects the businesses we own in ways that might influence my decision making. The fact that a general price index increases 10% has no bearing at all if the cost of the items we are buying goes up 80%. Or does it?"

"I'm going to the Paris air show next week, Chip, and while I'm away, I'd like you to establish an approach to analyzing which sub deserves the investment money. You'll have to tie it into ROI or no one around here will accept it. Have you worked out your thoughts on all this currency translation and inflation accounting stuff yet?"

Chip Nedder twisted in his chair and replied: "Well, I have thought some about one aspect of what you're proposing. We can either translate the currency to U.S. dollars first and then adjust for U.S. inflation, or we can adjust for inflation in the local currency first and then translate to U.S. dollars. These two approaches will normally yield quite different results. Based on our not repatriating foreign subs' earnings, the "adjust, then translate" approach seems conceptually superior to me. In other words, first adjust for foreign price-level changes and then translate for currency-exchange-rate differences."

"Yes," Glen Evans noted, somewhat absentmindedly, "that sounds fine, Chip. It does seem reasonable to adjust for local inflation and not the U.S. inflation in view of this repatriation business, so let's run with that approach. I'll want to finalize this decision when I return in about a week. Don't let me down!"

## NEDDER'S DILEMMA

During the next few days, Chip had his staff prepare schedules which are reproduced as Exhibits 3 to 16.[2] Feeling more than a bit bewildered at the mass of numbers and the lack of clear-cut conclusions, Chip prepared Exhibit 17 to summarize the analysis. After considering the summary exhibit at some length, he still felt he needed additional guidance and called Mr. Evans in Paris.

"I've done quite a bit of numerical analysis, Mr. Evans, and I think I'll need some input from you before I can wrap this up. As you know, we agreed that the "restate-translate" sequence for adjusting our statements seemed correct. But there are several other options. We can adjust for inflation using a general price level index or a specific index for the industries we're in. In the currency translation area there are at least four options! We can select the "monetary/nonmonetary" method, the "current/noncurrent" method, the "all current" method, or a hybrid. Each yields different answers. Which do you think is best?"

After a brief pause, Mr. Evans replied. "Chip, I think you have posed some interesting and important questions. Your staff and you represent our best corporate thinking on this type of analysis and I would like to hear your recommendations about which combination is most reasonable. You're our top analyst and I'll value your comments."

"I should be back on Saturday. Why don't you prepare a memo on the approach you select and attach it to the financials. I'll want to see it as soon as I get in. Be sure to explain clearly what differences the selection of a method makes—if any."

Chip Nedder remembered Harry Truman's adage about the buck stopping here as he tried to decide which numbers provided the most meaningful comparison of the Brazilian and West German operations.

## QUESTIONS

1   Which of the two subsidiaries has a better record of profitability over the past 5 years? What is the basis for your conclusion?

2   As Chip Nedder, how would you explain to Glen Evans why the analytic scheme you favor is superior to any of the others being considered?

---

[2] Exhibits 1 and 2 are "output" from the regular accounting system. They are the statements Mr. Evans would normally see.

**EXHIBIT 1**
**WEST GERMAN TELEPHONE COMPANY**

|  | 1970 | 1971 | 1972 | 1973 | 1974 |
|---|---|---|---|---|---|
|  | Translated Balance Sheets Monetary/Nonmonetary Method (Millions of Dollars) | | | | |
| Cash | $ 10 | $ 11 | $ 13 | $ 28 | $ 16 |
| Accounts Receivable | 16 | 19 | 22 | 32 | 29 |
| Property, Plant, and Equipment | 120.7 | 129.7 | 217.88 | 204.37 | 250.78 |
| Total Assets | $146.7 | $159.7 | $252.88 | $264.37 | $295.78 |
| Current Liabilities | $ 24 | $ 24 | $ 27 | $ 28 | $ 32 |
| Long-Term Debt | 69 | 61 | 116 | 92 | 75 |
| Retained Earnings | 53.7 | 74.7 | 109.88 | 144.37 | 188.78 |
| Total Equities | $146.7 | $159.7 | $252.88 | $264.37 | $295.78 |
|  | Translated Income Statements (Millions of Dollars) | | | | |
| Revenue |  | $147.261 | $188.062 | $215.079 | $244.861 |
| Operating Expenses |  | 82.586 | 99.933 | 97.699 | 133.746 |
| Depreciation |  | 7.0 | 7.82 | 13.51 | 13.51 |
| Interest |  | 4.871 | 9.798 | 7.819 | 5.846 |
| Profit before Taxes |  | 52.804 | 70.511 | 96.051 | 91.759 |
| Taxes |  | 26.063 | 34.659 | 47.234 | 43.920 |
| Translation Gain (Loss) |  | (5.741) | (.672) | (14.327) | (3.429) |
| Net Income |  | $ 21.00 | $ 35.18 | $ 34.49 | $ 44.41 |

## EXHIBIT 2
### BRAZILIAN EXPLORATION CORPORATION

|  | 1970 | 1971 | 1972 | 1973 | 1974 |
|---|---|---|---|---|---|
| Translated Balance Sheets | | | | | |
| Monetary/Nonmonetary Method | | | | | |
| (Millions of Dollars) | | | | | |
| Cash | $11 | $ 9 | $ 12.0 | $ 11.0 | $ 25.0 |
| Accounts Receivable | 12 | 13.00 | 22 | 21.0 | 49 |
| Property, Plant, and Equipment | 60.4 | 89.87 | 98.08 | 149.11 | 168.45 |
| Total Assets | $83.40 | $111.87 | $132.08 | $181.11 | $242.45 |
| Current Liabilities | $22 | $ 23.55 | $ 26.99 | $ 35.21 | $ 46.99 |
| Long-Term Debt | 7 | 17.00 | 16 | 24.0 | 34.00 |
| Retained Earnings | 54.40 | 71.32 | 89.00 | 121.90 | 161.46 |
| Total Equities | $83.40 | $111.87 | $132.08 | $181.11 | $242.45 |
| Translated Income Statements | | | | | |
| (Millions of Dollars) | | | | | |
| Revenue | | $105.91 | $130.98 | $160.98 | $179.31 |
| Operating Expenses | | 59.16 | 62.91 | 75.57 | 81.79 |
| Depreciation | | 7.56 | 11.68 | 13.90 | 21.12 |
| Interest | | 2.44 | 2.36 | 2.97 | 4.62 |
| Profit before Taxes | | 36.75 | 54.03 | 68.54 | 71.78 |
| Taxes | | 19.05 | 19.69 | 35.60 | 37.64 |
| Translation Gain (Loss) | | (.78) | (16.57) | (.13) | 5.42 |
| Net Income | | $ 16.92 | $ 17.77 | $ 32.81 | $ 39.56 |

## EXHIBIT 3
## WEST GERMAN TELEPHONE COMPANY

| | 1970 | 1971 | 1972 | 1973 | 1974 |
|---|---|---|---|---|---|
| | Balance Sheets (Millions of Deutsche Marks) | | | | |
| Cash | 36.48 | 35.948 | 41.626 | 75.684 | 38.56 |
| Accounts Receivable | 58.368 | 62.092 | 70.444 | 86.496 | 69.89 |
| Property, Plant, and Equipment | 470.85 | 496.3 | 744.5 | 730.3 | 829.8 |
| Total Assets | 565.698 | 594.34 | 886.57 | 892.48 | 938.25 |
| | | | | | |
| Current Liabilities | 87.552 | 78.432 | 86.454 | 75.684 | 77.12 |
| Long-Term Debt | 251.712 | 199.348 | 371.432 | 248.676 | 180.75 |
| Retained Earnings | 226.434 | 316.56 | 428.684 | 568.12 | 680.38 |
| Total Equities | 565.698 | 594.34 | 886.57 | 892.48 | 938.25 |
| | Income Statements (Millions of Deutsche Marks) | | | | |
| Revenue | 403.984 | 509.232 | 608.382 | 634.915 | 625.866 |
| Operating Expense | 239.824 | 285.583 | 323.285 | 288.410 | 341.854 |
| Depreciation | 20.35 | 26.55 | 29.15 | 44.55 | 44.55 |
| Interest | 20.064 | 16.847 | 31.699 | 23.083 | 14.942 |
| Profit before Taxes | 123.746 | 180.252 | 224.248 | 278.872 | 224.52 |
| Taxes | 61.873 | 90.126 | 112.124 | 139.436 | 112.26 |
| Net Income | 61.873 | 90.126 | 112.124 | 139.436 | 112.26 |

## EXHIBIT 4
### WEST GERMAN TELEPHONE COMPANY

|  | 1970 | 1971 | 1972 | 1973 | 1974 |
|---|---|---|---|---|---|
| **General Price-Level-Adjusted Balance Sheets** | | | | | |
| **(Millions of 1974 Deutsche Marks)** | | | | | |
| Cash | 46.18 | 43.22 | 47.43 | 80.65 | 38.56 |
| Accounts Receivable | 73.89 | 74.65 | 80.27 | 92.18 | 69.89 |
| Property, Plant, and Equipment | 684.60 | 700.70 | 965.97 | 909.814 | 998.26 |
| Total Assets | 804.67 | 818.57 | 1,093.67 | 1,082.64 | 1,106.71 |
| Current Liabilities | 110.84 | 94.30 | 98.52 | 80.65 | 77.12 |
| Long-Term Debt | 318.68 | 239.67 | 423.25 | 265.00 | 180.75 |
| Retained Earnings | 375.15 | 484.6 | 571.9 | 736.99 | 848.84 |
| Total Equities | 804.67 | 818.57 | 1,093.67 | 1,082.64 | 1,106.71 |
| **General Price-Level-Adjusted Income Statements** | | | | | |
| **(Millions of 1974 Deutsche Marks)** | | | | | |
| Revenue |  | 628.350 | 711.840 | 699.566 | 645.759 |
| Operating Expenses |  | 352.386 | 378.261 | 317.778 | 352.719 |
| Depreciation |  | 35.495 | 38.63 | 56.01 | 56.01 |
| Interest |  | 20.787 | 37.089 | 25.433 | 15.416 |
| Profit before Taxes |  | 219.682 | 257.86 | 300.345 | 221.614 |
| Tax |  | 111.208 | 131.191 | 153.634 | 115.828 |
| Price-Level Gain (Loss) |  | .976 | (39.369) | 18.379 | 6.064 |
| Net Income |  | 109.45 | 87.30 | 165.09 | 111.85 |

## EXHIBIT 5
### WEST GERMAN TELEPHONE COMPANY

|  | 1970 | 1971 | 1972 | 1973 | 1974 |
|---|---|---|---|---|---|
| **Specific Price-Level-Adjusted Balance Sheets** | | | | | |
| **(Millions of 1974 Deutsche Marks)** | | | | | |
| Cash | 46.18 | 43.22 | 47.43 | 80.65 | 38.56 |
| Accounts Receivable | 73.89 | 74.65 | 80.27 | 92.18 | 69.89 |
| Property, Plant, and Equipment | 462.63 | 488.10 | 763.99 | 720.05 | 820.57 |
| Total Assets | 582.70 | 605.97 | 891.69 | 892.88 | 929.02 |
| | | | | | |
| Current Liabilities | 110.84 | 94.30 | 98.52 | 80.65 | 77.12 |
| Long-Term Debt | 318.68 | 239.67 | 423.25 | 265.00 | 180.75 |
| Retained Earnings | 153.18 | 272.00 | 370.02 | 547.23 | 671.15 |
| Total Equities | 582.70 | 605.97 | 891.79 | 892.88 | 929.02 |

| | | | | | |
|---|---|---|---|---|---|
| **Specific Price-Level-Adjusted Income Statements** | | | | | |
| **(Millions of 1974 Deutsche Marks)** | | | | | |
| Revenues | | 628.350 | 711.840 | 699.566 | 645.759 |
| Operating Expenses | | 352.386 | 378.261 | 317.778 | 352.719 |
| Depreciation | | 26.125 | 28.91 | 43.89 | 43.94 |
| Interest | | 20.787 | 37.089 | 25.433 | 15.416 |
| Profit before Taxes | | 229.052 | 267.58 | 312.465 | 233.684 |
| Tax | | 111.208 | 131.191 | 153.634 | 115.828 |
| Price-Level Gain (Loss) | | .976 | (39.369) | 18.379 | 6.064 |
| Net Income | | 118.82 | 97.02 | 177.21 | 123.92 |

**EXHIBIT 6**

## WEST GERMAN TELEPHONE COMPANY

| | 1970 | 1971 | 1972 | 1973 | 1974 |
|---|---|---|---|---|---|
| | Translated General Price-Level-Adjusted Balance Sheets | | | | |
| | Monetary/Nonmonetary Method | | | | |
| | (Millions of 1974 Dollars) | | | | |
| Cash | $ 12.66 | $ 13.23 | $ 14.81 | $ 29.65 | $ 15.99 |
| Accounts Receivable | 20.25 | 22.84 | 25.07 | 34.10 | 28.99 |
| Property, Plant, and Equipment | 160.54 | 170.71 | 270.08 | 254.59 | 299.08 |
| Total Assets | $193.45 | $206.78 | $309.96 | $318.34 | $344.05 |
| | | | | | |
| Current Liabilities | $ 30.38 | $ 28.85 | $ 30.77 | $ 29.85 | $ 32.00 |
| Long-Term Debt | 87.36 | 73.34 | 132.18 | 98.04 | 74.99 |
| Retained Earnings | 75.71 | 104.59 | 147.01 | 190.45 | 237.07 |
| Total Equities | $193.45 | $206.78 | $309.96 | $318.34 | $344.06 |
| | | | | | |
| | Translated General Price-Level-Adjusted Income Statements | | | | |
| | (Millions of 1974 Dollars) | | | | |
| Revenue | | $181.709 | $220.043 | $236.980 | $252.644 |
| Operating Expenses | | 101.904 | 116.927 | 107.648 | 137.996 |
| Depreciation | | 7.871 | 10.021 | 15.491 | 15.491 |
| Interest | | 6.011 | 11.464 | 8.615 | 6.031 |
| Profit before Taxes | | 65.923 | 81.631 | 105.226 | 93.126 |
| Tax | | 32.159 | 40.553 | 52.044 | 45.316 |
| Price-Level Gain (Loss) | | .282 | (12.169) | 6.225 | 2.372 |
| Translation Gain (Loss) | | (5.166) | 13.511 | (15.967) | (3.562) |
| Net Income | | $ 28.88 | $ 42.42 | $ 43.44 | $ 46.62 |

**EXHIBIT 7**
WEST GERMAN TELEPHONE COMPANY

| | 1970 | 1971 | 1972 | 1973 | 1974 |
|---|---|---|---|---|---|
| | Translated Specific Price-Level-Adjusted Balance Sheets<br>Monetary/Nonmonetary Method<br>(Millions of 1974 Dollars) | | | | |
| Cash | $ 12.66 | $ 13.23 | $ 14.81 | $ 29.65 | $ 15.99 |
| Accounts Receivable | 20.25 | 22.84 | 25.07 | 34.10 | 28.99 |
| Property, Plant, and Equipment | 118.61 | 127.73 | 215.26 | 203.16 | 250.86 |
| Total Assets | $151.52 | $163.80 | $255.14 | $266.91 | $295.84 |
| | | | | | |
| Current Liabilities | $ 30.38 | $ 28.85 | $ 30.77 | $ 29.85 | $ 32.00 |
| Long-Term Debt | 87.36 | 73.34 | 132.18 | 98.04 | 74.99 |
| Retained Earnings | 33.78 | 61.61 | 92.19 | 139.02 | 188.85 |
| Total Equities | $151.52 | $163.80 | $255.14 | $266.91 | $295.84 |
| | Translated Specific Price-Level-Adjusted Income Statements<br>(Millions of 1974 Dollars) | | | | |
| Revenue | | $181.709 | $220.043 | $236.980 | $252.644 |
| Operating Expenses | | 101.904 | 116.927 | 107.648 | 137.996 |
| Depreciation | | 6.8 | 7.6 | 13.20 | 13.20 |
| Interest | | 6.011 | 11.464 | 8.615 | 6.031 |
| Profit before Taxes | | 66.994 | 84.052 | 107.517 | 95.417 |
| Taxes | | 32.159 | 40.553 | 52.044 | 45.316 |
| Price-Level Gain (Loss) | | .282 | (12.169) | 6.225 | 2.372 |
| Translation Gain (Loss) | | (7.287) | (.750) | (14.868) | (2.643) |
| Net Income | | $ 27.83 | $ 30.58 | $ 46.83 | $ 49.83 |

## EXHIBIT 8
### WEST GERMAN TELEPHONE COMPANY

| | 1970 | 1971 | 1972 | 1973 | 1974 |
|---|---|---|---|---|---|

Translated General Price-Level-Adjusted Balance Sheets
Current Method
(Millions of 1974 Dollars)

| | 1970 | 1971 | 1972 | 1973 | 1974 |
|---|---|---|---|---|---|
| Cash | $ 12.66 | $ 13.23 | $ 14.81 | $ 29.65 | $ 15.99 |
| Accounts Receivable | 20.25 | 22.84 | 25.07 | 34.10 | 28.99 |
| Property, Plant, and Equipment | 187.66 | 214.41 | 301.68 | 336.59 | 414.22 |
| Total Assets | $220.57 | $250.48 | $341.56 | $400.34 | $459.20 |
| | | | | | |
| Current Liabilities | $ 30.38 | $ 28.85 | $ 30.77 | $ 29.85 | $ 32.00 |
| Long-Term Debt | 87.36 | 73.34 | 132.18 | 98.04 | 74.99 |
| Retained Earnings | 102.83 | 148.29 | 178.61 | 272.45 | 352.21 |
| Total Equities | $220.57 | $250.48 | $341.56 | $400.34 | $459.20 |

Translated General Price-Level-Adjusted Income Statements
(Millions of Dollars)

| | | 1971 | 1972 | 1973 | 1974 |
|---|---|---|---|---|---|
| Revenue | | $181.709 | $220.043 | $236.980 | $252.644 |
| Operating Expenses | | 101.904 | 116.927 | 107.648 | 137.996 |
| Depreciation | | 10.86 | 12.06 | 20.72 | 23.24 |
| Interest | | 6.011 | 11.464 | 8.615 | 6.031 |
| Profit before Taxes | | 62.934 | 79.592 | 99.997 | 85.377 |
| Tax | | 32.159 | 40.553 | 52.044 | 45.316 |
| Price-Level Gain (Loss) | | .282 | (12.169) | 6.225 | 2.372 |
| Translation Gain (Loss) | | 14.403 | 3.450 | 39.662 | 37.327 |
| Net Income | | $ 45.46 | $ 30.32 | $ 93.84 | $ 79.76 |

## EXHIBIT 9
## WEST GERMAN TELEPHONE COMPANY

|  | 1970 | 1971 | 1972 | 1973 | 1974 |
|---|---|---|---|---|---|

Translated Specific Price-Level-Adjusted Balance Sheets
Current Method
(Millions of 1974 Dollars)

|  | 1970 | 1971 | 1972 | 1973 | 1974 |
|---|---|---|---|---|---|
| Cash | $ 12.66 | $ 13.23 | $ 14.81 | $ 29.65 | $ 15.99 |
| Accounts Receivable | 20.25 | 22.84 | 25.07 | 34.10 | 28.99 |
| Property, Plant, and Equipment | 126.81 | 149.35 | 238.59 | 266.39 | 340.48 |
| Total Assets | $159.72 | $185.42 | $278.47 | $330.14 | $385.46 |
| | | | | | |
| Current Liabilities | $ 30.38 | $ 28.85 | $ 30.77 | $ 29.85 | $ 32.00 |
| Long-Term Debt | 87.36 | 73.34 | 132.18 | 98.04 | 74.99 |
| Retained Earnings | 41.98 | 83.23 | 115.52 | 202.25 | 278.47 |
| Total Equities | $159.72 | $185.42 | $278.47 | $330.14 | $385.46 |

Translated Specific Price-Level-Adjusted Income Statements
(Millions of 1974 Dollars)

|  | 1971 | 1972 | 1973 | 1974 |
|---|---|---|---|---|
| Revenue | $181.709 | $220.043 | $236.980 | $252.644 |
| Operating Expenses | 101.904 | 116.927 | 107.648 | 137.996 |
| Depreciation | 7.16 | 8.846 | 16.24 | 18.23 |
| Interest | 6.011 | 11.464 | 8.615 | 6.031 |
| Profit before Taxes | 66.634 | 82.806 | 104.477 | 90.387 |
| Tax | 32.159 | 40.553 | 52.044 | 45.316 |
| Price-Level Gain (Loss) | .282 | (12.169) | 6.225 | 2.372 |
| Translation Gain (Loss) | (9.057) | 2.206 | 28.072 | 28.777 |
| Net Income | $ 25.70 | $ 32.29 | $ 86.73 | $ 76.22 |

## EXHIBIT 10
### BRAZILIAN EXPLORATION CORPORATION

| | 1970 | 1971 | 1972 | 1973 | 1974 |
|---|---|---|---|---|---|
| | Balance Sheets (Millions of Cruzeiros) | | | | |
| Cash | 54.45 | 50.715 | 74.58 | 68.42 | 170.425 |
| Accounts Receivable | 59.4 | 73.255 | 136.73 | 130.62 | 334.033 |
| Property, Plant, and Equipment | 262.9 | 438.495 | 506.695 | 841.095 | 964.890 |
| Total Assets | 376.75 | 562.65 | 618.005 | 1,040.135 | 1,469.348 |
| | | | | | |
| Current Liabilities | 108.9 | 132.695 | 167.800 | 219.04 | 320.389 |
| Long-Term Debt | 34.65 | 95.795 | 99.44 | 149.28 | 231.778 |
| Retained Earnings | 233.20 | 333.975 | 450.765 | 671.82 | 917.181 |
| Total Equities | 376.75 | 562.47 | 718.01 | 1,040.14 | 1,469.348 |
| | Income Statements (Millions of Cruzeiros) | | | | |
| Revenue | 350.100 | 560.287 | 776.722 | 999.712 | 1,168,748 |
| Operating Expenses | 179.895 | 312.948 | 373.07 | 469.262 | 533.094 |
| Depreciation | 32.9 | 32.9 | 56.1 | 69.9 | 114.8 |
| Interest | 4.475 | 12.889 | 13.972 | 18.44 | 30.132 |
| Profit before Taxes | 132.83 | 201.55 | 333.58 | 442.11 | 490.722 |
| Taxes | 66.415 | 100.775 | 116.790 | 221.055 | 245.361 |
| Net Income | 66.415 | 100.775 | 116.790 | 221.055 | 245.361 |

## EXHIBIT 11
### BRAZILIAN EXPLORATION CORPORATION

|  | 1970 | 1971 | 1972 | 1973 | 1974 |
|---|---|---|---|---|---|
| | General Price-Level-Adjusted Balance Sheets (Millions of 1974 Cruzeiros) | | | | |
| Cash | 109.98 | 85.37 | 107.61 | 87.47 | 170.425 |
| Accounts Receivable | 119.98 | 123.31 | 197.28 | 166.99 | 334.033 |
| Property, Plant, and Equipment | 647.71 | 917.71 | 977.10 | 1,354.11 | 1,395.39 |
| Total Assets | 877.67 | 1,126.39 | 1,281.99 | 1,608.57 | 1,899.848 |
| | | | | | |
| Current Liabilities | 219.98 | 223.37 | 242.11 | 280.03 | 320.389 |
| Long-Term Debt | 69.99 | 161.25 | 143.47 | 190.85 | 231.778 |
| Retained Earnings | 587.70 | 741.77 | 896.41 | 1,137.69 | 1,347.681 |
| Total Equities | 887.67 | 1,126.39 | 1,281.99 | 1,608.57 | 1,899.848 |
| | General Price-Level-Adjusted Income Statements (Millions of 1974 Cruzeiros) | | | | |
| Revenue | | 1,028.89 | 1,206.91 | 1,355.31 | 1,311.59 |
| Operating Expenses | | 574.69 | 579.69 | 636.18 | 598.25 |
| Depreciation | | 80.96 | 119.95 | 139.87 | 197.30 |
| Interest | | 23.67 | 21.71 | 24.99 | 33.81 |
| Profit before Taxes | | 349.57 | 485.56 | 554.27 | 482.23 |
| Taxes | | 185.06 | 181.47 | 299.69 | 275.35 |
| Price-Level Gain (Loss) | | (10.44) | (149.45) | (13.30) | 3.11 |
| Net Income | | 154.07 | 154.64 | 241.28 | 209.991 |

## EXHIBIT 12
### BRAZILIAN EXPLORATION CORPORATION

|  | 1970 | 1971 | 1972 | 1973 | 1974 |
|---|---|---|---|---|---|
| | | Specific Price-Level-Adjusted Balance Sheets (Millions of 1974 Cruzeiros) | | | |
| Cash | 109.98 | 85.37 | 107.61 | 87.47 | 170.425 |
| Accounts Receivable | 119.98 | 123.31 | 197.28 | 166.99 | 334.033 |
| Property, Plant, and Equipment | 1,359.95 | 1,558.95 | 1,533.03 | 1,822.95 | 1,730.79 |
| Total Assets | 1,589.91 | 1,767.63 | 1,837.92 | 2,077.41 | 2,235.358 |
| | | | | | |
| Current Liabilities | 219.98 | 223.37 | 242.11 | 280.03 | 320.389 |
| Long-Term Debt | 69.99 | 161.25 | 143.47 | 190.85 | 231.778 |
| Retained Earnings | 1,299.94 | 1,383.01 | 1,452.34 | 1,606.53 | 1,683.081 |
| Total Equities | 1,589.91 | 1,767.63 | 1,837.92 | 2,077.41 | 2,235.248 |
| | | Speific Price-Level-Adjusted Income Statement (Millions of 1974 Cruzeiros) | | | |
| Revenue | | 1,028.89 | 1,206.91 | 1,355.31 | 1,311.59 |
| Operating Expenses | | 574.69 | 579.69 | 636.18 | 598.25 |
| Depreciation | | 151.96 | 205.26 | 226.96 | 278.56 |
| Interest | | 23.67 | 21.71 | 24.99 | 33.81 |
| Profit before Taxes | | 278.57 | 400.25 | 467.18 | 400.97 |
| Taxes | | 185.06 | 181.47 | 299.69 | 275.35 |
| Price-Level Gain (Loss) | | (10.44) | (149.45) | (13.30) | 3.111 |
| Net Income | | 83.07 | 69.33 | 154.19 | 128.731 |

**EXHIBIT 13**
**BRAZILIAN EXPLORATION CORPORATION**

| | 1970 | 1971 | 1972 | 1973 | 1974 |
|---|---|---|---|---|---|
| Translated General Price-Level-Adjusted Balance Sheets | | | | | |
| Monetary/Nonmonetary Method | | | | | |
| (Millions of 1974 Dollars) | | | | | |
| Cash | $ 22.22 | $ 15.15 | $ 17.31 | $ 14.06 | $ 25.00 |
| Accounts Receivable | 24.24 | 21.88 | 31.74 | 26.85 | 49.00 |
| Property, Plant, and | | | | | |
| Equipment | 148.90 | 192.57 | 195.85 | 250.20 | 248.41 |
| Total Assets | $195.36 | $229.60 | $224.90 | $291.11 | $322.41 |
| | | | | | |
| Current Liabilities | $ 44.44 | $ 39.64 | $ 38.96 | $ 45.02 | $ 47.00 |
| Long-Term Debt | 14.14 | 28.62 | 23.08 | 30.68 | 34.00 |
| Retained Earnings | 136.78 | 161.34 | 182.86 | 215.41 | 241.41 |
| Total Equities | $195.36 | $229.60 | $244.90 | $291.11 | $322.41 |

Translated General Price-Level-Adjusted Income Statements
(Millions of 1974 Dollars)

| | | 1971 | 1972 | 1973 | 1974 |
|---|---|---|---|---|---|
| Revenue | | $194.50 | $203.53 | $218.25 | $201.23 |
| Operating Expenses | | 108.64 | 97.75 | 102.44 | 91.78 |
| Depreciation | | 18.61 | 25.53 | 28.74 | 37.97 |
| Interest | | 4.47 | 3.66 | 4.02 | 5.19 |
| Profit before Taxes | | 62.78 | 76.59 | 83.05 | 66.29 |
| Taxes | | 34.98 | 30.60 | 48.26 | 42.24 |
| Price-Level Gain (Loss) | | (1.97) | (25.00) | (2.14) | .48 |
| Translation Gain (Loss) | | (1.27) | .73 | (.10) | 1.47 |
| Net Income | | $ 24.56 | $ 21.52 | $ 32.55 | $ 26.00 |

## EXHIBIT 14
### BRAZILIAN EXPLORATION CORPORATION

|  | *1970* | *1971* | *1972* | *1973* | *1974* |
|---|---|---|---|---|---|
| Translated Specific Price-Level-Adjusted Balance Sheets Monetary/Nonmonetary Method (Millions of 1974 Dollars) | | | | | |
| Cash | $ 22.22 | $ 15.15 | $ 17.31 | $ 14.06 | $ 25.00 |
| Accounts Receivable | 24.24 | 21.88 | 31.74 | 26.85 | 49.00 |
| Property, Plant, and Equipment | 295.46 | 329.56 | 316.61 | 343.49 | 322.25 |
| Total Assets | $341.92 | $366.59 | $365.66 | $384.40 | $396.25 |
| | | | | | |
| Current Liabilities | $ 44.44 | $ 39.64 | $ 38.96 | $ 45.02 | $ 47.00 |
| Long-Term Debt | 14.14 | 28.26 | 23.08 | 30.68 | 34.00 |
| Retained Earnings | 283.34 | 298.33 | 303.62 | 308.70 | 315.25 |
| Total Equities | $341.92 | $366.59 | $365.66 | $384.40 | $396.25 |

Translated Specific Price-Level-Adjusted Income Statements
(Millions of 1974 Dollars)

|  | | | | | |
|---|---|---|---|---|---|
| Revenue | | $194.50 | $203.53 | $218.25 | $201.23 |
| Operating Expenses | | 108.64 | 97.75 | 102.44 | 91.78 |
| Depreciation | | 34.93 | 44.39 | 47.88 | 56.17 |
| Interest | | 4.47 | 3.66 | 4.02 | 5.19 |
| Profit before Taxes | | 46.46 | 57.73 | 63.91 | 48.09 |
| Taxes | | 34.98 | 30.60 | 48.26 | 42.24 |
| Price-Level Gain (Loss) | | (1.97) | (25.20) | (2.14) | ..48 |
| Translation Gain (Loss) | | 5.48 | 3.36 | (8.43) | .22 |
| Net Income | | $ 14.99 | $ 5.29 | $ 5.08 | $ 6.55 |

**EXHIBIT 15**
BRAZILIAN EXPLORATION CORPORATION

|  | 1970 | 1971 | 1972 | 1973 | 1974 |
|---|---|---|---|---|---|
| Translated General Price-Level-Adjusted Balance Sheets | | | | | |
| Current Method | | | | | |
| (Millions of 1974 Dollars) | | | | | |
| Cash | $ 22.22 | $ 15.15 | $ 17.31 | $ 14.06 | $ 25.00 |
| Accounts Receivables | 24.24 | 21.88 | 31.74 | 26.85 | 49.00 |
| Property, Plant, and | | | | | |
| Equipment | 95.01 | 134.62 | 143.30 | 198.60 | 205.39 |
| Total Assets | $141.47 | $171.65 | $192.35 | $239.51 | $279.39 |
|  | | | | | |
| Current Liabilities | $ 44.44 | $ 39.64 | $ 38.96 | $ 45.02 | $ 47.00 |
| Long-Term Debt | 14.14 | 28.62 | 23.08 | 30.68 | 34.00 |
| Retained Earnings | 82.89 | 103.39 | 130.31 | 163.81 | 198.39 |
| Total Equities | $141.47 | $171.65 | $192.35 | $239.51 | $279.39 |

Translated General Price-Level-Adjusted Income Statements
(Millions of 1974 Dollars)

|  | | 1971 | 1972 | 1973 | 1974 |
|---|---|---|---|---|---|
| Revenue | | $194.50 | $203.53 | $218.25 | $201.23 |
| Operating Expenses | | 108.64 | 97.75 | 102.44 | 91.78 |
| Depreciation (at current rate) | | 14.37 | 19.30 | 22.49 | 28.94 |
| Interest | | 4.47 | 3.66 | 4.02 | 5.19 |
| Profit before Taxes | | 67.02 | 82.82 | 89.30 | 75.32 |
| Taxes | | 34.98 | 30.60 | 48.26 | 42.24 |
| Price-Level Gain (Loss) | | (1.97) | (25.20) | (2.14) | .48 |
| Translation Gain (Loss) | | (9.57) | (.10) | (5.40) | 1.02 |
| Net Income | | $ 20.50 | $ 26.92 | $ 33.50 | $ 34.58 |

**EXHIBIT 16**
BRAZILIAN EXPLORATION CORPORATION

|  | 1970 | 1971 | 1972 | 1973 | 1974 |
|---|---|---|---|---|---|
| | Translated Specific Price-Level-Adjusted Balance Sheets | | | | |
| | Current Method | | | | |
| | (Millions of 1974 Dollars) | | | | |
| Cash | $ 22.22 | $ 15.15 | $ 17.31 | $ 14.06 | $ 25.00 |
| Accounts Receivables | 24.24 | 21.88 | 31.74 | 26.85 | 49.00 |
| Property, Plant, and | | | | | |
| Equipment | 178.33 | 226.33 | 224.88 | 259.74 | 253.88 |
| Total Assets | $224.79 | $263.36 | $273.93 | $300.65 | $327.88 |
| | | | | | |
| Current Liabilities | $ 44.44 | $ 39.64 | $ 38.96 | $ 45.02 | $ 47.00 |
| Long-Term Debt | 14.14 | 28.62 | 23.08 | 30.68 | 34.00 |
| Retained Earnings | 166.21 | 195.10 | 211.89 | 224.95 | 246.88 |
| Total Equities | $224.79 | $263.36 | $273.93 | $300.65 | $327.88 |

Translated Specific Price-Level-Adjusted Income Statements
(Millions of 1974 Dollars)

| | | | | | |
|---|---|---|---|---|---|
| Revenue | | $194.50 | $203.53 | $218.25 | $201.23 |
| Operating Expenses | | 108.64 | 97.75 | 102.44 | 91.78 |
| Depreciation (at current rate) | | 26.97 | 33.03 | 36.49 | 40.86 |
| Interest | | 4.47 | 3.66 | 4.02 | 5.19 |
| Profit before Taxes | | 54.42 | 69.09 | 75.30 | 63.40 |
| Taxes | | 34.98 | 30.60 | 48.26 | 42.24 |
| Price-Level Gain (Loss) | | (1.97) | (25.20) | (2.14) | .48 |
| Translation Gain (Loss) | | 11.42 | 3.50 | (11.84) | .29 |
| Net Income | | $ 28.89 | $ 16.79 | $ 13.06 | $ 21.93 |

**EXHIBIT 17**
Summary of Return-on-Investment Calculations
Under the Various Accounting Methods

| Accounting Basis | Currency | Translation Method | Case Exhibit | 1971 | 1974 |
|---|---|---|---|---|---|
| West German Telephone | | | | | |
| Historical | Marks | | 3 | 17.4 | 13.0 |
| Historical | Dollars | M/NM | 1 | 25.9 | 16.8 |
| GPI[a] | Marks | | 4 | 15.1 | 10.8 |
| SPI[b] | Marks | | 5 | 23.2 | 14.5 |
| GPI | Dollars | M/NM | 6 | 16.2 | 14.9 |
| SPI | Dollars | M/NM | 7 | 20.6 | 18.8 |
| GPI | Dollars | All current | 8 | 20.5 | 18.6 |
| SPI | Dollars | All current | 9 | 16.4 | 21.5 |
| Brazilian Exploration Corporation | | | | | |
| Historical | Cruzeiros | | 10 | 23.4 | 21.3 |
| Historical | Dollars | M/NM | 2 | 19.1 | 20.2 |
| GPI[a] | Cruzeiros | | 11 | 17.0 | 13.2 |
| SPI[b] | Cruzeiros | | 12 | 5.3 | 6.7 |
| GPI | Dollars | M/NM | 13 | 12.9 | 9.4 |
| SPI | Dollars | M/NM | 14 | 4.5 | 1.8 |
| GPI | Dollars | All current | 15 | 15.4 | 14.8 |
| SPI | Dollars | All current | 16 | 12.9 | 7.8 |

[a]General price index.
[b]Specific price index for this industry.

# Drago Chemical

In October 1974, Mr. Ralph Reeves, managing director of Drago Chemical, was reviewing his financial director's proposal for changes in the company's management control system. The proposed changes, prepared at Reeve's request, made explicit provision for inflation accounting.

Drago Chemical's manufacturing was centered in southern England. The company's major products included PVC, plasticizers, polyethylenes, surfactants, and herbicides. The heads of the five manufacturing divisions and the several staff departments reported to the managing director. Over 30% of the company's sales were outside the United Kingdom (although mostly within the EEC).

The capital investments of each division were carefully reviewed at the corporate level; in most respects, however, each division manager was free to pursue his business objectives. For control purposes, a division was organized as an investment center. Each was expected to steadily improve current performance while pursuing long-term viability. In August 1974, all divisions had a positive ROI. Nevertheless, there were wide variances in their returns; the two least profitable divisions had ROIs of 2% and 4%.

In mid-1974, although pleased with Drago's current financial performance (Exhibits 1 and 2), Ralph Reeves had become concerned about the impact of inflation on the firm's profitability (Exhibit 3). Accordingly, he had asked his financial director to study the internal impact of inflation. He knew the subject of external reporting was under active study in the U.K. (Exhibit 4). However, he felt that Drago's approach to this issue for management control and for per-

Copyright © 1974 by the President and Fellows of Harvard College. Reproduced by permission. This case was prepared by Professor F. Warren McFarlan as a basis for class discussion rather than to illustrate either effective or ineffective handling of an administrative situation.

formance appraisal should be independent of statutory requirements for external reporting and for the Inland Revenue Service.

Mr. Reeves was impressed by the simplicity and comprehensive approach of the financial director's report (Appendix A). Nonetheless, he wondered if the proposed procedures would adequately reflect what happened to his stocks of raw materials, works in process, and finished goods. During the last 18 months, this stock had dropped about 2% in tonnage, although the mix of products had remained almost the same. In the same 18 months, however, the rapid rise in the prices of raw materials had inflated the value of his stock from slightly over £6.6 million to £11.6 million (£8.5 million on February 28, 1974). (As was common in the U.K., stock was valued on a first-in, first-out basis.) This stock represented about 60 days of purchases.

Mr. Reeves was also mindful of a recent chance conversation with the head of Drago's most important union. The union head had been complimentary about the company's recent results (Exhibit 1), which he had just seen. Then he had expressed the hope that all who had helped to achieve those results could share amicably in the obviously ample rewards.

Of equal concern to Mr. Reeves was a recent letter that Drago's chairman had sent to the stockholders. The chairman had hailed the firm's record performance in sales and earnings; he added that he intended to pay an increased dividend for the year, "up to the maximum" then permitted. Mr. Reeves was partly reassured, since Drago's pretax profit of £2,960,000 came only after deduction of a special one-time contribution of £900,000 to the corporate pension fund. (This was to recognize the fund's increased liabilities, "an inevitable consequence of inflationary pressures upon remuneration.") For that reason, Mr. Reeves felt that the company's real earnings were somewhat higher than the announced figure.

Mr. Reeves had a further bit of relevant information: in the last 6 months, Drago had incurred a tax liability of £1,598,000 as a result of operations. However, the company had acquired considerable new equipment during the same period. Since the associated tax credits were large enough to balance the liability, no tax would have to be paid.

## QUESTIONS

1    How much inflation-adjusted profit do you believe Drago earned during the last 18 months?

2    Should this inflation-adjusted profit figure be the basis for calculating the firm's return on investment?

## EXHIBIT 1
### DRAGO CHEMICAL
Profit and Loss Statement
(Thousands of Pounds)

|  | *Full Year Ending February 28, 1974* | *Half-Year Ending August 31, 1974* |
|---|---|---|
| Turnover | £48,002 | £40,800 |
| Trading Profit before | | |
|    Following Deductions | 4,604 | 3,806 |
| Depreciation | 980 | 492 |
| Interest Charges | 802 | 354 |
| Profit before Taxes | 2,822 | 2,960 |
| Tax | 1,524 | 1,599 |
| Profit after Taxes | £ 1,298 | £ 1,361 |

## EXHIBIT 2
### DRAGO CHEMICAL
Balance Sheet
(Thousands of Pounds)

|  | *March 1, 1973* | *February 29, 1974* |
|---|---|---|
| **Assets** | | |
|   Cash | £ 103 | £ 158 |
|   Debtors | | |
|     (Accounts Receivable) | 9,614 | 11,413 |
|   Stock (Inventory) | 6,614 | 8,512 |
|   Fixed Assets | 8,684 | 9,103 |
| | £25,015 | £29,186 |
| **Liabilities and Net Worth** | | |
|   Accounts Payable | £ 8,276 | £12,109 |
|   Short-Term Debt | 2,010 | 1,400 |
|   Long-Term Debt | 5,040 | 5,040 |
|   Net Worth | 9,689 | 10,637 |
| | £25,015 | £29,186 |

EXHIBIT 3
DRAGO CHEMICAL
Inflation in the United Kingdom,
1963-1973

| Year | Retail Price Index | Annual Inflation (%) | Cumulative Inflation (%) |
|------|------|------|------|
| 1963 | 100 | | |
| 1964 | 103 | 3 | 3 |
| 1965 | 108 | 5 | 8 |
| 1966 | 112 | 4 | 12 |
| 1967 | 115 | 3 | 15 |
| 1968 | 121 | 5 | 21 |
| 1969 | 127 | 5 | 27 |
| 1970 | 135 | 6 | 35 |
| 1971 | 148 | 10 | 48 |
| 1972 | 158 | 7 | 58 |
| 1973 | 173 | 10 | 73 |

EXHIBIT 4
DRAGO CHEMICAL
The State of Inflation Accounting in the United Kingdom,
October 1974[a]

In London, the Sandilands Committee on Inflation Accounting is hard at work in an attempt to produce its recommendations by early 1975. Last May, the Institute of Chartered Accountants published its provisional statement of Standard Accounting Practice No. 7 (SSAP 7). This contains proposals for adapting conventional historic cost accounts to conditions of inflation. The statement supports the current-purchasing-power or general-price-level method of adjustment. *The accountants point out that management must be able to appreciate the effects of inflation on costs, profits, distribution policies, dividend cover, borrowing power, return on investment, and cash requirements.*

Although the Institute opinion supports the current-purchasing-power method, the Sandilands Committee is still analyzing the advantages and disadvantages of the replacement-cost method. The replacement-cost method has many supporters in industry who argue that it is better to use a more complex system in an effort to approach the truth than to use a rigid, easy-to-apply formula which will always be inaccurate.

The ease of applying the current-purchasing-power system for the company and the ease of auditing it for the accountant make the system an attractive one. Although the Sandilands Committee has made no disclosures on which way it is leaning, many feel that they will attempt a synthesis of the two methods. There is currently a loophole in SSAP 7 allowing companies to revalue assets as well as to apply a rigid index to their original purchase cost. If the Sandilands Committee decades to support this decision, the controversy over the two systems may become irrelevant.

[a]*Financial Times,* October 3, 1974.

To:     Mr. Ralph Reeves, Managing Director

From:   Mr. John Thompson

Date:   October 7, 1974

Pursuant to our discussion of last month, I have investigated the feasibility of incorporating an inflation accounting approach into our ongoing management control system. It is my opinion that while many aspects of an inflation accounting approach are counterbalancing insofar as their ultimate impact on the firm's profit, the overall impact on profits could be sufficiently significant that we should move to an inflation accounting approach for internal purposes, effective January 1. The rest of this memorandum details the approach I believe we should follow, with Exhibit A showing how these procedures would have impacted our stated earnings for the year ending February 28, 1974 and the half-year ending August 31, 1974, and Exhibit B showing the critical calculations in depth.

Debtors, creditors, stock, and fixed assets are all subject to inflation adjustments, which will affect the company's real profitability. Accordingly, I plan to process these items each quarter to take into account the impact of inflation during the quarter. The Economist Intelligence Unit's index (E.I.U.)[a] will be used on an annual basis to revalue our fixed assets. The Retail Price Index (R.P.I.) will be used on other assets and liabilities.

Quarterly, all assets and liabilities will be adjusted for inflation using only the Retail Price Index (the base value of fixed assets being the calculated E.I.U. values as of March 1 each year). If anything, we are understanding the specific effect of inflation on the company, since chemical industry raw material prices have soared in the past 12 months. The following table gives a brief feel for the magnitude of the changes in our plant values as a result of using the E.I.U. index.

---

[a]The E.I.U. Index is an industry replacement-value index created by The Economist Intelligence Unit of The Economist magazine. The E.I.U. produces 16 indices for various industries. An industry index is established by selecting a number of different types of standard equipment representative of the industry. The number of deliveries of a piece of equipment determines its relative importance. The change in the manufacturer's sale price over a certain period of time is then considered and weighted according to the relative importance of each piece of equipment to determine the E.I.U. The weighting of the various pieces of equipment is revised as the items become obsolete.

*Net Book Value*

| Plant | Historical (thousands) | Current Purchasing Power as of August 31, 1974 (thousands) |
|-------|------------------------|-------------------------------------------------------------|
| A | £1,538 | £2,392 |
| B | 452 | 820 |
| C | 360 | 604 |

The specific procedure for calculating the effect of inflation is as follows, and the impact worked out in detail for the year ending February 28, 1974, is given in Exhibit B.

A. *Net Monetary Assets (i.e., Debtors less Creditors)*

The closing Retail Price Index is divided by the opening Retail Price Index. The percentage uplift multiplied by the value of the opening net monetary assets is the loss (profit if net monetary liability) to be offset against the historically recorded profits.

B. *Stock*

The index to be used for the opening stock must be back-dated to allow for the period over which that stock was purchased (if 2 months' stock in hand, then the opening index is the average index of those two months). This index is divided into the closing index, etc., as above.

The closing stock, on a similar basis, would yield a constant purchasing power profit in the period:

$$\frac{\text{R.P.I. @ closing date}}{\text{R.P.I. @ average of last 2 months}} \times \text{value of closing stock}$$

$-$ value of closing stock = profit impact in period

C. *Fixed Assets*

The depreciation charge is to be uplifed by the proportion of historical costs to current value.

**EXHIBIT A**
Impact of Inflation on Company Accounts
(Thousands of Pounds)

|  | Year Ending February 28, 1974 | Half-Year Ending August 31, 1974 |
|---|---|---|
| Profits before Taxes per Conventional Accounts | £2,822 | £2,960 |
| − Taxes | 1,524 | 1,599 |
| = Profit after Taxes, Conventional Accounts | £1,298 | £1,361 |
| *Adjustments* | | |
| (1) Stocks (Restatement of Stocks at Beginning and End of Year) | £ (638) | £ (668) |
| (2) Depreciation (Additional Depreciation Due to Adjusting Fixed-Asset Values) | (457) | (304) |
| (3) Monetary Items (Gain Due to Excess of Monetary Liabilities over Monetary Assets) | 573 | 278 |
| Net Adjustments | (522) | (694) |
| Profit before Taxes Expressed in Pounds of Current Purchasing Power at the End of the Period | 2,300 | 2,266 |
| − Taxes | 1,524 | 1,599 |
| = Profit after Taxes in Pounds of Current Purchasing Power | £ 776 | £ 667 |

## EXHIBIT B
Calculation of Change in Corporate Profits Moving from
Historical-Cost Accounting to Inflation-Adjusted Accounting
(March 1, 1973–February 28, 1974)

1.  *Summary Balance Sheet Data from Exhibit 2*

|  | *March 1, 1973* | *February 28, 1974* |
|---|---|---|
| Net Monetary Assets (Cash + Debtors – Creditors – Short-Term Debt – Long-Term Debt) | (5,609) | (6,978) |
| Stock | 6,614 | 8,512 |
| Net Book Value–Fixed Assets | 8,684 | 9,103 |

2.  *Retail Price Index*

| | |
|---|---|
| December 31, 1972 | 158 |
| January 31, 1973 | 160 |
| February 28, 1973 | 160.6 |
| December 31, 1973 | 173 |
| January 31, 1974 | 175 |
| February 28, 1974 | 177 |

3.  *Fixed Assets Adjusted by E.I.U. Index*

| | |
|---|---|
| March 1, 1973 | 11,550 |
| February 28, 1974 | 12,106 |

4.  *Calculation of Impact of Inflation on Profits*     *Gain (Loss)*

*Net Monetary Assets*
$$5,609 \times \frac{177}{160.6} - 5,609 = 573$$

*Opening Stock*
$$6,614 \times \frac{177}{(158 + 160.6) \times .5} - 6,614 = (735)$$

*Closing Stock*
$$8,512 \times \frac{177}{(173 + 177) \times .5} - 8,512 = 97$$

*Depreciation*
$$\frac{11,550}{8,684} \times 980 \times \frac{177}{160.6} - 980 = 457$$

# part 3

# COST
# ACCUMULATION
# SYSTEMS

# Amos Carholtz Distillery, Inc.

In early August 1961, Mr. David Carholtz, president and chief operating executive of Amos Carholtz Distillery, Inc., of Oakwoods, Tennessee, sat in his office pondering the results of the previous day's meeting of the board of directors and wondering whether he should submit the 1961 financial statements (Exhibits 1 and 2) to the Ridgeview National Bank of Nashville, Tennessee, in support of a recent loan request for $1.5 million, or whether he should wait until next month's board meeting in the hope of obtaining clarification of some of the preceding day's discussion. A great deal of controversy had arisen over the 1961 reported loss of $407,000 and how this result should be reported to the bank. The controversy seemed to revolve principally around the accounting treatment of various expenses reported in the "other costs" section of the operating statement. Mr. Carholtz knew that a decision had to be reached quickly on these matters, for the company had reached a point where additional working capital was needed immediately if the company was to remain solvent.

## COMPANY HISTORY

Amos Carholtz began distilling whiskey in 1880. Amos had come to Oakwoods, Tennessee, from Germany the preceding year and had decided to carry on in the family tradition of beverage manufacture. He purchased a tract of land on a high

Copyright © 1961, by the President and Fellows of Harvard College; revised 1968 and 1969. Reproduced by permission. This case was prepared by R. H. Deming under the supervision of R. F. Vancil. Case material of the Harvard Graduate School of Business Administration is prepared as a basis for class discussion. Cases are not designed to present illustrations of either correct or incorrect handling of administrative problems. Distributed by the Intercollegiate Case Clearing House, Soldiers Field, Boston, Mass., 02163. All rights reserved to the contributors. Printed in the U.S.A.

knoll adjacent to a small stream fed by a limestone spring and began to distill bourbon whiskey in an old barn behind his home. His business grew from a trickling in 1880 to a million-dollar firm by 1911. He attributed this growth to the distinctive, high-quality bourbon whiskey which he produced. The quality of "Old Trailridge," Carholtz's only brand of whiskey, was claimed to be the result of the unusual iron-free spring water used in the distillation process, and the aging process, which took place in specially prepared fire-charred white oak barrels.

From 1911 to 1933, the years of prohibition in Tennessee, the distilling equipment lay dormant, and it was not until late in 1934 that the company began to operate once again in a newly constructed building. Sales rose from $500,000 in 1935 to nearly $5 million in 1941, when the plant was converted to defense production of commercial alcohol.

In 1946, Mr. David Carholtz, grandson of Amos, took over as chief operating executive of the company and doubled sales revenue during the next 10 years. Mr. Carholtz felt that the company had grown because of the stress it placed on marketing a distinctive, high-quality, high-price product and because of its concentration on one brand of fine bourbon whiskey, Old Trailridge. The company's advertising stressed the uniqueness of the cool, bubbling spring water used in the distillation of Old Trailridge and pointed to its use of "specially prepared and cured fire-charred white oak barrels." This type of promotion had been very effective in establishing a brand image of Old Trailridge in the consumer's mind that conveyed a concept of full-bodied mellowness, camaraderie, and old-fashioned, backwoods quality.

In 1960, the company produced approximately 1.5% of the whiskey distilled in the United States and thus was one of the smaller distillers in the industry. Since the mid-1950s the company's production had been stable; the financial statements for 1960 (Exhibits 1 and 2) were typical of the results of the preceding several years. After the initial postwar surge in demand, no special effort had been made to gain a larger share of the market; but at a board meeting in December 1960, a decision had been made to expand production to try to capture a larger than proportionate share of the increase in whiskey consumption which Mr. Carholtz had forecast, based on an industry research report. This report showed that the consumption of straight bourbon whiskey had increased (at the expense of blended whiskeys) from 15% of total whiskey consumption in 1947 to nearly 50% of total consumption in 1959. Based on this report and other industry forecasts, Mr. Carholtz had forecast a doubling of straight whiskey consumption from 1960 to 1968. In view of this, and because bourbon whiskey had to be aged for at least 4 years, the board had decided to increase the production of whiskey in 1961 by 50% of the 1960 volume (see Exhibit 2) in order to meet the anticipated increase in consumer demand for straight bourbon whiskey from 1964 to 1968.

## THE MANUFACTURING PROCESS

Old Trailridge was a straight bourbon whiskey and thus, by law, had to be made from a mixture of grains containing at least 51% corn and be aged in new (not reused) charred white oak barrels. The process began when the ground corn was mixed with pure limestone spring water in a large vat. To this mixture was added a certain amount of ground barley malt and rye. It was then heated slowly until the starches were converted to sugars, thus completing the "mashing" process. This mash was then pumped into a cypress fermenting vat, where yeast and certain other ingredients were added. This mixture was allowed to ferment for several days until the yeast had converted the sugars into alcohol, at which time the fermenting process was complete and the mash was pumped into a distillation tower (or still) where the alcohol was separated from the "slurry," or spent mash, through a series of distillation tanks and condensers. The distilled liquid was then mixed with limestone spring water to obtain the desired proof (percent of alcohol by volume, where one degree of proof equals one-half of 1% of alcohol). At this point the whiskey was a clear liquid with a sharp, biting taste and had to be mellowed before consumption. For this process, it was pumped into 50-gallon barrels and moved to an aging warehouse. The cost accumulated in the product prior to its entry into barrels, including all direct and indirect materials and labor consumed in the production process, was approximately $.50 per gallon (see Exhibit 2). The volume of production had been the same for each of the years 1957-1960, and all costs during this period had been substantially the same as the 1960 costs shown in Exhibit 2.

## MATURING OR AGING PROCESS

To mellow the whiskey, improve its taste, and give it a rich amber color, the new bourbon whiskey had to be matured or aged for a period of time of not less than 4 years under controlled temperature and humidity conditions. The new whiskey reacted with the charred oak and assimilated some of the flavor and color of the fire-charred oak during the period of aging.

Since the quality of the aging barrel was an important factor in determining the ultimate taste and character of the final product, Carholtz had his 50-gallon barrels manufactured under a unique patented process at a cost of approximately $31 per barrel. The barrels could not be reused for aging future batches of bourbon whiskey but could be sold to used barrel dealers for $.50 each at the end of the aging period.

The filled barrels were next placed in open "ricks" in an aging warehouse, rented by Carholtz, or in that half of the factory building which had been converted into warehousing space. The increased production in 1961 necessitated the leasing of an additional warehouse at an annual rental cost of $100,000. The temperature and humidity of the warehouse space had to be controlled, since the quality of the whiskey could be ruined by aging too fast or too slowly, a process determined by temperature and humidity conditions.

Every 6 months the barrels had to be rotated from a high rick to a lower rick or vice versa (because of uneven temperatures at different locations in the warehouse) and sampled for quality and character up to that point in the aging process. A small amount of liquid was removed from representative barrels at this time and sent to the sampling laboratory for quality inspection (usually performed by skilled tasters). If the quality of the whiskey was not up to standard, certain measures were taken, such as adjusting the aging process, to bring it up to standard. At the same time, each barrel was also checked for leaks or seepage and the required repairs were made.

At the end of the 4-year aging period, the barrels were removed from the ricks and dumped into regauge tanks, where the charred oak residue was filtered out and volume was measured. On the average, the volume of liquid in a barrel declined by 30% during the aging period because of evaporation and leakage. Thus a barrel originally filled with 50 gallons of new bourbon would, on the whole, produce only 35 gallons of aged bourbon. The regauge operation was supervised by a government liquor tax agent, since it was at this point that the federal excise tax of $10.50 per gallon was levied on the whiskey removed from the warehouse. Once the bourbon had been removed from the aging warehouse, it was bottled and shipped to wholesalers with the greatest speed possible because of the large amount of cash tied up in taxes on the finished product. During both 1960 and 1961, the company sold 30,000 *regauged* barrels of whiskey, equivalent to about 43,000 barrels of original production.

## EXCERPTS FROM BOARD OF DIRECTORS MEETING AUGUST 3, 1961

**DAVID CARHOLTZ:**   President

Gentlemen, I'm quite concerned over the prospect of obtaining the $1.5 million loan we need in light of our 1961 loss of $407,000. We have shown annual profits since 1948, and our net sales of $21.0 million this year is the same as last year and yet we incurred a net loss for the year. I think I understand the reason for this, but I'm afraid that the loan officers at the Ridgeview National Bank will hesitate in granting us a loan on the basis of our most recent performance. It appears that we are becoming less efficient in our production operation.

**JAMES DOUD:**   Production Manager

That's not quite so, David. You know as well as I do that we increased production by 50% this year, and with this increased production our costs are bound to increase. You can't produce something for nothing.

**ROBERT THOMPSON:**   Controller

Well, that's not quite so, Jim. Granted that our production costs must rise when production increases, but our inventory account takes care of the increased costs by deferring these product costs until a future period when the product is actually sold. As you can see by looking at our 1961 profit and loss statement, our cost of goods sold did not increase in 1961 since the volume of sales was the same in 1961 as in 1960. The largest share of the increase in production costs has been deferred until future periods, as you can see by looking at the increase in our inventory account of nearly half a million dollars. I believe that the real reason for our loss this year was the large increase in other costs, composed chiefly of warehousing costs. The "Occupancy Costs" category in our P & L is really the summation of a group of expense accounts, including building depreciation or rent, heat, light, power, building maintenance, labor and supplies, real estate taxes, and insurance. In addition, warehouse labor costs also rose substantially in 1961. Even administrative and general expenses went up, due primarily to higher interest expense on the additional money needed to finance our increase in inventory.

**DAVID CARHOLTZ**

Well, what's your explanation for the large increase in the warehousing costs, Jim?

**JAMES DOUD**

As I said before, Dave, we increased production, and this also means an increase in warehousing costs since the increased production has to be aged for several years. You just can't age 50% more whiskey for the same amount of money.

**DAVID CARHOLTZ**

But I thought Bob said that increased production costs were taken care of in the inventory account. Isn't that so, Bob?

**ROBERT THOMPSON**

Well, yes and no, David. The inventory account can only be charged with those costs associated with the direct production of whiskey, and our warehousing costs are handling or carrying costs, certainly not production costs.

**JAMES DOUD**

Now just a minute, Bob, I think that some of those costs are just as valid production costs as are the direct labor and materials going into the distillation of the new bourbon. The manufacturing process doesn't stop with the newly produced bourbon; why it isn't even marketable in that form. Aging is an absolutely essential part of the manufacturing process, and I think the cost of barrels and part of the warehouse labor should be treated as direct costs of the product.

**DAVID CARHOLTZ**

Great, Jim! I agree with you that warehousing and aging costs are an absolutely essential ingredient of our final product. We certainly couldn't market the bourbon before it had been aged. I think that all the costs associated with aging the product should be charged to the inventory account. I think that most of the "other costs" should be considered a cost of the product. Don't you agree, Bob?

**ROBERT THOMPSON**

Sure, Dave! Let's capitalize depreciation, interest expenses, your salary, the shareholders' dividends, our advertising costs, your secretary's salary—why, let's capitalize all our costs! That way we can show a huge inventory balance and small expenses! I'm sure Ridgeview and the Internal Revenue boys would be happy to cooperate with us on it! Why, we'll revolutionize the accounting profession!

**DAVID CARHOLTZ**

Now cool down, Bob. Be reasonable about this. I'm afraid I really don't see why we couldn't charge all of those costs you mentioned to the inventory account, since it seems to me that they are all necessary ingredients in producing our final product. What distinction do you draw between these so-called "direct" costs you mentioned and the aging costs?

**ROBERT THOMPSON**

By direct costs I mean those costs that are necessary to convert raw materials into the whiskey that goes into the aging barrels. This is our cost of approximately $.50 per gallon and includes the cost of raw materials going into the product such as grain, yeast, and malt; the direct labor necessary to convert these materials into whiskey; and the cost of any other overhead items that are needed to permit the workers to convert grain into whiskey. I don't see how aging costs can be included under this generally accepted accounting definition of the inventory cost of the finished product.

**DAVID CARHOLTZ**

I think we'd better defer further discussion of this entire subject until our meeting next month. In the meantime I am going to try to get this thing squared away in my own mind. I have never really thought that financial statements had much meaning, but now I am not at all sure that they aren't truly misleading documents!

Well, let's turn next to the question of . . . .

**REQUIRED**

1    Calculate the effect on the financial statements in Exhibits 1 and 2 assuming that the accounting system was changed to incorporate the cost of barrels ($31.50 each) into the inventory accounts.

    *a*    What would pretax profit be in 1961?

    *b*    If the change were made retroactively as of July 1, 1959 (by adding the cost of barrels to all whiskey in inventory), what would be the effect on

        (1) The balance sheet at the end of 1960?

        (2) The balance sheet at the end of 1961?

        (3) The income statement for 1960?

2    Do you believe that Carholtz should show a lower profit in 1961 than in 1960, despite the fact that sales were the same and production increased in 1961?

3    Examine carefully the costs listed in the lower half of Exhibit 2. Which, if
     any, of these costs should be capitalized into inventory?

4    Would you recommend that Mr. Carholtz use this method of accounting
     in preparing the annual financial statements which were to be submitted
     to Ridgeview National Bank?

## Focus of the Class

The short label for the issue here is "product vs. period costs," but that's
really just a more realistic label for the "direct vs. full costs" issue. No company
operates a "completely full cost" system; some costs are always treated as costs of
the current operating period rather than loaded into the cost of the product.

The issue is not as simple as: *Which* costs should be product costs? The
practical issue is situational: Which costs should be treated as product costs in
*this* company? We'll try to answer that question for Carholtz and then see if we
can generalize a little bit beyond that.

## Preparation Hints

The calculations required for question 1 are not massive (it takes more
thinking than pencil-pushing), and working those calculations will help solidify
your understanding of cost accounting. You'll know you've got the right answers
if you conclude that the answer to part b(3) is "no effect." The question to ponder
then is *why* such a change in accounting doesn't affect the 1960 profit.

The important question is number 3. Don't fret the calculations in question
1 if they won't yield easily. Think about question 3 and try to frame an accounting
policy which you think would make sense for this company.

EXHIBIT 1

**AMOS CARHOLTZ DISTILLERY, INC.**
Balance Sheet
as of June 30, 1960 and 1962
(Thousands of Dollars)

|  | 1960 | 1961 |
|---|---|---|
| **Current Assets** | | |
| Cash | $ 1,274 | $ 316 |
| Accounts Receivable—Trade (Less Allowance for | | |
| Doubtful Accounts of Approximately $165,000 | 1,427 | 1,831 |
| Inventories: | | |
| Bulk Whiskey in Barrels at Average Production | | |
| Cost (no Excise Tax Included) | 4,506 | 5,030 |
| Bottled and Cased Whiskey, 175,000 Gallons in Each | | |
| year at an Average Cost of $11.25 per Gallon | | |
| (Including Excise Tax) | 1,969 | 1,969 |
| Inventory in Process | 101 | 101 |
| Raw Materials and Supplies | 400 | 236 |
| Prepaid Expenses | 441 | 389 |
| Total Current Assets | $10,118 | $ 9,872 |

Fixed Assets

|  | Cost | | Accumulated Depreciation | | Net | |  |  |
|---|---|---|---|---|---|---|---|---|
|  | 1960 | 1961 | 1960 | 1961 | 1960 | 1961 |  |  |
| Cash Surrender Value of Officers' Life Insurance |  |  |  |  | $ 32 | $ 35 |  |  |
| Land | $ 30 | $ 30 |  |  | 30 | 30 |  |  |
| Building[a] | 1,910 | 2,110 | $800 | $853 | 1,110 | 1,257 |  |  |
| Factory Equipment | 72 | 72 | 26 | 38 | 46 | 34 |  |  |
| Warehouse Equipment | 35 | 64 | 24 | 34 | 11 | 30 |  |  |
| Trademarks and Brands | 8 | 8 |  |  | 8 | 8 | 1,237 | 1,394 |
| Total Assets |  |  |  |  |  |  | $11,355 | $11,266 |

EXHIBIT 1 (continued)

|  | Net | |
|---|---|---|
|  | *1960* | *1961* |
| **Current Liabilities** | | |
| Notes Payable: | | |
| Short-Term to Banks | $ 1,100 | $ 1,500 |
| Current Maturities of Long-Term Debt | 230 | 483 |
| Accounts Payable | 860 | 419 |
| Accrued Liabilities | 199 | 115 |
| Provision for Federal Taxes on Earnings | 410 | – |
| Total Current Liabilities | $ 2,799 | $ 2,517 |
| **Noncurrent Liabiltieis** | | |
| Notes Payable (5½%) Secured by Deed of Trust on Warehouse Property (Less Current Maturities of $230,000 for 1960 and $245.000 for 1961) | $ 3,500 | $ 4,100 |
| **Stockholders' Equity** | | |
| Common Stock Held Principally by Members of the Carholtz Family | 1,800 | 1,800 |
| Earnings Retained in the Business | 3,256 | 2,849 |
| Total Liabilities and Capital | $11,355 | $11,266 |

aIn June 1961, payment was made for work that had been performed during the year in adding to and improving the warehousing space in the building owned by Carholtz Distillers.

# EXHIBIT 2

## AMOS CARHOLTZ DISTILLERY, INC.
### Statement of Income
### for the Years Ended June 30, 1960 and 1962
### (Thousands of Dollars)

| | 1960 | 1961 |
|---|---|---|
| **Net Sales** | | |
| Sale of Whiskey to Wholesalers | $21,000 | $21,000 |
| **Cost of Goods Sold** | | |
| Federal Excise Taxes—on Barrels Sold | 15,802 | 15,802 |
| Cost of Product Charged to Sales: | | |
| Bulk Whiskey Inventory July 1, of Each Year—172,000 Barrels | $4,506 | $4,506 |
| *Plus:* Cost of Whiskey produced to Inventory (43,000 Barrels in 1960 and 63,000 Barrels in 1961 at an Average Cost of $26.20 per 50-Gallon Barrel in Both Years) | 1,127 / $5,633 | 1,651 / $6,157 |
| Less: Bulk Whiskey Inventory June 30 of Respective Year (172,000 and 192,000 Barrels, at Average Production Cost) | 4,506 | 5,030 |
| Cased Goods and in Process July 1 of Respective Year | $2,070 | $2,070 |
| Cased Goods and in Process June 30, of Respective Year | 2,070 / $16,929 | 2,070 / — / $16,929 |

|  | 1960 | | 1961 | |
|---|---|---|---|---|
| Other Costs Charged to Cost of Goods Sold: | | | | |
| Cost of Barrels Used during Year at $31.50 per Barrel | | $1,354 | | $1,984 |
| Occupancy Costs | | | | |
| Factory Building | | 133 | | 149 |
| Rented Buildings | | 136 | | 286 |
| Labor Cost of Warehousemen and Warehouse | | | | |
| Supervisor | | 94 | | 167 |
| Labor and Supplies Expense of Chemical | | | | |
| Laboratory | | 68 | | 83 |
| Depreciation | | | | |
| Factory Equipment | | 12 | | 12 |
| Warehouse Equipment | | 6 | | 10 |
| Cost of Government Supervision and Bonding | | | | |
| Facilities | | 3 | | 7 |
| Cost of Bottling Liquor (Labor, Glass, and | | | | |
| Miscellaneous Supplies) | 229 | 2,035 | 229 | 2,927 |
| Total Cost of Goods Sold | | $18,964 | | $19,856 |
| Gross Profit from Operations | | 2,036 | | 1,144 |
| Less | | | | |
| Selling and Advertising Expenses | $934 | | $1,087 | |
| Administrative and General Expenses | 350 | 1,284 | 464 | 1,551 |
| Net Profit (Loss) before Tax | | $ 752 | | $ (407) |
| Less: Income Tax | | 290 | | – |
| Net Profit (Loss) after Tax | | $ 462 | | $ (407) |

# Petersen Pottery

Just outside of Elkins, West Virginia, high in the Appalachian Mountains, Clive Petersen had been making ceramic bathroom fixtures since 1960. Petersen fixtures (commonly called toilets) had become known over the years for their distinctive custom features, their high quality, and their long life. Petersen Pottery had grown from a two-man operation in 1960 to the present group of 20 master potters located in two huge old warehouses, converted from World War II storage depots. By 1980 Clive's business had expanded to the point where he felt he must institute some type of formal, systematic controls over his costs. Modern cost systems were becoming a prerequisite for the bank loans which funded Clive's expansion and continuing operations.

The manufacture of ceramic fixtures consists of three processes: molding, glazing, and firing. Raw clay is first molded into the desired shape and baked in a kiln to harden. It is then coated with a glaze mixture to give it its color and characteristic smooth finish. The fixture is then baked again (fired) to harden and fix the glaze to the clay. The finished product is then shipped to the various wholesale outlets around the state. The molding and firing of ceramics, although not highly complex, requires an experienced potter to assure the quality of the product. Excessive heat or excessive time in the kiln can ruin a fixture. The mixing and application of the glaze also requires a significant amount of skill. However, too much time cannot be spent on the molding and glazing processes because delays can cause a bottleneck in the whole production process.

The need for better cost control, coupled with a need for better overall production scheduling to meet the increases in demand, led Clive Petersen to

This case is adapted from a similar exercise written by Professor M. Edgar Barrett of Southern Methodist University. The case was written by Thomas Graham under the supervision of Professor John K. Shank.

adopt a standard cost system. After extended discussions with his most experienced master potters, Clive and his new cost accountant arrived at the following cost standards:

| Materials | | |
|---|---|---|
| Raw Clay | 25 lb @ $.95/lb | $23.75 |
| Glazing Mix | 5 lb @ $.75/lb | 3.75 |
| Direct Labor | | |
| Molding | 1 hr @ $15/hr | 15.00 |
| Glazing | .5 hr @ $15/hr | 7.50 |
| Indirect Costs: Absorbed @ $5 per Fixture | | 5.00[a] |
| | Total per Fixture | $55.00 |

[a]Normal volume per month for overhead allocation purposes was assumed to be 1,200 units. The estimated overhead budget equation was $3.98 per fixture plus $1,224 of fixed cost.

## ANALYSIS OF OPERATIONS

After 6 months of operations using the new cost system Clive was disturbed over the lack of attention paid to the standards. He felt that the potters were just too set in their ways to pay any attention to the "confusing" new system. As one of the potters observed, "I have been making these fixtures a lot longer than these new ideas had been around, and I don't see how a bunch of numbers that some hot-shot accountant puts together are going to help me make any better toilets." The result was that although the standards existed, they were seldom met.

In reviewing the June production results, the following actual costs for 1,145 fixtures were noted:

| Materials Purchased | |
|---|---|
| Clay | 30,000 lb @ .92/lb |
| Glaze | 6,000 lb @ .78/lb |
| Materials Used | |
| Clay | 28,900 lb |
| Glaze | 5,900 lb |
| Direct Labor | |
| Molding | 1,200 hr @ 15.25/hr |
| Glazing | 600 hr @ 15.00/hr |
| Overhead Incurred: $6,100 | |

Before proceeding with further analysis, Clive met with his most experienced master potter, Jim Sedgefield, to discuss the continued variances from the standards. He was seriously considering implementing a standard metal mold system to replace the existing manual system of shaping the fixtures. When Sedgefield arrived, Clive explained the problem: "Jim, you insist the standards are reasonable and yet you never meet them. It looks like we will have unfavorable variances again this month." Sedgefield was not impressed. "Well Clive," he said, "I don't understand this system at all. Why don't you ask that fast-talking accountant to explain the variances? He seems to know what these numbers mean. All I know is, we seemed to spend all month fussing with that new brand of clay you said was going to be cheaper for us."

## QUESTIONS

1    Analyze cost performance for June. Calculate all important variances.
2    What conclusions are suggested regarding cost performance for the month?
3    What suggestions can you make to Mr. Petersen regarding the implementation of the standard cost system?

# Graham, Inc.

The new president of Graham, Inc., was very pleased with himself. He had taken over the top job of a declining company and had almost single-handedly turned it around. Such turnarounds are the dream of every creative, ambitious executive. The August sales were $200,000 greater than those of July, so the president had every reason to expect the income statement to show a healthy profit. When the August report came it showed an $18,540 loss (Exhibit 1) as compared to a $14,036 profit for July. After the initial shock, the president, thinking there must be some mistake, called the controller, Mr. Derrow, for an explanation. Mr. Derrow assured him that the figures were correct. The reason for the loss was that the company had set back production below normal. This resulted in an unabsorbed burden charge which more than offset the increase in sales. He maintained that the rate of sales must equal the factory production or the same thing would happen every month. As it was, the factory operations were out of phase with the sales operations. As long as the company practiced the accounting method of charging or crediting the under- or overabsorbed factory overhead to the current income statement, the type of distortion which occurred in August would happen.

The president had recovered totally from his initial shock: "You always seem to be able to talk your way out of a jam. I don't care about your fancy accounting conventions. Common sense indicates to me that when sales go up, and other things are reasonably the same, profit will also rise. If your reports cannot reflect this simple fact, why do I pay you so much money?"

This case was suggested by a similar exercise written by Professor Robert Anthony of Harvard Business School. The case was written by Thomas Graham under the supervision of Professor John K. Shank.

Mr. Derrow was not even phased. He had been pondering the same question himself, but from a different angle. So he took the opportunity to suggest a different approach to the problem. He wanted to charge the fixed overhead cost for the current month to the income statement in a lump sum, the same as selling and administrative expenses. There would be no problem with variations in under- or overabsorbed overhead when the production volume changed. Cost of goods sold would now reflect variable costs, which Derrow called "direct costs."

To illustrate, he reworked the August statement and found that the loss turned into a profit (Exhibit 2). When he showed this to the president, the response was, "That's more like it!" But after some consideration about the increase in taxes, demands for wage increases, and dividends resulting from the increase in profits, the president said, "Maybe this idea isn't so good after all."

Mr. Derrow was in favor of the idea chiefly because it simplified accounting procedures. He was always one for simple methods. Omission of fixed overhead costs from the product cost would eliminate the tiresome and expensive task of determining an acceptable allocation of overhead to each product. The change was doubly desirable to Derrow, as the current prorations had become out of date and were due to be reconsidered anyway. He could neatly avoid the extra work by doing away with the system.

The president wondered whether the proposed system might have any impact on cost control efforts or on marketing efforts. Certainly, product costs would be lower now by the amount of fixed manufacturing cost previously assigned to each unit.

## QUESTIONS

1   What do you recommend?
2   Approximately how busy (relative to normal volume) was the factory in August?
3   Could the problem in the case ever arise with respect to *annual* statements of profit?
4   Be prepared to explain the profit differences shown in Exhibits 1 and 2 ($-22,928 vs. $+34,272) and in Exhibit 3 ($+14,036 vs. $-59,432).

EXHIBIT 1
GRAHAM, INC.
Condensed Income Statement
for August 1980

| | | |
|---|---:|---:|
| Sales | $1,347,000 | |
| Standard Cost of Goods Sold | 712,000 | |
| Standard Gross Margin | | $635,000 |
| Less Manufacturing Variances | | |
|   Labor | (17,200) | |
|   Material | 15,800 | |
|   Overhead | | |
|     Volume | 107,480 | |
|     Spending | 5,380 | 111,460 |
| Gross Profit | | 523,540 |
| Selling Costs: | | |
|   Sales Expenses | 338,056 | |
|   Sales Taxes | 13,900 | |
|   Freight Allowed | 28,750 | 380,736 |
| Administrative Costs | | |
|   General and Administrative | 82,560 | |
|   Research and Development | 25,500 | 108,060 |
| Operating Profit | | 34,744 |
| Other Income or (Expense) | | (57,672) |
| Current Profit (Loss) | | $ (22,298) |

## EXHIBIT 2
### GRAHAM, INC.
Condensed Income Statement (Proposed)
for August 1980

| | | |
|---|---:|---:|
| Sales | $1,347,000 | |
| Cost of Goods Sold (Standard "Variable" Cost) | 492,000 | |
| Standard Gross Margin | | $855,000 |
| Selling Expenses | | |
|   Sales Expenses | 338,056 | |
|   Sales Taxes | 13,900 | |
|   Freight Allowed | 28,780 | 380,736 |
| Merchandising Margin | | 474,264 |
| Administrative Expenses | | |
|   General and Administrative Expense | 82,560 | |
|   Research and Development Expense | 25,500 | 108,060 |
| Fixed Factory Expense | | |
| Factory Overhead | 270,280 | |
| Manufacturing Variances | | |
|   Labor | (17,200) | |
|   Material | 15,800 | |
|   Overhead Spending | 5,380 | 274,260 |
| Operating Margin | | 91,944 |
| Other Income or (Expense) | | (57,672) |
| Net Profit (Loss) | | $ 34,272 |

## EXHIBIT 3
### GRAHAM, INC.
Condensed Income Statement
for July 1980

| | As Actually Prepared | Under Proposed Method |
|---|---|---|
| Sales | $1,132,112 | $1,132,112 |
| Cost of Sales at Standard | 610,416 | 418,648 |
| Gross Margin | 521,696 | 713,464 |
| Less Manufacturing Variances | | |
| Labor | (21,704) | (21,704) |
| Material | 20,324 | 20,324 |
| Overhead | | |
| Volume | (1,788) | – |
| Spending | 8,692 | 8,692 |
| Fixed Factory Overhead | – | 263,448 |
| Subtotal Overhead and Variances | 5,524 | 270,760 |
| Profit before Administrative and Selling Expenses | 516,172 | 442,704 |
| Selling Expenses (Total) | 341,928 | 341,928 |
| Administrative Expenses (Total) | 104,104 | 104,104 |
| Total Administrative and Selling Expenses | 446,032 | 446,032 |
| Operating Profit | 70,140 | (3,328) |
| Other Income or (Charges) | (56,104) | (56,104) |
| Net Profit (Loss) for Current Month | $ 14,036 | $ (59,432) |

# Battelle's
# Columbus Laboratories

Battelle's Columbus Laboratories is the original research center of Battelle Memorial Institute, a nonprofit corporation established in 1925 as a charitable trust that now has laboratories and offices throughout the world. The corporation's ultimate purpose is to utilize scientific research, creativity, and education for the benefit of mankind. Its primary activity is the sale of research and development on a contract basis to industry, state and federal government agencies, and associations. Any gain from operations is used to acquire or replace facilities and equipment or to cover any other expenses necessary to carrying out its purpose. In addition, a certain proportion of Battelle's income is required to be distributed directly to charities. The payment of dividends or bonuses to trustees, officers, employees, or other individuals is not allowable.

Battelle's Columbus Laboratories (BCL) began operations in Columbus, Ohio, in 1929 with a staff of 30 specializing in metallurgy. In 1979, BCL has over 2,700 staff members and performs research and development in many fields. Sponsored research volume in 1978 was about $90 million. Exhibit 1 shows the current upper management organization. Below the associate directors for research are 13 research departments. Exhibit 2 shows the breakdown of the departments by fields of specialization.

BCL operates its research departments as profit centers. Each department has a research volume goal. Research volume is the sum of all reimbursable charges to sponsored contracts. Each contract is assigned a project number which is used to collect all costs associated with or allocated to it. These costs can be summarized as follows:

Copyright © 1979 by Professor Felix Kollaritsch of the Ohio State University.

*1*   Labor (salaries plus fringe benefits of personnel working on the project)
*2*   Use of BCL equipment and technical facilities (charged either as a percentage of labor dollars on a departmental basis or as a rate per unit used)
*3*   All direct purchases on behalf of project activities
*4*   General overhead (charged to the project as a percentage of labor dollars)
*5*   Research department burden (charged to the project as a percentage of labor dollars)
*6*   Cost of capital (as allowed by the CASB[1], charged to the project as a percentage of labor dollars; treated by BCL as fee income)
*7*   Fee (negotiated profit on each project)

Item 2 provides income to the research departments to cover the maintenance and upgrading of equipment and technical facilities. Item 5 provides income to the research departments to cover general, department-level administrative expenses: for example, the manager's time, office equipment, hiring, and staff development. The income and expense for these two types of department-level activities are budgeted to break even each calendar year.

Item 4, general overhead, provides income to cover the following:

*A*   *Direct operating expenses* of the research departments. Each department receives an annual budget to cover marketing costs, technical development costs, and project losses. In addition, this budget must cover any administrative and facility expenses that exceed the income earned by (5) and (2), above. The research department manager can use his discretion in deciding how to apply the money in this budget.
*B*   *Other direct expenses* of the research departments. These consist of special budgets that are provided by BCL upper management to cover special needs or to encourage special activities of the research departments. They include internal research and development funds for major research areas in which BCL wants to grow, extra financial support for marketing for large programs, funds to cover special publication expenses, and funds to cover any staff time devoted to major national technical association activities. These budgets are provided on request if BCL upper management considers the objective to be in the best interest of the company. Special allocations are also provided to cover costs that are considered to be extraordinary to be charged to a research department's normal direct operating budget.
*C*   *Indirect overhead expenses.* These include all costs associated with BCL buildings, utilities, insurance, taxes, service groups (personnel, legal, safety, accounting, etc.), and upper management.

Items 6 and 7 contribute to net income after overhead costs in excess of absorbed overhead income (2) are deducted. All of the above is shown schematically on the BCL dollar flowchart (Exhibit 3).

---

[1] The Cost Accounting Standards Board (CASB), a governmental agency charged with setting standards for allowable cost for reimbursement purposes under government contracts.

Until January 1979 direct expenses covered by the special budgets described in paragraph B above were not included on the departmental performance report, the summary of fiscal operations (SFO). Allocation of indirect overhead expenses (C) was also not made on the performance reports. Each department's income was estimated using the following proration formula:

$$\frac{\text{Research department labor on projects}}{\text{BCL total labor on projects}} \quad \times \quad \begin{matrix}\text{total BCL income (including} \\ \text{absorbed overhead, cost of} \\ \text{capital, and fee)}\end{matrix}$$

The difference between this prorated income and the department's direct operating expenses (A) was called the department's "contribution" to cover overhead costs and profit. Each department was given a "contribution" goal based on its individual research volume potential, and the attainment of this goal was a basic performance measure.

As of January, 1979, however, several significant changes have been made to the BCL SFO. (See Exhibit 4 for an annotated sample of the SFO.) First, each department is to be credited with the actual absorbed overhead cost of capital income, and fee income generated from its own projects (lines 13-16). Because all three of these income items vary between types of sponsors (government vs. industrial, government agency vs. government agency[2]) and between type of contract (fixed-price vs. cost-plus-fee[3]) the exact income contribution from each department may vary a great deal from the past prorated income. In general, departments doing fixed-price industrial work will show the most income. Those doing cost-plus-fixed-fee work with the Department of Health, Education and Welfare will show the least income because of the differences in the current allowable overhead rates and negotiated fees.

A second change to the SFO is the full allocation of costs to the research departments, including the special budgets for other direct expenses that previously were unaccountable subsidies to the departments (lines 26-33). Indirect overhead expenses are allocated on the following bases:

Facility Costs (line 35)

1    Building depreciation and property taxes will be allocated based on square footage occupied by specific building. Research departments located in the newer buildings will, therefore, be charged more than those assigned to the older buildings.

---

[2]Some branches of the federal government disallow certain types of overhead costs, and the overhead rate charged to their projects is lower than that charged to others.

[3]Fixed-price contracts carry higher fees to reward the contractor for assuming the risk of cost overruns. Cost-plus-fixed-fee contracts carry a lower fee, because the contractor is reimbursed for the actual costs incurred.

2    The actual total cost of janitorial services, maintenance and alterations, and utilities will be prorated to the research departments based on the square footage that they occupy.

General and Administrative Costs (line 36)

All actual costs will be prorated to the research departments based on their total labor dollars for project and nonproject labor.

The final net income is to be compared to research volume as a type of return-on-sales measure (line 42).

A third change is the addition of cash flow information to the summary of fiscal operations (lines 39-41). Depreciation from the department's research facilities and equipment is added to the net income to show total cash generated, and then the department's current expenditures for capital equipment are subtracted to show the department's net cash flow.

The research departments are somewhat troubled by all of the above-described changes in the performance report. They feel that departments located in the newer buildings will be unnecessarily penalized because of the method of allocating building depreciation and property taxes. Allocation of other facility costs based on square-footage-occupied will penalize laboratory-intensive departments and favor those doing primarily paper studies. Basic laboratory research may eventually be discouraged. The cash flow measure may also discourage investment in new and better equipment. The research departments also feel that charging the other direct expenses to a department's SFO that were previously unaccountable subsidies will discourage the requesting of special funds for internal research and development, publications, and technical society activities, all of which are important in developing new technical capabilities and/or maintaining BCL's reputation in the scientific community.

Although the allocation of general and administrative expense is not objected to in principle, the allocation of actual expenses instead of budgeted expenses is thought to be unfair, because it might cause perturbations in net income percentages that are not a result of the research department's performance. Allocation based on total labor dollars rather than on number of staff members is questioned because it implies that the more highly paid staff members cause more general and administrative overhead expenses to be incurred. Credit for actual income earned is considered fair, but it is felt that departments will be penalized for doing business with certain government agencies which allow lower overheads and fees than other sponsors. In addition, it is believed that regardless of how well a department manages its operations, given the type of research that it does and the types of sponsors that it sells to, it may have a low or negative net income percentage, which may ultimately cause its research area to be dropped as a line of business.

Upper management claims that the per-square-foot-occupied charge for facility overhead costs will cause more efficient utilization of space; that it will discourage the hoarding of empty offices in contemplation of expansion and the retention of old, idle laboratory space while new laboratories are being built or requested. Upper management claims that department performance will really be measured by line 25 of the SFO, which is the equivalent of the old "contribution" measure. The net income percentage is an economic indicator of the viability of the various research areas. It will help upper management be aware of the degree of extra support some research areas require.

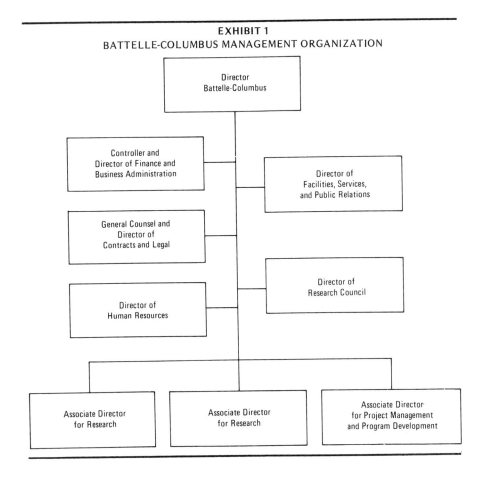

**EXHIBIT 1**
**BATTELLE-COLUMBUS MANAGEMENT ORGANIZATION**

# EXHIBIT 2
## ORGANIZATION OF
## BATTELLE-COLUMBUS RESEARCH DEPARTMENTS

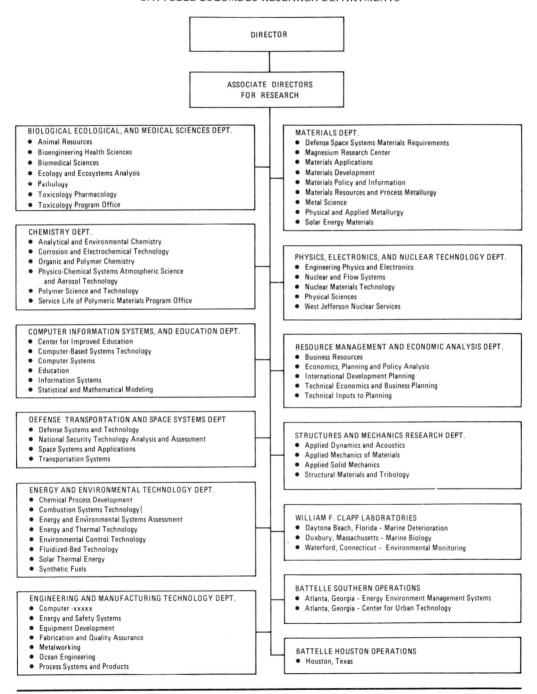

DIRECTOR

ASSOCIATE DIRECTORS FOR RESEARCH

**BIOLOGICAL ECOLOGICAL, AND MEDICAL SCIENCES DEPT.**
- Animal Resources
- Bioengineering Health Sciences
- Biomedical Sciences
- Ecology and Ecosystems Analysis
- Pathology
- Toxicology Pharmacology
- Toxicology Program Office

**CHEMISTRY DEPT.**
- Analytical and Environmental Chemistry
- Corrosion and Electrochemical Technology
- Organic and Polymer Chemistry
- Physico-Chemical Systems Atmospheric Science and Aerosol Technology
- Polymer Science and Technology
- Service Life of Polymeric Materials Program Office

**COMPUTER INFORMATION SYSTEMS, AND EDUCATION DEPT.**
- Center for Improved Education
- Computer-Based Systems Technology
- Computer Systems
- Education
- Information Systems
- Statistical and Mathematical Modeling

**DEFENSE TRANSPORTATION AND SPACE SYSTEMS DEPT**
- Defense Systems and Technology
- National Security Technology Analysis and Assessment
- Space Systems and Applications
- Transportation Systems

**ENERGY AND ENVIRONMENTAL TECHNOLOGY DEPT.**
- Chemical Process Development
- Combustion Systems Technology[
- Energy and Environmental Systems Assessment
- Energy and Thermal Technology
- Environmental Control Technology
- Fluidized-Bed Technology
- Solar Thermal Energy
- Synthetic Fuels

**ENGINEERING AND MANUFACTURING TECHNOLOGY DEPT.**
- Computer -xxxxx
- Energy and Safety Systems
- Equipment Development
- Fabrication and Quality Assurance
- Metalworking
- Ocean Engineering
- Process Systems and Products

**MATERIALS DEPT.**
- Defense Space Systems Materials Requirements
- Magnesium Research Center
- Materials Applications
- Materials Development
- Materials Policy and Information
- Materials Resources and Process Metallurgy
- Metal Science
- Physical and Applied Metallurgy
- Solar Energy Materials

**PHYSICS, ELECTRONICS, AND NUCLEAR TECHNOLOGY DEPT.**
- Engineering Physics and Electronics
- Nuclear and Flow Systems
- Nuclear Materials Technology
- Physical Sciences
- West Jefferson Nuclear Services

**RESOURCE MANAGEMENT AND ECONOMIC ANALYSIS DEPT.**
- Business Resources
- Economics, Planning and Policy Analysis
- International Development Planning
- Technical Economics and Business Planning
- Technical Inputs to Planning

**STRUCTURES AND MECHANICS RESEARCH DEPT.**
- Applied Dynamics and Acoustics
- Applied Mechanics of Materials
- Applied Solid Mechanics
- Structural Materials and Tribology

**WILLIAM F. CLAPP LABORATORIES**
- Daytona Beach, Florida – Marine Deterioration
- Duxbury, Massachusetts – Marine Biology
- Waterford, Connecticut – Environmental Monitoring

**BATTELLE SOUTHERN OPERATIONS**
- Atlanta, Georgia – Energy Environment Management Systems
- Atlanta, Georgia – Center for Urban Technology

**BATTELLE HOUSTON OPERATIONS**
- Houston, Texas

# EXHIBIT 3
## BCL Dollar Flowchart

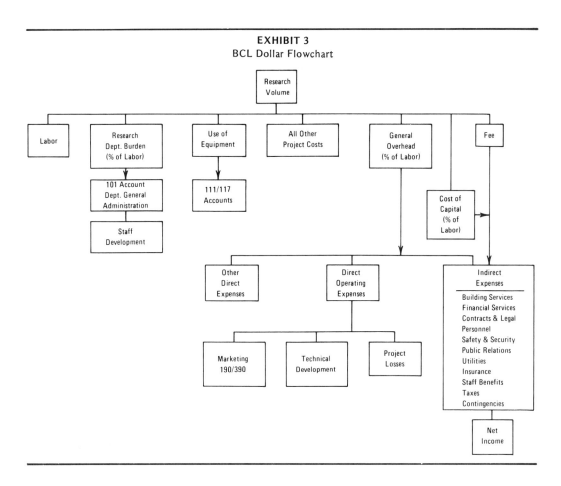

# EXHIBIT 4
## Summary of Fiscal Operations

| Month | | | Year-to-Date | | |
|---|---|---|---|---|---|
| | | | Goal | Budget | Actual |
| | 1 | Working Hours | | | |
| | 2 | Research Volume (W/O Major Subs – Includes Gov't Fee) | | | |
| | 3 | Research Volume (W/O Major Subs and Government Fee) | | | |
| | 4 | Government–Excludes Fee | | | |
| | 5 | Industrial–Includes Fee | | | |
| | 6 | Direct Labor | | | |
| | 7 | Government | | | |
| | 8 | Industrial | | | |
| | 9 | Project Factor–Government (Line 4/7) | | | |
| | 10 | Project Factor–Industrial (Line 5/8) | | | |
| | 11 | Project Labor (Line 17, Page 2) | | | |
| | 12 | B Accounts–Gross Expenditures | | | |
| | 13 | Subaccount Income:   Overhead | | | |
| | 14 | Government Fee and Cost of Capital | | | |
| | 15 | Industrial Fee | | | |
| | 16 | Total Income | | | |
| | 17 | Less: Direct Expenses | YTD Expenses | YTD Income | |
| | 18 | Net 101 (Department Administration) | | | Should Net |
| | 19 | Net 111 (General Support Facilities) | | | to "Zero" |
| | 20 | Net 117 (Special Technical Facilities) | | | by Year End |
| | 21 | Project Write–Offs and Reserve for Contingencies | | | |
| | 22 | 190s, 390s (Marketing) | | | |
| | 23 | Grants & IR&D (Technical Development) | | | |
| | 24 | Total Direct Expenses | | | |
| | 25 | Subtotal:   (Line 16 less 24)  (Contribution) | | | |
| | 26 | Less: Major Research Area Funds | | | |
| | 27 | Large Project Funds | | | |
| | 28 | Director's Reserve | | | |
| | 29 | Assoc. Director's Discretionary | | | |
| | 30 | Associations and Publications | | | |
| | 31 | Disposal of Equipment | | | |
| | 32 | Industrial Marketing Office | | | |
| | 33 | Total Other Direct | | | |
| | 34 | Subtotal:   (Line 25 less 33) | | | |
| | 35 | Less: Facility Costs | | | |
| | 36 | General and Administration | | | |
| | 37 | Total Indirect Expense Allocation | | | |
| | 38 | Net Income (Loss)  (Line 34 less 37) | | | |
| | 39 | Add: Depreciation of Dept. Equip. and Amort. of Prepaids | | | |
| | 40 | Less: Dept. Capital Equip. Expenditures | | | |
| | 41 | Net Cash Flow  (Line 38 plus 39 less 40) | | | |
| | 42 | Net Income  (Loss)  as % of Res. Volume (Line 38 ÷ 2) | | | |

# Mogul Paper Company (A)

Jim Andrews, manager of the Cincinnati region of the Containers Division of Mogul Paper Company, one of the largest integrated companies in the industry, cited the following incident in discussing Mogul's problems with profit center measurement systems.

*One of my customers is a furniture company in Mansfield, Ohio. I supply 80 percent of their shipping cartons. I can ship to that customer from our container plant in Columbus, which is 60 miles from Mansfield, or from our plant in Cincinnati, which is 170 miles from Mansfield. That choice seems easy until I tell you that my reported costs will be cheaper if I use the Cincinnati plant! Our Columbus plant is actually supplied with paperboard by a competitor under an exchange agreement[1], whereas our Cincinnati plant is supplied by our own Middletown board mill. It turns out that*

---

[1] Under a long-standing agreement in the paperboard industry, the major firms regularly exchange "board" (which is all essentially identical), on a barter basis, to supply competitor's corrugated container plants in certain locations. For example, suppose Company A has a board mill near Cincinnati and Company B has a mill near Atlanta. Both A and B have container plants in both Cincinnati and Atlanta. Company A's Cincinnati mill might supply Company B's container plant in Cincinnati while Company B's Atlanta mill might supply Company A's container plant in Atlanta. Both companies thereby save the freight costs on shipping paperboard between Cincinnati and Atlanta. A complex record-keeping system among the companies keeps track of all such transfers. No cash changes hands except for net imbalances each quarter.

This case was written by Professor John K. Shank with the cooperation of a major firm, which prefers to remain anonymous. It is intended for classroom discussion rather than to illustrate either effective or ineffective handling of an administrative situation.

*Mogul repays the product supplied to Columbus by supplying the exchange partner's Chicago container plant out of our Portage, Indiana, board mill. No problem yet. However, Mogul's cost accounting system, which is based on actual costs, charges board to my Columbus plant at the actual cost of the board shipped out of Portage to repay the exchange deal. That way, sales out of Columbus get charged a raw material cost based on what it costs Mogul to produce board in Portage, Indiana, since Portage actually ships the tonnage which repays the exchange deal under which Columbus is supplied. Well, as it turns out, our Portage mill is technologically obsolete and is one of the ten highest cost board mills in the western world. Portage is so expensive to operate that my reported cost to supply Mansfield is lower out of Cincinnati with a 170-mile freight haul than out of Columbus with only a 60-mile freight haul. Since Portage's overall production doesn't change either way and no cash changes hands on the exchange deal, the incremental cost to Mogul has to be less if I supply the customer from the closer plant, but the accounting system doesn't show it that way. Now, I know that I should supply the Mansfield customer out of Columbus, and I probably will. What gripes me is that my region is supposed to be a profit center with my performance judged in terms of revenues minus costs. I really don't understand why headquarters uses an accounting system which penalizes my profits when I do something which makes more money for the company.*

When apprised of this anecdote, Bill Morton, vice president of the Containers Division for Mogul said that it was just one more incident in a long history of problems in measuring the profit performance of Mogul's production and marketing operations. He continued.

*We got into the container business initially as a way of providing a more stable market for our paperboard. The board business was viewed as a very profitable way of converting our timber holdings into cash, as long as we could sell the board. But all that was 30 years ago. Now, the board mills and the container plants and the Woodlands division (timber) are all competing for corporate resources, and each part of the business is expected to produce a good return on invested capital. Corporate management believes that a decentralized profit center structure is the best way to run our overall business in 1980. The problem is how to carve up the overall profit when our board mills buy their wood from the Woodlands division and our container plants buy their raw material from the board mills.*

Prior to 1974, the board mills and container plants of Mogul were both part of one organizational unit, the Board Products Division, with no attempt made to measure their profits separately. Costs were collected and reported where incurred and revenues were collected and reported where earned. Shipments of board from the mills to the container plants were reported on a tonnage basis but not a dollarized basis. The only accounting reports were for the Board Products Division as a whole. Although most of the output of Mogul's board mills goes to its own container plants, about 20 percent of board production is sold to customers outside the company and perhaps 25 percent of the board used by container plants is supplied by outside vendors.

In 1974, top management instituted a new reporting system within the Board Products Division to try to measure the separate profitability of the board mills versus the container plants. Under this new scheme, the accounting system was not changed, but a special "line of business profitability report" was prepared quarterly. For purposes of this report, the board mills were charged with their own costs, including wood purchases, and were given credit for the value of production based on quoted board prices from an industry trade letter, *Board Report,* which publishes average price data monthly for wood, paperboard, and corrugated containers. The container plants were charged with their own costs and with the value of raw material used based on the *Board Report* and were given credit for container sales at actual sales prices. This new reporting system was viewed very suspiciously by the managers of the board mills and container plants who were afraid the report would be used to evaluate their performance as much as to judge line of business profitability. They objected to the report because it was largely hypothetical.

The board mills were obliged to buy wood from Mogul's Woodlands Division even though the prices were normally higher than industry averages because of the mix of wood types and forest locations for Mogul's timber holdings. Yet, the board mills were only credited with industry average sales prices in the profitability report. The board mill managers considered this unfair. Since the report was hypothetical anyway, they argued, why not charge the mills for wood cost at industry averages per the *Board Report?* Before the discussions about the construction and uses of the new report had progressed very far, they were dropped when the corporation announced a reorganization under which the Board Products Division was split into the Board Mills Division and the Containers Division. This reorganization required a basic change in the accounting and reporting systems.

As of January 1975, separate accounts were maintained for the board mills and the container plants. The accounting system was based on actual costs. The board mill managers were told to concentrate on production quantity and quality while operating under production plans developed at corporate level. Board mill accounting reports focused on budgeted versus actual costs. The container plants were grouped into regions considered as profit centers and the regional managers were told to run their businesses accordingly. The container plants were charged for board at actual cost from the supplying board mill. As noted earlier, board supplied by a competitor under an exchange agreement was charged to the container plant at whatever it actually cost Mogul to repay the exchange partner from one of Mogul's board mills. The mix of board supplied to any given container plant was determined at corporate level.

The corporation used a very sophisticated computerized scheduling model to optimize its product mix at the board mills, based on wood sources, wood costs, operating costs in the individual board mills and container plants, projected sales demand by product categories, projected sales prices, and standard freight rates for shipping wood, paperboard, and containers throughout the system. This scheduling model used mathematical programming to determine the optimal production and shipping schedule by product by mill. The model was constantly being refined, and it was run monthly as a basis for establishing master production and shipping schedules. The Container's regional managers were given board supply figures from the model and told to maximize the profit from that board in the given selling area. For a typical corrugated container product, gross margin might be 10 percent of sales price. Total cost would be broken down as 60 percent for wood, 25 percent for board mill conversion costs, and 15 percent for conversion costs and selling costs in the Containers Division.

In 1977, top management became concerned that container prices generally were not high enough to earn an adequate return on the capital invested in the board mills as well as the container plants. They felt that this problem was partially due to the fact that costs in the Containers Division did not reflect any profit margin for the board mills. Actual board mill costs were being recovered but not any increment over cost to allow for a return on the invested capital at the board mills. One possibility considered at this time was to make the board mills profit centers. This idea was rejected in favor of a modification in the accounting system to charge container plants with actual board mill costs plus a capital surcharge. The surcharge was designed to allow each board mill to earn a 20 percent pretax return on invested capital each year if it met its overall production targets.

During 1975 and 1976 the company had adjusted the charges to the container plants each month for actual board mill costs that month. This approach was extremely complex and cumbersome for the corporate accounting center, since board mill costs and production levels varied month by month. The additional complications of estimating the appropriate capital surcharge for each mill each month caused this system to break down in 1977 with delays up to four months in the cost reports. In 1978, the accounting system was changed so that board shipments from January through November were charged at standard rates for the shipping mill. These rates were designed to recover estimated actual costs plus a 20 percent return on the capital employed. In December, each Containers region was charged for an adjustment to its board cost for the year to pick up cost variances at the board mills and to correct the capital surcharge. Several of the Containers regional managers expressed shock at the magnitude of the "adjustment" to their reported profits when the board mill cost variances were passed "downstream" in December of 1978.

When the overall financial reports for 1978 were completed, they showed the board mills making approximately a 20 percent return on their invested capital and the container plants, as a whole, losing money. One corporate executive who looked at the reports said it was ironic that the cost centers were making all the profit while the profit centers couldn't cover their costs.

In an effort to improve the profitability of the container plants, another refinement to the information system was added in 1979. For use in short-term decision making, the Containers regions were supplied with corporate incremental cost data on all products. This incremental cost data, generated by the mathematical mill scheduling model, reflected the net cost to the corporation of selling incremental tonnage of the specific product. This information was based on the cost differential between the optimal overall production schedule with the incremental tonnage and the optimal schedule without it. This information was felt to be the most accurate reflection of the incremental profit contribution of tonnage added at the margin. All the marketing regions were encouraged to solicit incremental business by using this marginal cost data in developing price quotes.

The incident described at the beginning of the case was mentioned during interviews in late 1979 concerning the effectiveness of the divisional accounting control systems at Mogul. At that time, the top management of Mogul was still very concerned about how to account for the board mills and container plants. The accounting system not only was intended to facilitate local decision making but also was used to measure managerial performance and to monitor business unit "attractiveness." The current system of mathematically derived incremental cost information was viewed as very useful for facilitating short-run decision making when supply exceeded demand. However, the actual cost system for reporting subunit performance seemed to create as many problems as it solved. The system was challenged by Containers division managers who resented having their profit performance influenced by poor cost control performance in the board mills and by what they viewed as arbitrary corporate decisions as to which regions to supply from low-cost mills and which from high-cost mills. They also did not feel that the system was fair in guaranteeing the board mills an assured return on investment, regardless of sales demand and market conditions.

Top management was also concerned about using this reporting system to measure business unit profitability. Containers regions could readily be expanded or contracted. For purposes of decisions about adding or dropping container plants, the actual cost and profit data did not seem as useful as the old line of business profitability reports used in 1974. However, those reports had also been challenged vigorously at the time they were being produced. No clearly appropriate reporting system had yet been found.

## QUESTIONS

1    What action should Jim Andrews take regarding the incident cited at the beginning of the case?
2    Evaluate the various different management control systems used by Mogul for the board mills and container plants between 1974 and 1979.
3    What are the main strengths and weaknesses of the control system in use in 1979?
4    Would you recommend any further changes?

# part 4

# NOT FOR PROFIT ORGANIZATIONS

# Amesburg School District

The Amesburg School District is in a suburban area near the twin cities. At one time, total enrollment for the district was over 25,000, but it had fallen to 22,000 by 1975. Further drops in enrollment were projected in the next few years. The economy in Amesburg was booming and support for education was strong. However, the population of school-age children was dropping almost as fast as the economy was growing.

Because of declining enrollment, the Amesburg district was operating under severe budgetary pressures. The superintendent, Bob Andrews, was discovering, much to his discomfort, that those cost increases which had come quite "naturally" as enrollments grew seemed to require almost supernatural power to reverse as enrollments subsequently shrunk. Cost cutting was imperative, but *where* to cut was a very difficult question involving many complex, value-laden trade-offs.

Elementary enrollment stood at 10,250 in 20 schools in 1975. Enrollment was projected to decline to 9,440 the following year and to continue declining for several years after that. Over 11,000 elementary pupils had been enrolled in 1974. School closings were an obvious cost-cutting step. One elementary school (Maple Grove School) had already been closed in 1974. It was a very old, six-room school which was very expensive to maintain and operate. The building had been sold to a church group which wanted to expand a small private school they operated. The location and size were ideal for them.

The decision to close the Maple Grove School had been a very easy one for Bob Andrews. Not only was there a ready buyer for the building, but also most of

This case was prepared by Professor John K. Shank of the Ohio State University. The names and financial data in the case are disguised, but the situation described is factual.

the Maple Grove parents were unhappy about the cramped, out-of-date facilities there. Changing to a newer school was viewed positively by almost all the Maple Grove families. In contemplating which school to close next, Bob Andrews observed wistfully that there were no more easy choices.

Each of the remaining 20 elementary schools was *the* school for some neighborhood within the district. Feelings always seem to run high about closing a "neighborhood school," and Amesburg was no exception in this regard. "Capacity" for the 20 schools was about 12,000 pupils, with individual schools having maximum enrollments ranging from about 400 to about 800. All the schools had been built since 1955. The current enrollments across the district ranged from about 300 pupils to about 700. Most of the smaller schools tended to be more nearly full than the larger ones.

Bob Andrews felt confident that another elementary school should be closed in 1975 (for the 1975-1976 school year) but that was as far as his confidence extended. Because further closings were likely in future years, he thought he would take this opportunity to try to develop formal criteria to be applied in deciding which school(s) to close first. He decided to recommend to the school board that they appoint a committee to develop recommendations for criteria for school closings. This way, he thought he might be able to get out of the line of fire from the flak that was bound to fly once any school-closing decision was announced. If the choice were dictated by the recommendations of a blue ribbon committee, how could anyone blame the superintendent?!

The committee idea was approved by the board. The composition was two school board members, two teachers, and four citizens, three of whom were *not* parents of elementary children. Bob Andrews sat in on their meetings as an ex-officio member. A 3-month timetable was established for their deliberations.

During the same period that the committee was deliberating, Bob Andrews also began to pull together an analysis of the potential cost savings if either the Brookview or Randall Ridge schools were closed. He thought that these were probably the two most likely candidates for closing, based on such "obvious" criteria as excess capacity, negative enrollment trends and projections, maintenance and operating costs, and minimized disruption from changed placement assignments. He wanted to have some figures already developed when the committee considering criteria for closings got around to exploring the cost-saving aspects of a closing decision.

The 1974-1975 budgets for Brookview and Randall Ridge are shown in Exhibit 1. Some comments regarding the cost items are shown in the notes to Exhibit 1.

The report of the Committee on School Closing Criteria is summarized in Exhibit 2. The Board of Education accepted this report and passed it on to Bob Andrews for implementation. Bob then computed the score for each of the 20 elementary schools in the District. The results are summarized in Exhibit 3. The superintendent was impressed by the "softness" of his 1 to 5 judgments on many of the factors. He noted that the overall score for a school could be changed by

28 to 35 points by using 3 instead of 4 or 2 instead of 3 for four or five of the "high-weight" factors. He was not even sure that the committee had intended for him to compute the scores himself. This had never been discussed by the committee, to his knowledge.

After looking at the results shown in Exhibit 3, Bob Andrews wondered which school to recommend closing. Both Brookview and Randall Ridge were in the bottom quintile on the weighting scale, but neither was at the bottom. The superintendent also wondered about the impact on the decision of one other criterion that wasn't in the committee's report. The chairman of the board of education had two elementary-age children in the Brookview School. The very vocal editor-publisher of the local newspaper had three children in the Ferncroft School.

## QUESTIONS

1    What do you think about the idea of the School Closing Criteria Committee?
2    What is your reaction to the committee report shown in Exhibit 2?
3    How much could the Amesburg School District save if the Randall Ridge or Brookview School were closed?
4    Should Bob Andrews close another elementary school? If so, which one?

## EXHIBIT 1
### 1974-1975 Budgets

|  | Randall Ridge School (456 Pupils) | Brookview School (423 Pupils) |
|---|---|---|
| Direct Costs[a] |  |  |
| Elementary and Kindergarten Teachers | $214,978 | $188,627 |
| Principal[b] | 23,900 | 26,514 |
| Secretary[c] | 7,513 | 7,552 |
| Media | 17,904 | 14,114 |
| Resource Center Secretary[d] | 2,192 | 2,298 |
| Physical Education Teacher (¼ equivalent) | 4,739 | 4,740 |
| Music Consultant (½ equivalent) | 7,736 | 6,643 |
| Instructional Materials and Supplies[e] | 15,515 | 14,393 |
| Building Costs[f] | 54,200 | 47,370 |
| School Nurse[g] | 4,576 | 4,576 |
| Lunch Program[h] | 39,672 | 36,801 |
| Allocated Costs[i] |  |  |
| District Administration | 11,856 | 10,998 |
| Central Instructional Services | 7,296 | 6,768 |
| General Services | 48,336 | 44,838 |
| Central Buildings Administration | 1,824 | 1,692 |
| Special Education | 33,744 | 31,302 |
| Total | $495,981 | $449,216 |

EXHIBIT 1 (continued)

ª"Direct" costs are those which can specifically be identified with the particular School.

ᵇIf the school were closed, the principal would revert to teacher status, at a salary of about $19,000, and one teacher would be dropped from the payroll. Currently, the lowest-seniority teachers were paid about $12,500 per year.

ᶜIf the school were closed, the principal's secretary would take about an $800 per year pay cut due to a reduction in job grade. Also, a "beginning"-level secretary would be dropped. Beginning secretaries received about $6,500 per year.

ᵈIf the school were closed, a part-time resource center secretary would not be needed.

ᵉThese expenses are budgeted, district-wide, at $34 per pupil per year.

ᶠFollowing is the breakdown of the direct building costs for the two schools:

|  | Randall Ridge | Brookview |
| --- | --- | --- |
| Head Custodian | $12,500 | $13,400 |
| Regular Custodians | 25,400 | 13,860 |
| Gas, Electric, and Oil | 11,400 | 10,360 |
| Repairs, Maintenance, and Miscellaneous | 3,500 | 8,750 |
| Water and Sewer | 1,400 | 1,000 |
| Total | $54,200 | $47,370 |

If a school were closed, annual custodial expenditures for basic surveillance and grass cutting would be about $800. Minimum gas and electric expenses for a closed school would run about $2,050 for Brookview and $3,030 for Randall Ridge. No water and sewer expense is required for a closed school. Basic repair and maintenance for a closed school would run about $1000 per year.

ᵍProfessional nurses are paid a set free to be available at a school during certain hours each week.

ʰThe lunch program expense includes kitchen help and food costs. If Randall Ridge or Brookview were closed, net labor cost savings to the district would be about 12½ labor hours each day for 190 days per year. Kitchen help is currently paid $3.63 per hour.

ⁱ"Allocated" costs are those costs which are only identifiable at a district-wide level. For budget reports they are prorated or allocated to each school location within the district on a per pupil basis. That is, the total district-wide cost for a certain item is first divided by the number of pupils in the district to get a cost per pupil. This cost is then multiplied by the pupils in a given school to get the allocated cost charged to that school.

EXHIBIT 2
Weighted Criteria for School Closing Decisions

|  |  | *Weight* |
|---|---|---|
| A. | **Student, Staff, and Community Factors** | |
| | Displacement of students | 10 |
| | Educational Program | 7 |
| | Anticipated Attendance Area Growth | 7 |
| | Community Use and Support of School | 6 |
| | Staff Displacement and Disruption | 5 |
| | School/Neighborhood Geographic Relationships | 5 |
| | Proximity to Secondary Schools | 5 |
| | Historical Value of Location | 1 |
| B. | **Physical Facilities Factors** | |
| | Special Supportive Facilities | 9 |
| | Classroom Facilities | 7 |
| | Life Safety of Building | 7 |
| | Site Size and Condition | 7 |
| | Building Capacity | 6 |
| | Building Condition | 6 |
| | Adaptability to Remodeling and Expansion | 6 |
| | School Site Location | 4 |
| C. | **Financial Factors** | |
| | Maintenance Cost per Square Foot | 6 |
| | Operation Cost per Square Foot | 4 |
| | Transportation Cost per Pupil | 4 |
| | Fixed Costs per Pupil | 3 |
| | Mothballing Costs | 3 |
| | Alternate Use as District Facility | 3 |

To identify the particular building to be closed, the committee suggests that a 5-point rating scale be used in applying each of the weighted criteria to each of the 20 existing elementary school buildings. Application of the rating scale is diagrammed below:

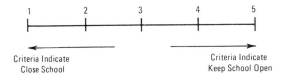

EXHIBIT 2 (continued)

Multiplying the criteria weight times the assigned rating will yield products which, when summed, will indicate that the school to be closed is the school with the least sum.

Further Definition

A   Student, Staff, and Community

   1   *Displacement of Students*—the number of students displaced by building closing, the "ripple effect," perimeter versus centralized building closing.

   2   *Educational Program*—the existing educational program is to be evaluated through a conference between the administrators applying the criteria with each building principal and representative staff.

   3   *Anticipated Attendance Area Growth*—the potential growth in numbers of students in a particular area as judged by the amount of undeveloped land, current zoning, area's current and future types of housing, population characteristics, remaining schools' ability to accommodate growth or continued decline.

   4   *Community Use and Support of School*—the amount of use of the school facility by the community, demonstrated parent interest and involvement in school activities, community efforts in school projects, PTO/PTA involvement, and so on.

   5   *Staff Displacement and Disruption*—the number of relocations and amount of disruption of staff in closed building, the stability and longevity of building faculty.

       *School/Neighborhood Geographic Relationship*—the physical makeup of the attendance area, accommodation of "natural" neighborhoods, neighborhood school concept, the school tradition and school "family" feeling, consideration of eventual closing of another elementary building.

   7   *Proximity to Secondary Schools*—closeness to secondary schools for sharing of facilities, secondary students assisting at elementary level.

   8   *Historical Value of Location*—the school's proximity to or location in historical setting, access to historical sites.

B   Physical Facilities Factors

   1   *Special Supportive Facilities*—the number, size, and adequacy of special facilities, such as physical education stations, music

EXHIBIT 2 (continued)

and reading rooms, resource centers, teacher workrooms, lunchroom facilities, etc. Also, carpenter shop, storage space, and other special non-instruction-related facilities.

2 *Classroom Facilities*—feature of classrooms, such as size, heating, lighting, appearance, arrangement, and "comfort."

3 *Life Safety of Building*—fire safety, conformance to present and future code regulations (electrical, fire, ventilation, and handicapped), type of construction, single- versus multiple-story building, and so on.

4 *Site Size and Condition*—the size of school site, maintenance needed on site (lawns, sidewalks, parking lot, playground facilities, etc.)

5 *Building Capacity*—consideration of building capacities as related to projected short-term and long-term enrollment projections and enrollment/capacity analyses.

6 *Building Condition*—the age and future useful life, planned building improvements, short-range and long-range maintenance requirements.

7 *Adaptability to Remodeling and Expansion*—the ease with which a building can be remodeled or expanded to accommodate changing educational program requirements.

8 *School Site Location*—access to school, location relative to highways, bridges, creeks, residential versus nonresidential setting.

C Financial Factors

1 *Maintenance Cost per Square Foot*—custodial/maintenance salaries, maintenance supplies, snow and refuse removal, security, maintenance equipment.

2 *Operation Cost per Square Foot*—electricity, gas, water/sewer, and telephone.

3 *Transportation Cost per Pupil*—the total cost of transportation per elementary student assuming each of the different schools were to be closed.

4 *Fixed Costs per Pupil*—the fixed instructional salaries other than classroom teachers *on a per pupil basis* by building.

5 *Mothballing Costs*—the costs of maintaining a closed building (utilities to be maintained, site maintenance, boarding windows, security, etc.)

6 *Alternative Use as District Facility*—the use of closed building as district warehouse, office area, portions of building used (physical education stations, resource centers, etc.) while classrooms closed, and so on.

**EXHIBIT 3**
Elementary School Rankings Under
the Weighted School Closing Criteria System

| | School | Weighted Score |
|---|---|---|
| 1. | Woodcrest | 482 |
| 2. | Bowman | 451 |
| 3. | Bridge | 420 |
| 4. | Estabrook | 416 |
| 5. | Muzzey | 387 |
| 6. | Clark | 380 |
| 7. | Diamond | 374 |
| 8. | Franklin | 372 |
| 9. | Parker | 361 |
| 10. | Hancock | 358 |
| 11. | Westgate | 349 |
| 12. | Catalpa | 337 |
| 13. | Broadmoor | 335 |
| 14. | Windemere | 327 |
| 15. | Indian Ridge | 314 |
| 16. | Normandy Farms | 302 |
| 17. | Bellbrook | 297 |
| 18. | Brookview | 288 |
| 19. | Randall Ridge | 278 |
| 20. | Ferncroft | 270 |

# Bernard School

John Theodore, business manager of the Bernard School, had just returned from the most recent meeting of the school's building committee with a ream of papers and a worried expression on his face. The committee had been considering a new classroom building, and had deferred its decision, upon Theodore's recommendation, until a thorough analysis could be made. The committee was torn between conflicting views. On the one hand, a group including Mrs. Irving, the headmistress, felt that minimizing the construction costs and the cash drain was paramount in the current climate of very tight school finances. On the other hand, a group agreed with the architect, Mr. Abrams, that an important consideration was future plans as well as current costs.

The Bernard School was a coed independent day school in a large west coast city for children in grades K-8. Enrollment had surged to 270 recently due to the community's dissatisfaction with the public school system. Seven months ago, Mrs. Irving, with the trustee's approval, engaged Mr. Abrams' firm to come up with architectural plans for a new classroom building.

Mr. Abrams' firm had designed school buildings in the past and he was aware of the new techniques being employed in school construction. Abrams proposed two possible plans allowing for Bernard's specific problems. Bernard's existing classroom building had 10 classrooms. The need for an additional 10 was immediate and the 10 existing rooms would need to be replaced in no more than 10 years. Abrams' cost estimate on a single 20-room building was $1.6 million. His estimate for a 10-room building was $900,000. He noted, with costs rising as they are, in 10 years the 10-room building would probably cost $1.8 million. It was clear

Copyright © 1973 by the National Association of Independent Schools.

that in 10 years the existing building would have to be replaced. If the larger building were built, the existing building would not have to be used at all.

Mr. Theodore was aware that one large building would be more economical because it could be fully utilized now (moving classes from the old building), which would facilitate lower heating and maintenance costs.

A building was virtually maintenance-free for 10 years, and approximately $1,000 per year could be saved through modern heating techniques. Maintenance costs for the existing building were $10,000 per year. A new 10-classroom building would be maintenance-free for 10 years and then a level of $7,500 per year would be needed. Twice that was planned for a 20-classroom building.

Theodore drew up Exhibit 1 to clarify the "size" decision for himself. He was unsure how to compare an outflow of $1.6 million now versus $900,000 now and $1.8 million in 10 years.

Not only did Mr. Theodore have to form a recommendation on the size of building to be constructed, but he also had to consider financing of this project. It would not be easy to raise $1 or $2 million. Before the school could commit itself to a design and let bids to contractors, the financing had to be arranged. Mr. Theodore had contacted other school business managers to get their suggestions and also had listened to members of the building committee, who proposed some good ideas. He had reduced the list to three possible alternatives and he had mentioned these at the building committee meeting just completed. Because he had not analyzed each alternative fully, he was unable to make a recommendation to the group. Therefore, he decided to suggest that the committee hold off its decision until he could analyze each possibility, and prepare a report. This met with the committee's approval. Theodore knew that he would have to work hard to get finished by next week's session, but he had agreed to that at the meeting.

He knew that he would have to be very careful about the interest rate, final construction costs, payback period, and the loan-repayment period in order not to overlook a potential drawback or advantage in each possibility. He felt that an old college friend, Joel Nance, who was now a loan officer in a nearby bank, could help him. He decided to get in touch with Nance, hoping they would be able to work out a solution. Nance said he was happy to be of help and they agreed to get together the next evening at Theodore's home. After a short dinner the two men adjourned to Theodore's study to analyze the three proposals.

## PROPOSAL 1—ENDOWMENT

The simplest idea of all was to take the money from the endowment fund. "After all," reasoned Nance, "what is this money for, if not school improvements." The endowment fund balance was about $1 million (at market values) at the present time. This would totally finance the smaller construction and would cover more than half of the larger building. Nance seemed to feel that it would be no trouble to arrange a "term loan" for the balance with his bank, given a plan for eventual repayment of the loan through a fund drive. This seemed to be the lowest-cost alternative to Mr. Theodore. He wondered, however, what the reaction of the rest of the building committee and the trustees would be to an idea that would eventually eliminate the endowment fund, which had taken so long to develop. Income from the endowment ran at about 4%, and the management company had been able to realize an annual appreciation of 5% for the past 12 years.

## PROPOSAL 2—MORTGAGE: NEW, 15 OR 25 YEARS

Mr. Nance favored the idea of taking a mortgage on the new building. He felt that the building committee and the trustees would not mind taking a down payment from the endowment. He felt that a school such as Bernard would probably only have to raise 25% ($400,000 for large construction, $225,000 for small) as a downpayment. A long-term mortgage (either 15 or 25 years) could be easily arranged for the balance at an 8% rate of interest.

## PROPOSAL 3

Nance suggested another option of mortgaging the new building, which would not necessitate withdrawal from the endowment. By mortgaging the existing physical plant (administration building, gymnasium, and land), Bernard could get enough cash to pay for either construction alternative. Using the same 25% rule in reverse, Nance said buildings and land worth $2.2 million (recently appraised value) would net Bernard $1.65 million, which would cover completely either of the construction options. Of course, this would entail paying back either $900,000 (small) or $1,600,000 (large) over a period of either 15 or 25 years at 8%.

It was clear to Theodore that although the rates were the same, each method did yield a different total cost. A longer payback period gave smaller annual payments but a much larger total cost. He had to weigh the merits of each before reaching a conclusion. Exhibit 2 of the case summarizes these differences.

## ADDITIONAL DOWN PAYMENT OPPORTUNITY

The most novel idea proposed by the building committee, although by no means a complete financing alternative, was to establish a revolving parent bond fund. This would enable Bernard to raise a permanent cash fund that could be used to pay the down payment. The fund was "permanent" in the sense that the money needed to repay the parents whose children were leaving the school each year would come from the bonds sold to the parents of the next incoming class. By having each family buy a $1,000 bond at a low interest rate, such as 5%, the school could raise $270,000, which would more than cover a $225,000 down payment. If the larger building were built, the bond could be for $1,500, giving the school $405,000 to cover the down payment. This would, of course, necessitate interest payments of $50 per thousand per year. This idea could be combined with any other financing method selected if the trustees felt it was acceptable to "use" the parents in this way.

As Theodore and Nance proceeded through each possibility, they analyzed the time frame, payback period, interest rate, total cash repayment, and annual cash repayment. As the evening wore on, they prepared a summary of the relative cash flows of each alternative (see Exhibit 3). They felt this would be the most graphic way of explaining the options to the building committee.

Clearly, there were two decisions: the size of construction, and, independent of this, how to finance the building.

Theodore was unsure what he should recommend to the committee.

## QUESTION

1    As a school head, how would you analyze this situation, and what would you recommend to the building committee? Be prepared to support your decision with the relevant quantitative analysis.

---

**EXHIBIT 1**
The "Size" Decision

| *Small* | *Large* |
|---|---|
| Build one 10-room building now | Build one 20-room building now |
| Use existing building for 10 years | Eliminate existing building[a] |
| Build one 10-room building in 10 years | No further construction foreseen |
| Scrap existing building in 10 years[a] | |

| | *Small* | *Large* |
|---|---|---|
| Construction | $ 900,000 now<br>1,800,000 in year 10 | $1,600,000 now |
| Maintenance | $10,000 years 1-10<br>7,500 years 11-20 | -0- years 1-10<br>$15,000 years 11-20 |

[a]The land could be sold for enough to cover demolition costs; therefore, the net removal cost was zero.

**EXHIBIT 2**
Mortgage Payments Schedule

| | | 15 Years | | 25 Years | |
| --- | --- | --- | --- | --- | --- |
| *Option* | *Mortgage Amount* | *Monthly Payment* | *Total Payments* | *Monthly Payment* | *Total Payments* |
| 2—Small | $ 675,000 | $ 6,480 | $1,166,400 | $ 5,220 | $1,566,000 |
| 3—Small | 900,000 | 8,640 | 1,555,200 | 6,960 | 2,088,000 |
| 2—Large | 1,200,000 | 11,520 | 2,073,600 | 9,280 | 2,874,000 |
| 3—Large | 1,600,000 | 15,360 | 2,764,800 | 12,373 | 3,712,000 |

**EXHIBIT 3**
Summary of Proposals

Proposal 1—Use Endowment Funds

| *Small* | *Large* |
| --- | --- |
| $900,000 from endowment | $1,000,000 from endowment<br>$ 600,000 term loan at 8% |

*Costs:*

1    Lost endowment income.
2    Interest at 8% on borrowed funds.

*Question:*

| Where does the $1,800,000 come from in year 10? | How can the school repay the $600,000? |
| --- | --- |

Proposal 2—Mortgage the new building over 15 or 25 years

| *Small* | | *Large* |
| --- | --- | --- |
| $225,000 | Down payment[a] | $ 400,000 |
| 675,000 | Mortgage | 1,200,000 |

*Costs:*

1    Interest at 8% on mortgage.
2    Lost endowment income or 5% borrowing cost on parent bonds.

Proposal 3—Mortgage the existing physical plant over 15 or 25 years

| *Small* | | *Large* |
| --- | --- | --- |
| $900,000 | Mortgage amount | $1,600,000 |

*Costs:*

1    Interest at 8% on the mortgage.

[a]The down payment could be taken from endowment funds or provided by the revolving parent bond fund.

# Lincoln Academy

"We can't drop the summer day camp program!" objected an art teacher. "I depend on that program for additional income each year."

"Dropping the summer program won't be very popular with the parents" another faculty member added. "Who's going to take care of their kids?"

"The fact of the matter," repeated Lincoln's new business manager, "is that our summer-day-camp program is operating at a substantial loss. Lincoln Academy cannot continue extracurricular programs which result in having to charge higher tuitions to students enrolled in the regular school year."

The maintenance supervisor added: "My summer repair program would sure be easier without having to worry about all the kids. We waste a lot of money in terms of overtime and idle time trying to squeeze a certain sequence of jobs in between and around the various class schedules."

"You can't measure a program in dollars and cents" retorted another disgruntled teacher. "The summer program is an integral part of the Academy's image."

Following a stormy faculty meeting, Mr. Clark, Lincoln's headmaster, retired to his office to piece together the day's arguments and to consider what action he should take regarding the continuance of Lincoln's summer program.

## BACKGROUND

Lincoln Academy was one of 10 independent boys schools located in a major eastern metropolitan area. In exchange for tuition of $2,400 per full (9-month) year, it offered educational programs and facilities which Lincoln administrators

Copyright © 1974 by the National Association of Independent Schools.

felt were markedly superior to those offered by the public schools. The regular-school-year program offered 525 boys in grades 6 to 12 opportunities to study such subjects as Russian, calculus, and political science. Athletic facilities included extras such as sailboats, a hockey rink, and a swimming pool. With a 70-member faculty, classes ranged in size from 5 to 20 students. Tutoring was arranged for students interested in subjects which did not attract at least 5 students.

Lincoln's administrative staff included the headmaster, assistant headmaster, development officer, bursar, business manager, and several secretaries. There was also a 14-man maintenance staff and a 4-person kitchen staff. Some teachers doubled as admissions and guidance counselors.

The only summer activity was the summer-day-camp program, which offered primarily arts and crafts classes to boys and girls aged 5 to 13. An average of 600 children participated each summer on weekly contracts for 1 to 12 weeks. Although kitchen facilities were closed for the summer, students were provided daily milk distribution and one hot cookout per week. The school also owned some land by a lake about 90 miles from the city, which was used as a field station for overnights and country recreation.

Mr. Anderson had been hired in January 1971 as business manager and had immediately delved into the school's financial statements (Exhibits 1 and 2) to learn the school's operations in a school environment. Inasmuch as the time was rapidly approaching when plans for summer 1971 would have to be finalized, he addressed himself in particular to the financial implication of these plans. He was not satisfied with the way accounts were lumped together, disguising what might be useful information. When he separated the revenues and expenditures of the summer-day-camp program from the aggregate (Exhibit 3), he found that the summer program was operating at a significant loss. He calculated that each student in the regular school program was forced to pay $72 more than would be necessary without the summer program's loss. He immediately reported his findings to Mr. Clark, who suggested that he present his analysis for discussion at the faculty meeting that afternoon.

## THE SEARCH FOR ALTERNATIVES

Mr. Clark had been surprised by the strong emotional reaction of the faculty to Mr. Anderson's analysis. Although he desired to act in response to faculty wishes, he felt that he could not ignore his responsibility for the school's financial well-being. He was particularly concerned that tuition for regular school students was, in effect, being used to help support the summer program.

As an alternative to dropping the summer program, Mr. Clark considered the possibility of raising summer tuition and cutting summer costs. Summer tuition increases seemed impossible because Lincoln's summer tuition was already slightly above that of competing independent schools, and parents were continually complaining about the high cost of summer programs. Although some cost savings could be realized without crippling the summer program, Mr. Clark did not feel that significant inroads could be made on the $37,800 loss.

Perhaps a more viable alternative would be to increase the utilization of facilities by submitting a bid for one of the educational enrichment programs for handicapped children and disadvantaged minority groups. Mr. Clark had previously compiled a file on the Head Start Summer Day Care Program in response to several trustees' concerns about the school's image in terms of social responsibility. He now reviewed this file as a financial alternative to the current summer program.

## THE HEAD START ALTERNATIVE

Mr. Clark had interviewed Mike Oakland, who was budget administration director of the Head Start Program in a nearby city. He found that he could apply for federal funding through the Department of Public Welfare under Title IV-A, Section 24, of the Economic Opportunity Act. The Act provided for refunding payments of up to $50 per week per child. Lincoln Academy would be required to submit comprehensive plans for the program it expected to provide, detailing its provisions for administration, career development, education services, social services, health services, and nutrition services. Detailed census data on each enrollee was required, such as race, family size, and family income. All program needs, such as staff services, equipment, physical facilities, and materials were to be itemized and costed. Lincoln Academy would be required to provide 25% of the program costs, and the federal government provided 75%. Typically, the local 25% was provided "in kind" (i.e., fair rental value of buildings and equipment, and equivalent salaries of volunteer workers).

Mr. Oakland admitted quite frankly that it was common practice to meet the 25% local contribution by reporting equivalent market value of the services of imaginary volunteers and by inflating fair market rental values of property. But Mr. Oakland cautioned that compilation of a program proposal required extraordinary patience with the maze of administrative details. Mr. Oakland's latest 12-month program proposal had exceeded 500 pages in length and had required 3 months of his full-time effort to compile. He estimated that compilation of a 3-month program would require at least 4 weeks of full-time effort. In addition, there could be no guarantee that federal funds would be available even if the program was found to be acceptable. The proposal would be due by March 15 in order to receive federal funds beginning in June.

Lincoln Academy had a "capacity" of 525 students and could operate the program for a maximum of 12 weeks. All direct costs and any indirect costs which could be estimated and itemized would be reimbursable. By properly juggling "fair rental values" and "fair market value of volunteers' services," a break-even program, even after allowance for a fair share of overhead costs, could be realized.

But there would be great difficulty in recruiting 525 Head Start enrollees. In order to qualify, the enrollees had to be eligible for kindergarten or the first grade and had to be attending school for the first time in the coming fall. Thus, each child could attend only one summer; there would be no returnees in following years. In addition, a parent of each enrollee had to be currently receiving Aid for Dependent Children or be participating in some kind of job-training program.

Recruitment of 525 such children would be a long, painstaking effort requiring a massive volunteer organization. The fewer the students recruited, the greater the "juggling" that would have to be done to break even.

There were also certain ethical questions to be resolved. Mr. Clark was not certain he wanted to become involved in inflating rental values charged to the government and in reporting nonexistent volunteers. Perhaps the social benefits to the Head Start enrollees justified such a practice. But Mr. Oakland had argued that "little of value can be accomplished in a 3-month program. By the time enrollees become acclimated to the new environment and ready to learn, the program is over and they're gone." Mr. Clark also wondered if maintenance costs would increase because of the increased exposure of facilities to large numbers of inner-city children. He knew some parents of tuition-paying regular students would object to violations of the "exclusivity" they thought they were buying for their children at Lincoln Academy.

## DECISION REGARDING CONTINUANCE OF THE SUMMER PROGRAM

As Mr. Clark pondered what he felt would be major strategic choices for the future of Lincoln Academy, he reviewed the specific figures used in Mr. Anderson's analysis. He noticed that several revenue and expenditure items, such as rental income and general institutional, had been identified with the summer program even though they would continue whether or not the summer program was dropped. Although he wanted the summer program to carry a fair share of the school's costs, he was not certain what basis should be used to allocate each revenue and expenditure item. For example, he knew that only about 10% of the time of the administrative staff was spent on the summer program, even during the summer. Mr. Anderson had allocated 25% (3 months out of 12) of office administration to the summer program. In considering salary and wage expenses, Mr. Clark questioned whether it would be advisable or even possible to employ maintenance staff and secretaries on a 9-month work year rather than a 12-month year.

On the other hand, there were some cuts which were not included in the analysis which would be incurred only if the summer program was dropped. For example, full-time security guards would be needed to prevent vandalism. A total additional cost of $5,000 would be incurred during the summer for guards providing 24-hour surveillance. Perhaps the local taxing authorities would question the tax exemption on Lincoln Academy's land in the country if it was not used as a field station in an educational program. If so, a new annual tax liability of approximately $4,000 would be incurred. It would certainly be difficult to justify the $4,500 annual repair and maintenance expense of the sailboats and swimming pool if they were not used in the summer programs.

Moreover, there were several noneconomic advantages to running a summer program. Considerable goodwill was generated with parents and the community through creation of "something to do" for many idle children, and summer jobs for a select few. In addition, the summer program provided Lincoln Academy exposure to younger children and their parents and therefore served as an important recruiting tool for potential students.

Mr. Clark wondered whether these noneconomic factors might be important enough to overshadow the loss, if in fact the summer program was operating at a loss. He wanted to be very careful that the financial dimension to the problem was carefully evaluated. He did not feel fully comfortable with Mr. Anderson's analysis of the net gain or loss to the school from operating the summer program. He wanted to rethink the question of whether the program was a net contributor or a net drain for the school.

He also wanted to seriously consider the possibility of substituting the summer Head Start Program. He was not sure whether this represented a better use of the school's facilities in terms of straight economics or not. This seemed to hinge on what fee would be charged to the government, which in turn hinged on how many enrollees could be recruited.

## QUESTIONS

1   What is the annual dollar gain or loss to the Lincoln Academy from operating the summer camp program?

2   Assuming a bid were going to be submitted for a Head Start summer program, what would be the maximum bid allowable under the terms specified in the Economic Opportunity Act? What would be the maximum allowable bid if only 250 enrollees could be recruited?

3   As Mr. Clark, what action would you recommend to the board of trustees regarding a summer program for 1971?

EXHIBIT 1
LINCOLN ACADEMY
Balance Sheet
as of September 30, 1970
(Thousands of Dollars)

| Assets | | | Liabilities | | |
|---|---|---|---|---|---|
| Current Fund Assets | | | Current Fund Liabilities | | |
| Unrestricted | | | Unrestricted | | |
| Cash | $ | 50.6 | Accounts Payable and Accruals | $ | 19.6 |
| Investments | | 8.2 | Enrollment Deposits | | 114.8 |
| Accounts Receivable | | 44.8 | Total Unrestricted | $ | 134.4 |
| Inventories | | 9.8 | | | |
| Other Current | | 21.0 | Restricted | | |
| Total Unrestricted | $ | 134.4 | Special Funds, etc.— | | |
| | | | Unexpended | | 49.6 |
| Restricted | | | Total Restricted | $ | 49.6 |
| Cash | $ | .5 | | | |
| Investments | | 49.1 | Total Current | $ | 184.0 |
| Total Restricted | $ | 49.6 | | | |
| | | | | | |
| Total Current | $ | 184.0 | | | |
| | | | | | |
| Endowment Fund Assets | | | Endowment Fund | | |
| Investments | $ | 420.2 | Scholarship Fund | $ | 303.1 |
| Cash | | 42.6 | Faculty Salary Fund | | 99.8 |
| | | | Other Funds | | 59.9 |
| Total Endowment | $ | 462.8 | | | |
| | | | Total Endowment | $ | 462.8 |
| | | | | | |
| Plant Assets | | | Plant Funds | | |
| Cash | $ | 78.4 | Mortgage and Other Notes Payable | $ | 196.0 |
| Furniture and Equipment | | 168.0 | Property and Plant Contingency | | |
| Land and Buildings | | 2,994.6 | Funds—Unexpended | | 78.4 |
| | | | Net Investment in Plant | | 2,966.6 |
| Total Plant | | $3,241.0 | | | |
| | | | | | $3,241.0 |
| | | | | | |
| Total Assets | | $3,887.8 | Total Liabilities | | $3,887.8 |

EXHIBIT 2
LINCOLN ACADEMY
Statement of Revenues, Expenditures, and Transfers
October 1, 1969-September 30, 1970[a]

| Revenues | | |
|---|---|---|
| Student Tuition and Fees—Note 1 | $1,414,000 | |
| Bookstore Sales—Note 2 | 35,000 | |
| Rental Income—Note 3 | 30,800 | |
| Investment Income Applied—Note 4 | 35,000 | |
| Gifts Applied—Note 4 | 152,000 | |
| Other—Note 3 | 2,800 | |
| Total Revenues | | $1,670,200 |
| | | |
| Expenditures | | |
| Program Salaries and Wages—Note 5 | $ 701,400 | |
| Program Supplies, Expenses, and Equipment—Note 6 | 245,000 | |
| Scholarships and Financial Aid—Note 7 | 100,700 | |
| Operation and Maintenance of Facilities—Note 8 | 204,400 | |
| Office Administration—Note 9 | 183,400 | |
| General Institutional—Note 10 | 212,800 | |
| Total Expenditures | | $1,647,800 |
| | | |
| Transfers to plant and investment fund balances—Note 11 | | $ 22,400 |

[a]See Exhibit 4 for the notes to this table.

---

EXHIBIT 3
LINCOLN ACADEMY—SUMMER PROGRAM
Statement of Revenues, Expenditures, and Transfers
July 1, 1970-September 30, 1970[a]

| Revenues | | |
|---|---|---|
| Student Tuition and Fees—Note 1 | $140,000 | |
| Rental Income—Note 3 | 15,400 | |
| Investment Income Applied—Note 4 | 5,600 | |
| Gifts Applied—Note 4 | 25,200 | |
| Other—Note 3 | 1,400 | |
| Total Revenues | | $187,600 |
| | | |
| Expenditures | | |
| Program Salaries and Wages—Note 5 | $ 57,000 | |
| Program Supplies, Expenses, and Equipment—Note 6 | 18,200 | |
| Operation and Maintenance of Facilities—Note 8 | 51,100 | |
| Office Administration—Note 9 | 45,900 | |
| General Institutional—Note 10 | 53,200 | |
| Total Expenditures | | $225,400 |
| | | |
| Transfers to plant and investment fund balances[b] | | $ (37,800) |

[a]See Exhibit 4 for the notes to this table.

[b]Mr. Anderson's conclusions: $37,800 in revenues must be taken from the regular school year program to cover this loss. Virtually all of these revenues must be obtained from students in the form of tuition. Tuition cost per student equals $37,800 divided by the 525 regular-school-year students, or $72 per student.

EXHIBIT 4
LINCOLN ACADEMY
Notes for Exhibits II and III

Note 1 – Breakdown of tuition and fees:

| | |
|---|---:|
| Regular School Year | $1,274,000 |
| Summer Program | 140,000 |
| Total | $1,414,000 |

Note 2 – Bookstore operates only during the regular school year.

Note 3 – Rental income is accrued primarily from the rental of athletic facilities. Approximately half of "rental" ($15,400) and "other" ($1,400) income is accrued during the summer.

Note 4 – About one-third ($12,600) of the investment income is restricted to use during the regular 9-month year. Unrestricted investment income is realized evenly over the full 12 months ($35,000 minus $12,600 leaves $22,400 unrestricted; 3/12 of this amount, or $5,600, is applied to the 3-month summer program).

Similarly, about one-third ($51,800) of the gifts are restricted to use during the regular 9-month school year. Unrestricted gifts are realized evenly over the full 12 months ($152,600 minus $51,800 leaves $100,800; 3/12 of this amount, or $25,200, is applied to the 3-month summer program).

Note 5 – Breakdown of salaries and wages:

| | |
|---|---:|
| Regular-School-Year Faculty | $618,800 |
| Kitchen Staff | 25,600 |
| Summer-Program Faculty | 57,000 |
| Total | $701,400 |

Regular-school-faculty salaries are paid in 12 equal monthly installments. This remuneration is in exchange for a 9-month work contract.

Note 6 – Breakdown of supplies, expenses, and equipment:

| | |
|---|---:|
| Regular School Year | $ 65,800 |
| Kitchen, Including Food | 65,800 |
| Bookstore Purchases | 30,800 |
| Publications | 5,600 |
| Athletics | 58,800 |
| Summer-Camp Expense | 18,200 |
| Total | $245,000 |

EXHIBIT 4 (continued)

Note 7 — Scholarships and financial aid are awarded only to students in the regular school year.

Note 8 — Maintenance staff is employed on the basis of 12-month contracts. Their salaries and wages represent 55% ($112,400) of the expenditures for operation and maintenance of the facilities. The remainder ($92,000) consists of utilities, repair and maintenance expense, transportation (including $15,400 summer camp transportation) and interest. Summer camp is allocated 3/12, or $51,100 of the total operation and maintenance of facilities account.

Note 9 — Office administration expenditures include staff salaries ($132,000), executive expenses ($22,000), public relations ($9,200), and office supplies, telephone, and miscellaneous office expense ($20,200). Administrative staff personnel work 12 months per year. Summer camp is allocated 25%, or 3 months out of 12, of the total office administration account (3/12 of $183,400 is $45,900).

Note 10 — General institutional expenditures include faculty pensions, retirement plan contributions, social security contributions, Blue Cross premium expense, development office expense, professional fees, insurance, interest, bad debts (including $1,400 of summer camp bad debts), and sabbaticals. Summer camp is allocated 25%, or 3 months out of 12, of the total institutional account, or $53,200.

Note 11 — Breakdown of transfers to plant and other fund balances:

| | |
|---|---:|
| Principal Payments on Real Estate Mortgage | $ 2,800 |
| Additional Investments in Plant Facilities | 1,400 |
| Replacement of Plant Investments | 8,400 |
| Additions to Investment Fund Balances | 9,800 |
| | $22,400 |

# St. Augustine School (A)

During an NAIS seminar held in the summer of 1973, Joan Bullock, headmistress of the St. Augustine School, became intrigued with the cost estimation model (CEM) developed by the Western Interstate Commission for Higher Education (WICHE). The model has been successfully used at the Tuskegee Institute as a tool in long-range planning and financial decision making. Variations of it had also been used by a few independent schools. Ms. Bullock acknowledged that the complex, computerized WICHE system would be too costly and sophisticated for her 600-student school. But she believed she could devise a manual version of the system which would help her evaluate the impact of alternative uses of resources at St. Augustine.

The principles of the WICHE planning system are simple: various categories of data are systematically gathered, segmented by the cost center, and then cross-tabulated against one another to yield certain measures of "resource productivity" and cost. The value of the model rests on the usefulness of these productivity and cost measurements in making financially related educational policy decisions. Consideration of these measures is intended to facilitate allocation of limited resources to cost centers in proportion to the benefits to be derived. In practice, of course, the quantitative analysis must be tempered by an appreciation for differing educational objectives and for such "unquantifiables" as the quality of the resource inputs.

The WICHE cost estimation model is "enrollment driven"; that is, the primary category of data input is enrollment projections by cost center. Enrollment is chosen as the primary data category because the tuition and fees associated with enrollment represent the major share of annual revenues. Furthermore, enroll-

Copyright © 1973 by the National Association of Independent Schools.

ments in various courses, departments, and programs (cost centers) impose the needs for faculty staffing, and faculty salaries represent the major proportion of annual expenditures. Thus, projected enrollment in a cost center represents the primary "demand" for services, which justifies and "drives" allocation of financial resources to that particular cost center, primarily in the form of faculty salaries. One major goal of the model is to evaluate the balance between faculty staffing and the faculty work load imposed by enrollment patterns.

In devising a simplified version of the WICHE model for her own school, Ms. Bullock selected "departments" as cost centers because St. Augustine's budget was allocated by department. She then summarized the input data required for such a model:

1    Enrollment projections by department.
2    Faculty mix in each department in terms of "pay steps" and salary at each pay step.
3    Desired faculty work load in terms of teaching hours and student contact hours. (20 teaching hours per week times 10 students per teaching hour = 200 student contact hours.) Alternatively, this could be stated at 40 student contacts per day.

The model would then provide projections of:

1    Direct faculty costs for each department (total, per teaching hour, and per student contact hour).
2    Departmental work load and the variances by department from desired faculty "productivity" levels.
3    Hiring (and "de-hiring") requirements by department to correct departmental work-load inequities.

## IMPLEMENTATION OF THE MODEL

### Data Inputs

Ms. Bullock began her implementation of the WICHE concepts by gathering the appropriate input data. After obtaining a summary of the school's basic data (Exhibit 1) from St. Augustine's annual report to parents, she sought enrollment projections by department. She soon discovered that St. Augustine had never made explicit enrollment projections by department. Ms. Bullock therefore had to gather actual enrollment data by department for 1971-1972 and combine these statistics with the partial preregistration returns for 1972-1973 to estimate the 1972-1973 enrollments (Exhibit 2). An example of how this schedule is prepared for any given department is also shown in Exhibit 2. Data on the faculty mix by department and the salaries at each pay step were more readily available. Ms. Bullock summarized these data in Exhibits 3 and 4.

St. Augustine had never had any explicit faculty work-load standards, but Ms.

Bullock reasoned that the achieved work load was implicit in current staffing deisions. With 600 students, each enrolled in six 5-day courses per week, a total of 3,600 student contacts per day (600 students × 6 courses) were "produced." Thus, the average faculty member was responsible for 45 student contacts per day (3,600 daily contacts ÷ 80 teachers). Since St. Augustine wanted to average 12[1] students per class, 45 contacts per day implied a course load of 3¾ sections, or an average of 18.75 weekly teaching hours per teacher. Ms. Bullock concluded that the historical "desired faculty load" was 18.75 weekly teaching hours and 45 student contacts per day.

## Model Outputs

The first model output Ms. Bullock sought was direct faculty costs for each department in total and per student contact hour. She multiplied the number of teachers in each pay step (Exhibit 3) by the average salary for that pay step (Exhibit 4) to produce the schedule of total direct faculty costs by pay step and by department (Exhibit 5).

Ms. Bullock found direct faculty costs per student contact hour (Exhibit 6) by dividing the departmental costs in Exhibit 5 by current and projected credit hour enrollments (Exhibit 2). She was disturbed by the large range in costs per hour and made a notation that she should investigate the reasons behind the spread.

The second model output Ms. Bullock sought was work load by department. She found this by dividing student contact hours in each department (Exhibit 2) by the number of faculty members. This information is shown in Exhibit 7. Ms. Bullock noted that the social science department had a higher work load than the other departments. At the other end of the spectrum, the English department had a comparatively light load.

The final model output which Ms. Bullock sought was a schedule of staffing requirements by department. She divided the 1972-1973 projected student credit hours in Exhibit 2 by the desired work load (225 contact hours per teacher) to arrive at 1972-1973 teacher requirements by department. She subtracted from these quotients the current number of teachers in each department to arrive at the hiring (or firing) requirements (Exhibit 8) to bring each department in line with the desired faculty load and productivity ratios.

Ms. Bullock felt that the quickest, most effective means of identifying the questionable assumptions and implications of the model would be to distribute the preliminary version of the model to department heads, members of the board of trustees, and other key personnel and solicit their comments.

---

[1]To Ms. Bullock's knowledge, no one had ever really analyzed why 12 was an "appropriate" class size or how this "standard" should vary from department to department, but she decided to use this well-known figure for her initial calculations.

## QUESTIONS

*1*  Be sure that you understand the mechanical aspects of the CEM. How many independent sources of data are fed into the model? How many output measurements does the model yield, and how are they interrelated?

*2*  What is the potential usefulness of the WICHE model? What are its limitations in terms of its mechanical structure and current assumptions? What comments on the model might one expect from members of the board of trustees? From the business manager? From various department heads?

---

**EXHIBIT 1**
ST. AUGUSTINE SCHOOL
Basic Data

| | |
|---|---|
| Enrollment | 600 students |
| Grades Offered | 6-12 |
| Lower School | 6-8  (136 students) |
| Upper School | 9-12 (464 students) |
| Total Full-Time Faculty | 80 |
| Faculty/Student Ratio | 1:7.5 (600 students ÷ 80 teachers = 7.5 students/teacher) |
| Annual Tuition | $2,400 |
| Student Course Load | Six 5-day courses |

---

## EXHIBIT 2
### Enrollment Projections by Department (Credit Hours)
### (1 Credit Hour = 1 class hr/student/week)

|  | Total | Lower | English | Math | Soc. Sci. | Nat. Sci. | Fine Arts | Foreign Language | Phys. Ed. |
|---|---|---|---|---|---|---|---|---|---|
| 71-72 Actual | 17,940 | 4,260 | 2,760 | 1,980 | 2,160 | 1,870 | 1,560 | 1,320 | 2,040 |
| 72-73 Projected | 18,000 | 4,080 | 2,640 | 1,980 | 2,460 | 1,920 | 1,560 | 1,320 | 2,040 |

As an illustration of how these numbers are derived, the following data show the calculations for the English department (1972-1973 projected):

| Courses Offered | Projected Enrollment | Student Credit Hours per Week[a] |
|---|---|---|
| English 9 | 114 | 570 |
| English 10 | 116 | 580 |
| English 11 | 90 | 450 |
| English Literature I[b] | 120 | 300 |
| English Literature II[b] | 110 | 250 |
| The Short Story[b] | 95 | 240 |
| The American Novel | 24 | 120 |
| Poetry | 9 | 45 |
| Drama | 6 | 30 |
| The Novel as Social Commentary[b] | 12 | 30 |
| Creative Writing Workshop[b] | 6 | 15 |
| The Writings of Shakespeare[b] | 4 | 10 |
| Total | | 2,640 |

[a]Each course meets five times per week.
[b]One-half year only.

## EXHIBIT 3
Faculty Mix by Department (Number of Teachers in Each Pay Step)

| | Total | Lower | English | Math | Soc. Sci. | Nat. Sci. | Fine Arts | Foreign Language | Phys. Ed. |
|---|---|---|---|---|---|---|---|---|---|
| Pay Steps 1-3 | 43 | 13 | 7 | 4 | 4 | 2 | 4 | 4 | 5 |
| Pay Steps 4-6 | 22 | 6 | 4 | 2 | 3 | 1 | 2 | 1 | 3 |
| Pay Steps 7-9 | 7 | 1 | 2 | 0 | 1 | 2 | 0 | 1 | 0 |
| Pay Steps 10-12 | 8 | 0 | 1 | 2 | 0 | 3 | 1 | 0 | 1 |
| Total | 80 | 20 | 14 | 8 | 8 | 8 | 7 | 6 | 9 |

**EXHIBIT 4**
ST. AUGUSTINE SCHOOL
Faculty Mix of Salaries

|  | Average Salary | Number of Teachers | Total Salaries |
|---|---|---|---|
| Pay Steps 1-3 | $ 8,000 | 43 | $344,000 |
| Pay Steps 4-6 | 10,000 | 22 | 220,000 |
| Pay Steps 7-9 | 13,000 | 7 | 91,000 |
| Pay Steps 10-12 | 16,000 | 8 | 128,000 |
| Total |  | 80 | $783,000 |

## EXHIBIT 5
### Total Direct Faculty Costs by Department (thousands of dollars)

|  | Total | Lower | English | Math | Soc. Sci. | Nat. Sci. | Fine Arts | Foreign Language | Phys. Ed. |
|---|---|---|---|---|---|---|---|---|---|
| Pay Steps 1-3 | 344 | 104 | 56 | 32 | 32 | 16 | 32 | 32 | 40 |
| Pay Steps 4-6 | 220 | 60 | 40 | 20 | 30 | 20 | 20 | 10 | 30 |
| Pay Steps 7-9 | 91 | 13 | 26 | 0 | 13 | 26 | 0 | 13 | 0 |
| Pay Steps 10-12 | 128 | 0 | 16 | 32 | 0 | 48 | 16 | 0 | 16 |
| Total | 783 | 177 | 138 | 84 | 75 | 110 | 68 | 55 | 86 |
| Average | 9,788 | 8,850 | 9,857 | 10,500 | 9,375 | 12,500 | 9,714 | 9,167 | 9,556 |

## EXHIBIT 6
### Direct Faculty Costs per Student Contact Hour (by Department)

| | Total | Lower | English | Math | Soc. Sci. | Nat. Sci. | Fine Arts | Foreign Language | Phys. Ed. |
|---|---|---|---|---|---|---|---|---|---|
| 71-72 Actual | 43.65 | 41.54 | 50.00 | 42.42 | 34.72 | 53.76 | 43.59 | 41.67 | 42.15 |
| 72-73 Projected | 43.50 | 43.38 | 52.27 | 42.42 | 30.49 | 52.08 | 43.59 | 41.67 | 42.16 |
| % of Tuition[a] | 54 | 54 | 65 | 53 | 38 | 65 | 54 | 52 | 53 |

[a]Since each student takes 30 credit hours per week, tuition per student credit hour = $80 (2,400 ÷ 30). In a school for which tuition covers 90% of total costs and faculty salaries account for 50% of total costs, faculty salaries will average 55% of tuition (1/2 × 10/9).

**EXHIBIT 7**

Departmental Work load

(desired work load = 225 weekly contact hours/teacher)

| | Lower | English | Math | Soc. Sci. | Nat. Sci. | Fine Arts | Foreign Language | Phys. Ed. | Total |
|---|---|---|---|---|---|---|---|---|---|
| 71-72 Actual | 213 | 197 | 247.5 | 270 | 232.5 | 222.9 | 220 | 226.7 | 224.3 |
| 72-73 Projected | 204 | 188.6 | 247.5 | 307.5 | 240 | 222.9 | 220 | 226.7 | 225 |
| 72-73 Projected Variance | (21) | (36.4) | 22.5 | 82.5 | 15 | (3.1) | (5) | 1.7 | 0 |

**EXHIBIT 8**

Hiring Requirements to Correct Variances

|  | Lower | English | Math | Soc. Sci. | Nat. Sci. | Fine Arts | Foreign Language | Phys. Ed. | Total |
|---|---|---|---|---|---|---|---|---|---|
| Teaching Requirements, 72-73 | 18.1 | 11.7 | 8.8 | 10.9 | 8.5 | 6.9 | 5.9 | 9.1 | 80 |
| Current Number of Teachers | 20 | 14 | 8 | 8 | 8 | 7 | 6 | 9 | 80 |
| Hiring (Firing) Requirements | (1.9) | (2.3) | .8 | 2.9 | .5 | (.1) | (.1) | .1 | 0 |
| Recommended Hiring (Firing) | (2) | (2) | 1 | 3 |  |  |  |  |  |

# St. Augustine School (B)

The following are excerpts from letters received in response to feedback requested by Ms. Bullock regarding the WICHE model:

From Mr. McCoy of the board of trustees:

> *This is the greatest management tool that I have seen in this school in 10 years. It raises questions that scream to be answered.*

From Mr. Hendricks of the board of trustees:

> *It will help identify areas in which excessively large classes are having a detrimental effect on St. Augustine's quality of education.*

From the business manager:

> *It will serve as a decision-making aid in pinning down areas where our budget is taking a beating because classes are too small.*

From the Foreign Languages Department head:

> *It will serve as an independent forecast of faculty needs which will provide an objective yardstick for evaluating the hiring needs submitted by department heads. It will bring fairness and efficiency to an area that has previously known the influence of seniority and internal politics.*

Copyright © 1973 by the National Association of Independent Schools.

From the English Department head:

> *It is absurd to use a mechanical model to make decisions about a qualitative issue. I am hurt deeply by the prospect of using an adding machine to determine the quality of education that a student at St. Augustine will receive. To suggest that two teachers be dropped from the English Department strikes at the heart of the discipline that made St. Augustine strong, created its reputation, and currently serves as a main source of its pride and dignity. If there are "adjustments" to be made, let us bring the other disciplines up to the standards set long ago by the English Department.*

From the head of the Lower School:

> *I have become increasingly aware in the last two or three years of the leveling off and perhaps even the downturn of enrollment trends. I am afraid your model points clearly to the fact that the Lower School has become somewhat overextended in hiring. But the real question is what we do about it. I would personally prefer to wait until normal attrition reduces our number than to fire anybody outright. Or perhaps we could transfer somebody to one of the departments in the Upper School.*

From Mr. Marsh of the board of trustees:

> *The faculty load measurements, which are potentially useful, essentially aim at providing the largest number of weekly credit hours at the lowest overall cost. It must not be used as the only or even the most important measure of a department's performance on which to base budget action. A strong immediate effort must be made on the much more difficult task of measuring the "value" of a department.*

From Mr. Roberts of the board of trustees:

> *I strongly urge that department heads always have the right to audit their departmental figures before a final report is prepared for management purposes. Even in the simplest model there will be enough inaccuracies to render it almost meaningless unless department heads validate the data.*

From Mr. Pierce of the board of trustees:

> *I am concerned about the selection process for the ratios chosen. They seem to be both arbitrary and artificial. Can they objectively evaluate and compare departments within the school? How do they relate to the educational process? How do they measure the effectiveness of the education taking place?*

From the Fine Arts Department head:

> *After thorough consideration I can say categorically that it gives a totally false impression of what the Fine Arts Department is doing. It cannot hope to give an accurate picture unless everything we do is included. For instance, our faculty spends a tremendous amount of time in private tutelage of our art students. Also, most of our music payroll is to part-time instructors and I don't think the part-time people are included in your figures. Our average class size is less than 12, and it should be! We would prefer to keep it at 5 or 6, but I think it averages out about 8. In addition, input data can be interpreted in many ways. For example, when I direct a play, is that teaching or something else?*

From the Social Sciences Department head:

> *I knew we were overworked and overloaded, but, up until this point, we haven't had an objective way of demonstrating it. I never would have had the nerve to ask for three additional teachers, but the figures clearly show that that's what we need. I guess enrollment is up because of the new interest in urban affairs and environmental problems, which fall into our domain.*

From the Mathematics Department head:

> *Our department's reaction is generally favorable to the ideas that seem to lie behind the model. We think they are potentially useful. But I personally fear that cost/effectiveness analyses are somewhat misleading for measuring the quality of a school and its departments for, ideally, we are not turning out a product for popular demand in quite the same sense as does General Motors. My apprehension is that these figures may eventually be misused at some level. But we are, at least, now getting some concrete data that ought to be taken into account in examining our operations. Also, if the data are used to draw questionable conclusions, we will at least have something definite to argue about.*

From the Physical Education Department head:

> *When I coach the basketball team after school, is that teaching or some other classification? My assistant coach is from the Math Department. Is his coaching salary charged to Math or PE? It's nice to see that we're a low-cost department according to the direct cost figures in Exhibits 7 and 8. But realistically, that's just because all students are required to take PE and because we have a lot of young teachers. Our costs would appear to be a lot lower if the model took into consideration that all our*

*classes have 20 students rather than 12. And happily it doesn't charge us anything for the new gymnasium or the new athletic equipment. The model may have some usefulness at St. Augustine, but certainly not to us in its current form.*

From the Natural Sciences Department head:

*I suppose the model is correct in pointing out that direct faculty costs per credit hour produced for the Natural Science Department are the highest in the school. The reasons for this are not very subtle or startling: we simply have a greater proportion of senior faculty than other departments. These senior teachers bring more experience and teaching quality to the classroom and therefore command a higher salary. The quality of instruction per credit hour produced in the Natural Sciences Department is higher, and so is the cost. The model yields no decision rules useful for management except that to get more experience and quality in the classroom, the cost is higher. We did not need a model to learn that.*

From Mr. Hardeman of the board of trustees:

*I see tremendous managerial applications for the model. It can answer questions I've had on my mind for ages. I didn't know how to begin to answer them, but this model provides an analytical framework for doing so. For example, what would be the impact of a 10% increase or decrease in enrollment in each of the next 5 years? Although the aggregate effect is not likely to be that large, we could see that much change through shifts in student interest from one department to another. How much would it cost us to increase the rate of faculty promotion from one step to another? How much would it cost us to increase faculty salaries 5% across the board? What if we increased salaries but cut the rate of promotion? If we assume that tuition should at least cover direct faculty costs, how much would we have to increase tuition to cover these changes in faculty salary structure? How much would tuition have to rise if we first increased the average class size from 12 to 16? What if by increasing the average class size to 16, we lost 3% of our enrollment to other schools? Then how much would tuition have to rise? What if we stopped offering Latin and expanded the drama area of the Fine Arts Department? How would projected enrollment changes alter our overall costs? What could we save by using team teaching in the Lower School? How much would it cost to increase teaching quality by hiring more senior faculty? What could we save by not allowing electives in the freshman year of the Upper School? What if we dropped the credit hours per student per week from 30 to 27?*

*I'm not sure if all of these questions can be answered with the model, but I'm sure that many of them can. Of course, there are some parts of the program that are necessary and must be retained in spite of what they cost. But there are a number of ways of improving our financial position without materially degrading the quality of education. The model provides a decision-making aid which can help us sort out the alternatives.*

As Ms. Bullock studied the feedback she had received regarding the simplified WICHE cost estimation model, she was astonished both by the possible applications of the model and by the potential problems in perfecting a model that would be acceptable in terms of the opposing demands on its accuracy, simplicity, and usefulness.

She had resolved that the cost estimation model would be more useful in studying the implications of alternative decisions than in actually choosing from the available options. But, hopefully, the capability of exploring alternatives more fully would improve the planning and decision making at St. Augustine.

Ms. Bullock felt a note of irony as she noted that the only hiring request she had approved to date for the coming school year was a replacement for a step 2 English teacher who was moving to California. She doubted that she would have hired the replacement if she had known what she currently knew about comparative faculty loads between departments. But what could or should she do about it at this point?

## QUESTIONS

1   Sort out the arguments for and against the use of a cost estimation model. What can the system tell you? What can't it tell you? What are some of the potential misuses or misunderstandings which can arise out of its use?

2   There are many "adjustments" which can be made to the preliminary model to make it better represent the real world. For example, the average class size of eight students could be used to revise the desired faculty load and productivity for teaching in the Fine Arts Department. Provision could be made for nonteaching costs such as the gymnasium. But Ms. Bullock believes that a simple model which explains 80% of what she wants to know is more valuable than a complex model which explains 85% of what she wants to know. What adjustments should Ms. Bullock make to the CEM? Be specific.

3   If you were in Ms. Bullock's position, would you attempt to use a version of the WICHE cost estimation model? Why or why not?

# part 5

# TECHNICAL NOTES

# A Note on
# Steel Sheet Finishing

One form of output from a steel mill is a coil called a "hot band." The coil is hot because it is formed by applying extreme pressure to a slab of raw steel which has been heated to an intense temperature. This coil of hot-rolled steel can be sold as is or processed further. A sheet finishing mill converts the hot-rolled coil (hot band) into cold-rolled products, which sell at a higher margin. Exhibit 1 depicts the flow of products through such a plant. The process starts by removing rust and corrosion from the hot bands by passing them through a sulfuric acid bath (pickling process). Next, the coils pass through a cold-reduction mill (a tandem mill), which decreases the gauge (thickness) of the steel by stretching it and applying pressure. The term "cold" is used because the coil is not heated first. This operation stretches the microscopic grains of the steel, leaving the steel brittle. To eliminate the brittleness, the steel is next annealed. Annealing is the process of allowing the steel grains to contract again by elevating the temperature of the steel for a certain length of time. Cold-rolled steel can be annealed using a batch or a continuous process. In batch annealing the steel is heated while still wrapped in coil form. This can take up to a week for each coil. Continuous annealing is a much faster process because the coils are unrolled, allowing the heat to reach the steel more easily. Due to highly technical factors, batch-annealed steel is metallurgically distinguishable from continuous-annealed steel. Because most customers require consistent metallurgical properties in the steel they use, only a few products are transferable between the two processes. After annealing, the steel is further processed into one of three main products.

This note was prepared by Professor John K. Shank of The Ohio State University.

*Galvanized steel*—zinc-coated steel used for such products as garbage cans, snow shovels, and grain bins.

*Tin-plated steel*—very thin steel coated with tin for use in manufacturing steel beverage and food cans.

*Cold-rolled steel*—basic sheet steel for use in such products as automobiles, appliances, or farm machinery.

Since the galvanizing line has its own continuous-anneal equipment, galvanized products are not processed through the separate batch- or continuous-anneal facilities (except for some specialized products which require additional annealing).

Finished products are sold in coil form or in sheet form. Sheets are made by cutting (shearing) a coil into lengths (cuts) specified by the customer.

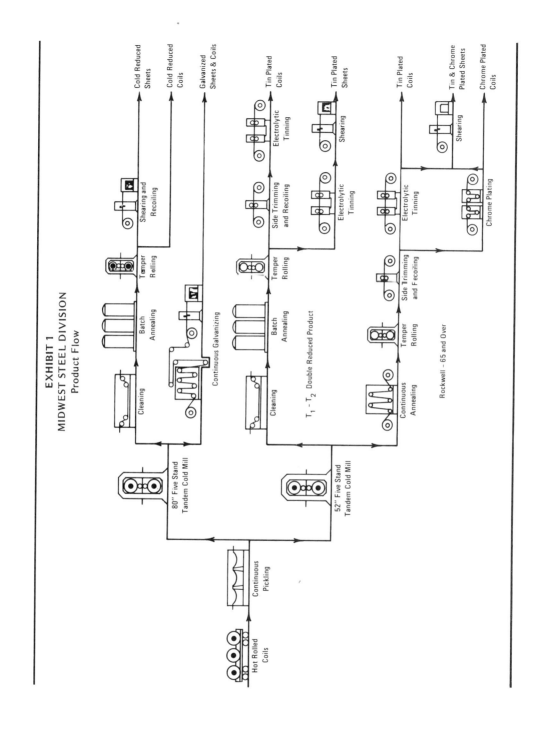

EXHIBIT 1
MIDWEST STEEL DIVISION
Product Flow

# Some Comments on Costing Alternative Choices

It is sometimes useful to decompose the decision-making process into the following four steps:

*1*   Identify the problem.
*2*   Enumerate the alternative courses of action.
*3*   Evaluate all the alternatives in terms of both quantitative and qualitative factors.
*4*   Choose the "best" alternative.

This note explains the notion of "differential cost" and its use in evaluating alternatives. We will illustrate the use of the differential cost concept in three common business situations:

*A*   Make or buy
*B*   Pricing
*C*   Temporary plant shutdown

Although this note emphasizes quantitative analysis, you should not assume that qualitative factors are less important in reaching a decision. We have also ignored here the impact of income taxes so as to simplify the calculations.

Copyright © 1975 by the President and Fellows of Harvard College. Reproduced by permission. This note was prepared by Vijayaragavan Govindaragan under the supervision of Associate Professor John Shank as a basis for class discussion rather than to illustrate either effective or ineffective handling of an administrative situation.

## A. MAKE OR BUY

*Facts Relating to Company A*

The company manufactures Part No. 580 in its own plant. The monthly production of this part is 10,000 units. The cost per part at the present level of activity is as follows:[1]

| | | |
|---|---|---|
| Direct Material | $ 5.50 | |
| Direct Labor | 3.00 | |
| Variable Overhead | 2.00 | |
| Fixed Overhead | 4.00 | ($40,000 ÷ 10,000 units) |
| | $14.50 | |

An outside manufacturer offers to supply similar parts at a price of $12.50 per part. It is determined that out of the total fixed costs of $40,000, only $10,000 could be saved if the company stopped manufacturing Part No. 580.

At first sight, it might seem that the parts should be purchased from outside because that would save the company $2.00 on every part purchased.

| | |
|---|---|
| Unit Cost of Making Part No. 580 | $14.50 |
| Unit Cost of Purchasing Part No. 580 | 12.50 |
| Per Unit Savings Resulting from Buying | $ 2.00 |

Differential (or relevant) cost analysis, however, tells a different story. Compared to the "base case" of making Part No. 580 in-house, the differential costs are those that would be different under the alternative of buying the part. Any cost that would have to be incurred under the base case as well as under the "buy" alternative is irrelevant (nondifferential) for the decision at hand. In the Company A situation, fixed costs amounting to $30,000 (total fixed costs $40,000 minus fixed costs that can be avoided under the "buy" alternative of $10,000) are irrelevant for the decision at hand because this amount ($30,000) would continue to be spent irrespective of whether the parts are made or bought. The differential cost computations following illustrate the dangers of using full-cost information in make-or-buy decisions.

---

[1] *Variable* overhead refers to those manufacturing costs other than material and labor for which the amount of cost is directly related to the amount of production. As the level of production varies, the amount of variable overhead varies proportionately. *Fixed* overhead refers to those manufacturing costs for which the amount of cost does not vary as production varies. The amount is fixed, regardless of the number of units produced. A more elegant way of stating the distinction is to say that fixed costs are variable at the unit cost level and variable costs are fixed at the unit cost level.

| | Make Part No. 580 (Base Case) | Buy Part No. 580 (Case II) | Incremental Cost in Case II As Compared to The Base Case |
|---|---|---|---|
| Cost of Purchase Parts | -0- | $125,000 (10,000 units × $12.50) | $125,000 |
| Direct Material (10,000 units × $5.50) | $ 55,000 | 0 | (55,000) |
| Direct Labor (10,000 units × $3.00) | 30,000 | 0 | (30,000) |
| Variable Overhead (10,000 units × $2.00) | 20,000 | 0 | (20,000) |
| Fixed Overhead That Can Be Avoided by Buying | 10,000 | 0 | (10,000) |
| | $115,000 | $125,000 | |
| Net Differential Cost in Case II | | | $ 10,000 |

Any decision based on the above calculations is subject to the following conditions:

1　Direct laborers can be laid off if production of Part No. 580 is discontinued. If laborers can neither be laid off nor transferred to other jobs, direct labor cost would be irrelevant because it would have to be incurred under both the alternatives.

2　The productive capacity released by discontinuing the manufactur of Part No. 580 does not have alternative use and will remain idle. Suppose that the released capacity can be leased for $11,000 a month. Then this alternative has to be considered and the relevant computations would be:

| | Make Part No. 580 (Base Case) | Buy Part No. 580 (Case II) | Buy Part No. 580 and Lease Plant Facilities (Case III) |
|---|---|---|---|
| Differential Cost | $115,000 | $125,000 | $114,000 ($125,000 minus lease income of $11,000) |
| Net Differential Cost (Compared to Base Case) | | $ 10,000 | ($1,000) |

Based on these computations, the decision would be to buy the parts and lease the plant premises.

## B. PRICING

*Facts Relating to Company B*

The company has a monthly production capacity of 50,000 units and is operating at a volume of 40,000 units at present. The revenue and cost data at the present volume are as follows:

|  | Per Unit | Total |
|---|---|---|
| Sales | $8 | $320,000 |
| Direct Material | 2 | $ 80,000 |
| Direct Labor | 1 | 40,000 |
| Variable Overhead | 1 | 40,000 |
| Fixed Overhead | 2 | 80,000 |
|  | 6 | 240,000 |
| Profit | 2 | $ 80,000 |

The company has received a special order for 10,000 units at a price of $5.00 per unit.

It might first seem that the special order would result in a loss of $1.00 per unit.

|  | Per Unit |
|---|---|
| Special-Order Price | $ 5.00 |
| Cost of Production | 6.00 |
| Loss | $(1.00) |

However, differential cost analysis leads to a different conclusion:

|  | Without Special Order 40,000 units (Base Case) | With Special Order 50,000 units (Case II) | Incremental Profit from Special Order |
|---|---|---|---|
| Sales | $320,000 | $370,000[a] | $ 50,000 |
| Direct Material | $ 80,000 | $100,000 | $(20,000) |
| Direct Labor | 40,000 | 50,000 | (10,000) |
| Variable Overhead | 40,000 | 50,000 | (10,000) |
| Fixed Overhead | 80,000 | 80,000 | 0 |
| Total Cost | $240,000 | $280,000 | $(40,000) |
| Profit | $ 80,000 | $ 90,000 | |
| Net Differential Profit | | $ 10,000 | $ 10,000 |

[a]40,000 units at $8 per unit and 10,000 units at $5 per unit.

The foregoing calculations of course depend on the following assumptions:

1    The unused plant capacity of 10,000 units will remain idle if the special order is rejected.
2    The special-order quotation of $5.00 per unit will not upset the market price for the other 40,000 units.
3    No additional fixed overhead will be incurred when the volume of production is increased from 40,000 units to 50,000 units.

## C. PLANT SHUTDOWN

*Facts Relating to Company C*

The company operates at a monthly volume of 100,000 units. The unit selling price and unit cost under the present operating conditions are as follows:

| | |
|---|---:|
| Selling Price | $10 |
| Direct Material | $ 2 |
| Direct Labor | 2 |
| Variable Overhead | 1 |
| Fixed Overhead | 3 |
| | $ 8 |
| Profit | $ 2 |

Due to a slump in the market, the unit selling price has fallen to $5.25. The company expects the selling price to return to normal after 2 months. The company is considering the possibility of a shutdown of the plant for a period of 2 months. Plant shutdown costs are expected to be $25,000. It would require $15,000 to recruit and train new workers and restart activity in the plant after 2 months. Monthly fixed overhead of $300,000 includes depreciation, interest, taxes, and insurance amounting to $250,000. This amount would have to be incurred even during the shutdown period. However, the remaining $50,000 per month could be avoided if the plant is shut down completely.

The relevant cost analysis would be as follows:

## SUNK COSTS

Sunk costs are costs that have already been incurred or committed. No decision made now can avoid these costs since the outlay has already been made. Sunk costs are, therefore, not relevant in considering future decisions. Consider the following illustration.

|  | Continue Operation (Base Case) | Shut Down for 2 months (Case II) |
|---|---|---|
| Sales (100,000 units per month X 2 months X $5.25) | $(1,050,000) | -0- |
| Variable Costs (200,000 units X $5) | 1,000,000 | -0- |
| Profit Contribution | $ (50,000) | |
| Fixed Costs that Could Be Saved, if Plant Is Shut Down ($50,000 per month X 2 months) | | $(100,000) |
| Costs Associated with Plant Shut Down: | | |
| Shutdown costs $25,000 | | |
| Costs to Restart 15,000 | | 40,000 |
| Differential Profit Contribution | $ (50,000) | $ (60,000) |
| Net Differential Profit, if Plant Is Shut Down (As Compared to the Base Case) | | $ 10,000 |

*Facts Relating to Company D*

The company has incurred $25,000 in test-marketing a new product. The company is now considering whether to introduce the product or not. The product, if introduced, would have a life of 2 years. The total revenue from the product in the 2 years is expected to be $200,000. Total costs are expected to be $180,000.

In this situation, the test market expense of $25,000 is a sunk cost. This amount has already been spent and no part of it can be recovered, whether the new product is introduced or not. Test market expense is, therefore, not relevant to the present decision. The differential cost analysis is as follows:

| | Introduce New Product (Base Case) | Don't Introduce New Product (Case II) | Incremental Profit (Loss) in Case II |
|---|---|---|---|
| Sales | $ 200,000 | -0- | $(200,000) |
| Costs | (180,000) | -0- | 180,000 |
| Profit | $ 20,000 | -0- | |
| Differential Loss in Case II (as Compared to the Base Case) | | | $ (20,000) |

The use of the differential cost concept is not restricted to the four situations discussed in this note.

The following observations may prove helpful to you in all decision problems:

*1*   For different decisions, different costs are relevant. The approach to every problem should be to determine which costs are relevant and to use them in the quantitative analysis. One way to think about differential costs is as follows. Let $X_1$ represent the total cost at the $L_1$ level of activity and $X_2$ the total cost at the $L_2$ level of activity. Then $(X_2 - X_1)$ is the incremental or differential cost for the $(L_2 - L_1)$ change in the level of activity. If we introduce the notion of fixed and variable costs, then the total cost at $L_1$ and $L_2$ levels of activity can be expressed as the following linear equations:

$$X_1 = a + bL_1$$
and
$$X_2 = a + bL_2$$
where   $a$ = total fixed costs
$b$ = unit variable cost

Then the differential cost for the change in level of activity is given by:

$$X_2 - X_1 = bL_2 - bL_1$$
$$= b(L_2 - L_1)$$

*2*   It is erroneous to conclude that fixed costs are always irrelevant. If the time span is long enough, even fixed costs could be changed. Within the time frame of the decision, the test of "relevance" is to find out whether costs—variable or fixed—would be altered by the decision at hand.

*3*   In alternative-choice problems, it is usually better to work with total amounts rather than with unit costs because of the slippery nature of the concept "fixed cost per unit."

This note is intended to be a very simple, straightforward introduction to the concept of differential costs. The examples are simplistic and you should not try to analyze them in depth. You will get many chances in your other courses to incorporate more complicated cost analyses into the evaluation of real business problems. All such cost analyses will make use of the differential costing concept.

# Some Comments on Computing Prime Cost Variances

The term "prime" costs refers to the material and labor costs which can be directly related to a unit of product. You will often hear the terms "direct" material cost or "direct" labor cost. "Indirect" material and "indirect" labor costs are considered to be part of manufacturing overhead or "burden" rather than part of prime cost. Examples of these four cost categories are shown below:

| Cost Category | Cost Classification | Example |
|---|---|---|
| Direct Labor | Prime Cost | Cost for a worker's time spent assembling a product |
| Indirect Labor | Overhead Cost | Cost for a worker's time spent repairing manufacturing equipment |
| Direct Material | Prime Cost | Cost of steel used in manufacturing an automobile |
| Indirect Material | Overhead Cost | Cost of material used in maintaining manufacturing equipment |

This commentary deals only with prime costs.

The standard for any element of prime cost involves two components: a price component and a quantity component. The standard cost is the standard quantity to be used multiplied by the standard price per unit of measure. For example, if an

Copyright © 1975 by the President and Fellows of Harvard College. Reproduced by permission. This note was prepared as a basis for class discussion by Associate Professor John K. Shank.

electric motor contains four bushings and each bushing should cost $.25, then the standard cost for bushings is $1.00 (standard quantity of 4 × the price per unit of $.25). Variances are usually computed for each of the two components for both material and labor costs. The formulas for calculating the variances are as follows:

$$\text{Price variance (PV)} = (\text{SP} - \text{AP}) \times \text{AQ}$$
$$\text{Quantity variance (QV)} = (\text{SQ} - \text{AQ}) \times \text{SP}$$
$$\text{Total variance (TV)} = \text{PV} + \text{QV}$$

where  SP = standard price
       AP = actual price
       SQ = standard quantity
       AQ = actual quantity

Since the total variance is the difference between the standard cost allowance (SP × SQ) and the actual cost incurred (AP × AQ), you should be able to verify for yourself that the price and quantity variance in the above formulas do sum to the total variance.

We can illustrate these calculations with the following example:

*Calculation*

| | |
|---|---|
| **Standard per Unit** | |
| Material | 2 pounds per unit at $1.00 per pound = $2.00 per unit |
| Labor | 3 hours per unit at $4.00 per hour = $12.00 per unit |
| Production | 10 units. Therefore, the standard cost allowance is $20 for material and $120 for labor. |
| **Actual Costs** | |
| Material | Used 25 pounds which were purchased at a cost of $.80 per pound, for a cost of $20. |
| Labor | Used 25 hours at an average rate of $5.00 per hour, for a cost of $125. |
| **Prime Cost Variances** | |
| Material | Price variance: ($1.00 − $.80) × 25 lb = $5 Favorable |
| | Quantity variance: (20 − 25) × $1.00/lb = $5 Unfavorable |
| | Total variance: $5F + $5U = 0 = $20 − $20 |
| Labor | Price variance: ($4 − $5) × 25 hr = $25  Unfavorable |
| | Quantity variance: (30 − 25) × $4/hr = $20  Favorable |
| | Total variance: $25U + $20F = $5U = $120 − $125 |

*Note:* We suggest that you not worry about whether to put standard or actual first in the formulas or about trying to keep track of whether a negative result is favorable or unfavorable. Instead, just think about whether the direction of the variance is good or bad and forget about algebraic signs.

## SOME COMPLICATIONS

You may have wondered why the quantity variance is computed using *standard* prices while the price variance is computed using *actual* quantities. Most people feel that price fluctuations should not be considered when measuring the variance due to quantity fluctuations—vary only one component at a time. However, most people also feel that the price variance should be measured over the actual quantities for which the price difference obtains, not the standard quantities. Some people do not like this logical inconsistency. They prefer to vary only one component at a time in both the price and quantity variance calculations. They then set up a third variance (joint variance) caused by the joint fluctuation in both prices and quantities. Under this approach the formulas are as follows:

$$PV = (SP - AP) \times SQ$$
$$QV = (SQ - AQ) \times SP$$
$$JV = (SP - AP) \times (SQ - AQ)$$
$$TV = PV + QV + JV$$

This can be illustrated graphically as follows, assuming both price and quantity variations are unfavorable:

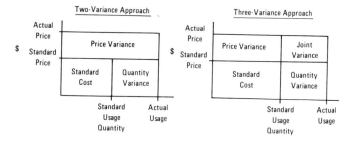

It is difficult, if not impossible, to give a commonsense interpretation to the joint variance when one of the two components varies favorably and the other varies unfavorably. Furthermore, we believe that purchasing agents should be assessed for price variations on quantities actually purchased but that production managers should be assessed for quantity difference times standard prices, ignoring price fluctuations. For these reasons, we favor the simpler, two variance approach.

The logically consistent framework we have set up in this note that PV + QV = TV is often violated in practice in regard to material variances. Many firms prefer to compute the price variance over quantities *purchased* and the quantity variance over quantities *used*. Since purchase and usage quantities often differ in any given period, the two variances cannot be summed algebraicly. They can, however, still be combined for cost reporting purposes to get a picture of purchasing and usage variances together.

Suppose, for example, that in our earlier illustration material purchases totaled 30 pounds at $.80 even though only 25 pounds were used in production. The material variance calculations could then be as follows:

Price variance: ($1.00 − $.80) × 30 lb = $6    Favorable
Quantity variance: (20 − 25) × $1.00/lb = $5    Unfavorable
Total variance: $6F + $5U = $1F ≠ $20 − $20

A labor price variance is often called a labor rate variance and a labor quantity variance is often called a labor efficiency variance. A material quantity variance is often called a material usage variance and a material price variance is often called a purchase price variance.

# Some Comments on Computing Manufacturing Overhead Cost Variances

## OVERHEAD BUDGETS

Budgets for prime costs hinge on unit-level standard costs. Once standard prime costs per unit are determined, the budget for any given period is just the standard per unit times the number of units produced. A simple approach like this works because prime costs are variable costs. The cost allowance or budget thus varies directly as production volume varies. Because manufacturing overhead costs do not all vary directly with volume, it is a more difficult task to determine allowable overhead at any given level of production.

One approach to overhead budgeting ignores the volume dependence issue entirely. This approach is called *fixed* overhead budgeting. Under a fixed-budget approach, management determines the amount of overhead which should be incurred at the normal or most likely production level. This expense total becomes the budget against which cost performance is measured regardless of the level of production output actually achieved. To the extent that manufacturing overhead costs vary with production, the fixed-budget approach yields less and less meaningful variance data, the more that actual output varies from planned or normal output. There is no conceptual support for a fixed-budget approach to manufacturing overhead. We would not bother to mention this approach except that many companies still use it.

The more conceptually sound approach to determining overhead standards is called *flexible* budgeting. A flexible manufacturing overhead budget specifies

Copyright © 1975 by the President and Fellows of Harvard College. Reproduced by permission. This note was prepared as a basis for class discussion by Associate Professor John K. Shank.

allowable cost at each possible output level. Once a period is completed and the actual production volume is known, the budget standard is determined by reference to the flexible budget for that level of output. This is a direct parallel to the way a budget for direct material and direct labor is determined. If all manufacturing overhead is assured to be either pure "variable" or pure "fixed," a flexible budget is just a formula of the following type:

$$\text{Budget allowance} = a + bx$$

where $a$ = fixed overhead costs for the period
$b$ = variable overhead costs per unit
$x$ = units produced during the period

Overhead cost behavior is not assumed to be this simplistic in most businesses today.

An example of a more complicated but still simplified flexible budget is as shown on page 315.

## OVERHEAD ABSORPTION

Because manufacturing overhead costs are considered to be product costs, it is necessary to find some way of charging or "absorbing" them into inventory. However, the simple approach of charging actual manufacturing overhead directly to work-in-process (WIP) inventory is usually not considered to be an acceptable approach, for two reasons:

1    Overhead variances are not usually considered to be product costs. Variances do not "add value" to the inventory. Thus, only *allowable* overhead is to be "inventoried."

2    Volume considerations also affect the decision of how much overhead to absorb in inventory. Suppose, for example, the depreciation is $1,000 per period and that 1 unit is produced in period 1 and 1,000 units are produced in period 2. It doesn't seem "fair" to most accountants to say that a period 1 unit carries a cost of $1,000 for depreciation (1 unit/$1,000 depreciation) and a period 2 unit only $1 (1,000 units/$1,000 depreciation). A unit can't really be "more valuable" just because fewer were produced that month. "Fair" allocation of depreciation to inventory seems to require a concept of "normal" volume. The $1,000 depreciation expense is incurred as a "reasonable" charge on the assumption that some reasonable or normal number of units will be produced on the equipment. It is this normal volume level over which the planned overhead should be spread, so the argument goes.

For these two reasons, "standard practice" for charging manufacturing overhead into inventory is to set an "absorption rate" computed as planned overhead costs at normal production volume (per the flexible budget) divided by that normal

A Flexible Budget

| Capacity Utilization: | 40%[a] | 60% | 70% | 80% *"Normal"* → | 100% | Cost Behavior |
|---|---|---|---|---|---|---|
| Labor Cost (Piece Rate): | $4,000 | $6,000 | $7,000 | $8,000 | $10,000 | |
| Allowed Overhead | | | | | | |
| Depreciation | $1,000 | $1,000 | $1,000 | $1,000 | $1,000 | Pure non-variable or "fixed" |
| Supervision | 500 | 1,000 | 1,000 | 1,000 | 1,500 | "Step" cost[b] |
| Supplies | 400 | 600 | 700 | 800 | 1,000 | Pure variable at 10% of labor |
| Power | 600 | 700 | 750 | 800 | 900 | Semivariable: $400 + 5% of labor |
| Total | $2,500 | $3,300 | $3,450 | $3,600 | $4,400 | |

[a] It is assumed that volume would never fall below 40% of capacity.

[b] A "step" cost is one which doesn't vary directly with production but does increase in lump-sum jumps when volume rises substantially. An example would be adding a second foreman when volume rose to the level that a second shift was needed.

volume. In the example shown above, the normal volume is 8,000 direct labor dollars (80% of capacity). At this level of output, budgeted overhead is $3,600. The overhead absorption rate is thus $3,600/$8,000, or $.45 per direct labor dollar. In single-product firms, output can be expressed in units of product. In multiproduct firms, however, it is necessary to set some other measure of capacity utilization, such as labor hours, labor dollars, or machine hours. The choice of a volume measure in a particular business should be based on which variable best measures the level of capacity utilization for that business.

The accounting works as follows. A T-account is established in the books of account called "factory overhead" or "burden" or something equivalent. Actual manufacturing overhead expenses are charged (debited) to this T-account. Overhead is absorbed into inventory by crediting the "factory overhead" account and debiting the work-in-process inventory. The amount of absorbed overhead is equal to the absorption rate times the actual volume attained. In our example, if actual volume was 7,000 direct labor dollars, $3,150 of overhead would be charged to WIP ($7,000 × $.45).

You will note that this absorption process will only "clear" the factory overhead account if two conditions are both met.

1    *If actual volume equals normal or planned volume.* Manufacturing overhead does not vary directly with production. The absorption rate, however, is a pure variable rate. Thus, absorbed overhead will only equal planned overhead at one particular volume level—that level used in computing the absorption rate.

2    *If actual overhead expenses equal planned expenses per the flexible budget.* Since only budgeted overhead is absorbed, any differences between budgeted costs and actual costs will not be "cleared" from the factory overhead T-account.

At the end of any accounting period, therefore, any residual balance in the factory overhead account results from failure to meet one or both of these two conditions. This end-of-period residual in the factory overhead T-account is sometimes called the "book" overhead variance because it is what shows up in the books of account. It is also sometimes called the total overhead variance.

Normal accounting practice is to charge this variance to cost of goods sold for the month as a period expense.

## ANALYZING THE TOTAL OVERHEAD VARIANCE

For purposes of evaluating cost control performance, the relevant comparison is actual overhead versus allowed overhead per the flexible budget. Assuming actual overhead expenses as follows, this calculation for our example would be:

| Cost Item | *Flexible Budget Allowance at Actual Volume of 7,000 direct Labor dollars* | *Actual Expense at Actual Volume* | *Spending Variance* |
|---|---|---|---|
| Depreciation | $1,000 | $1,100 | $100U |
| Supervision | 1,000 | 1,050 | 50U |
| Supplies | 700 | 690 | 10F |
| Power | 750 | 770 | 20U |
| Total | $3,450 | $3,610 | $160U |

As shown in the table, the difference between actual overhead incurred and the flexible budget at this level of output is called the overhead "spending" variance. It measures cost control performance.

You will remember that the total variance which shows up in the T-account is equal to the difference between actual overhead (the debits) and absorbed overhead at actual volume (the credit). The variance which is useful in measuring cost control effectiveness (the spending variance) is equal to the difference between actual overhead and allowed overhead at actual volume. In order to present an analysis which "balances" cost accountants need to have some name for the difference between the total variance (actual OH[1] – absorbed OH) and the spending variance (actual OH – allowed OH). Using a little algebra, you can see that the quantity for which we need a name is allowed OH – absorbed OH. Then, this quantity plus the spending variance equals the total variance:

(Actual OH – allowed OH) + (allowed OH – absorbed OH) = (actual OH – absorbed OH)
Spending variance        +              "plug"          =          total variance

Regarding the plug, we have already observed that allowed OH will only equal absorbed OH when the firm operates at normal volume. Why? Because budgeted overhead does not vary directly as production varies, but absorbed overhead is purely variable, by convention. The absorption rate is set to just absorb into inventory the planned overhead when the firm actually operates at its normal volume. Standard (absorbed) overhead cost per unit, for purposes of valuing inventories, is thus equal to a proportional share of budgeted overhead when production volume is at normal levels. This means that the difference between allowed OH and absorbed OH relates to the difference between normal production volume and actual production volume.

Because the plug variance (allowed OH – absorbed OH) results from the difference between planned and actual production volume, it is called a "production volume variance." The dollar amount of this production volume variance has

[1]OH, overhead.

no particular management significance whatsoever. The dollar amount is just the plug required to reconcile a managerially significant number (the spending variance) to a number which shows up in the income statement (the total variance). The production volume variance *does* result from variation between planned and actual production volume. In this sense, the name is appropriate. However, the amount is not managerially useful—the amount is just a plug. For our example the amount is computed as follows:

Total variance = actual OH − absorbed OH = $3,610 − $3,150 = $460 Unfavorable
Spending variance = actual OH − allowed OH = $3.610 − $3,450 = $160 Unfavorable
Production volume variance = total variance − spending variance = $460U − $160U = $300U
*or*                                          = allowed OH − absorbed OH = $3,450 − $3,150 = $300 Unfavorable

Going one step further, we can talk about what comprises the plug. In a nutshell, it is made up of under- or overabsorbed fixed manufacturing overhead. It does not include any variable overhead because items which are directly variable with production are treated identically in the absorption rate and in the flexible budget. They thus cancel out in computing the difference between allowed and absorbed cost. In our illustration, for example, the absorption rate of $.45 per direct labor dollar includes $.15 of variable cost and the flexible budget also includes $.15 per direct labor dollar of variable cost ($.10 for supplies and $.05 for power). At actual volume of $7,000 direct labor dollars, therefore, the allowed OH of $3,450 includes $1,050 of variable cost and the abosrbed OH of $3,150 also includes $1,050 of variable cost. This $1,050 thus does not contribute anything to the difference between $3,450 and $3,150. The difference is the fixed-cost absorption rate ($.30) times the unfavorable volume fluctuation of $1,000 direct labor dollars, or $300 Unfavorable. The $.30 fixed-cost absorption rate is equal to the $2,400 of planned fixed overhead at normal volume divided by the volume measure of 8,000 direct labor dollars. The overall absorption rate of $.45 is just the sum of the variable part and the nonvariable part.

# Some Comments on "Absorption" Costing and "Direct" Costing

So far in the course, raw material, direct labor, and factory overhead have been treated as *product costs* and assigned to units sold as cost of goods sold or to inventory cost for units still on hand. All nonproduction costs have been treated as *period expenses* and charged against revenues in the accounting period in which they are incurred. Common examples of period expenses are selling, general, and administrative expenses. This traditional approach to product costing classifies costs by *function* (i.e., production, selling or administration).

By reclassifying production costs according to their *behavior* rather than their *function,* factory overhead costs that don't vary with production could be included with the traditional period costs such as selling and administration expenses. Product costs would then include direct material, direct labor, and *variable* factory overhead. The distinction between the traditional product costing system, which is known as *full absorption* or simply *absorption* or *full* costing, and this alternative product costing system, known as *direct, variable,* or *marginal* costing, is the treatment of fixed factory overhead costs. Absorption costing treats *all* factory overhead as product costs, ignoring the fixed/variable distinction. Direct costing includes as product costs only those manufacturing costs that vary directly with production units. Direct costing considers fixed factory overhead to be a period expense.

The following table emphasizes the major differences between the two alternative treatments of product costs.

Copyright © 1975 by the President and Fellows of Harvard College. Reproduced by permission. This note was prepared as a basis for class discussion by Professor Joseph G. San Miguel and Professor John K. Shank.

|  | Absorption Costing | | Direct Costing | |
|  | Product | Period | Product | Period |
|---|---|---|---|---|
| Direct Material | X | | X | |
| Direct Labor | X | | X | |
| Variable Factory Overhead | X | | X | |
| Fixed Factory Overhead | X | | | X |
| Selling | | X | | X |
| Administrative | | X | | X |
| General | | X | | X |

From the table you should verify for yourself that if all production costs are variable, absorption and direct costing yield identical results.

What difference does this make to a manager? A short example will help illustrate the effects on earnings and inventories of using the two alternative methods of product costing.

EXAMPLE

Assume that a firm called the All-Fixed Company has discovered a new process that transforms air into a new product called Super-air. The manufacturing process consists of a specialty built machine that is fully automated and requires no labor or purchased materials. The only ingredient required in the production process is air. We can assume no costs for air consumed by the process. Therefore, the annual production costs are $12,000 of fixed factory overhead costs for factory rental, machine depreciation, and maintenance. These fixed costs are assumed to be constant within a range of 0 to 25,000 units of production. The normal level of production is 16,000 units per year. The standard fixed overhead absorption rate is $.75 per unit ($12,000 of factory overhead costs divided by the normal volume of 16,000 units). The following data pertain to the first 3 months of operations:

|  | Jan. | Feb. | Mar. | 3-Month Total |
|---|---|---|---|---|
| Units Sold | 1,000 | 1,000 | 2,000 | 4,000 |
| Units Produced | 2,000 | 1,000 | 1,000 | 4,000 |
| Production Costs (All Fixed Overhead) | $1,000 | $1,000 | $1,000 | $3,000 |
| Selling and Administrative Expenses | $ 200 | $ 200 | $ 200 | $ 600 |

Under an absorption standard costing system, cost of goods sold and ending inventories consist of the fixed factory overhead. The ending inventory is always valued at standard cost of $.75 per unit. Under direct costing, there are no product costs to assign to cost of goods sold or inventories, because there are no variable costs of production. Exhibit 1 illustrates the differences between absorption and direct costing for the foregoing data. You should study Exhibit 1 now.

Over the 3-month period, it is obvious that both product costing alternatives result in the same total earnings of $400 and no ending inventories. However, in January, absorption costing shows a profit of $550, whereas direct costing results in a loss of $200. In February, absorption costing shows the same loss as direct costing. In March, absorption costing profits are only $50, while direct costing shows $800 profits, Why the different results?

The key to understanding the alternatives and their effects on earnings and inventories is in the accounting for *fixed* factory overhead. Under direct costing, the income statement each period includes the fixed manufacturing overhead actually incurred that period. Under absoption costing, the situation is more complicated. The income statement will include the fixed manufacturing costs which are part of the standard cost of goods sold (standard fixed overhead costs per unit times units sold). However, the income statement will also include the production volume variance for the period, which, as you know, represents under or over absorbed fixed manufacturing overhead during the period. The difference between profit reported under the two systems is always equal to the difference in the amount of fixed manufacturing costs charged in the income statement. For our example in Exhibit 1, this can be illustrated as follows:

| | *Period* | | | |
| | *1* | *2* | *3* | *Total* |
|---|---|---|---|---|
| Profit under Direct Costing | $ (200) | $ (200) | $  800 | $  400 |
| Profit under Absorption Costing | 550 | (200) | 50 | 400 |
| Profit Difference | $  750 | -0- | $ (750) | -0- |
| | | | | |
| Fixed Manufacturing Cost Included in the Income Statement: | | | | |
| Direct Costing | $1,000 | $1,000 | $1,000 | $3,000 |
| Absorption Costing | | | | |
| Standard Cost of Goods Sold | $  750 | $  750 | $1,500 | $3,000 |
| Production Volume Variance | (500) | 250 | 250 | 0 |
| | $  250 | $1,000 | $1,750 | $3,000 |
| Fixed-Cost Difference | $  750 | -0- | $ (750) | -0- |

Must Be Equal for Each Period

Under direct costing, profit varies directly with sales volume. Since cost of goods sold includes only variable manufacturing costs, gross margin is really the same as profit contribution.[1] Reported profit thus equals total profit contribution (contribution per unit times units sold) less total fixed costs.

Under absorption costing, reported profit varies partly with sales and partly with production. For every unit sold, reported profit goes up by the difference between sales price per unit and standard manufacturing cost per unit (both fixed and variable). In addition to this "sales effect," for every unit produced the production volume variance is reduced by the amount of fixed cost absorbed for that unit. This means, in effect, that every unit produced increases reported profit by the amount that the production volume variance is reduced. This amount for each unit produced is just the fixed-cost absorption rate. An alternative way of looking at absorption costing, therefore, is to say that reported profit equals the "sales profit" (standard profit margin per unit × units sold) plus the "production profit" (fixed-cost absorption rate × units produced) less the total fixed costs incurred. We can illustrate this for the All-Fixed Company as follows:

|  | Period | | |
|---|---|---|---|
|  | 1 | 2 | 3 |
| Sales Profit ($.25 per Unit Sold) | $ 250 | $ 250 | $ 500 |
| Production Profit ($.75 per Unit Produced) | 1,500 | 750 | 750 |
| Less Fixed Costs Incurred | (1,200) | (1,200) | (1,200) |
| Reported Profit[a] | $ 550 | $ (200) | $ 50 |

[a]The same as shown in Exhibit 1 for absorption costing.

## SUMMARY

Proponents of direct costing often argue that reported profit should vary only with sales, not with the level of production. They view this statement to be an argument in favor of direct costing over absorption costing. What do you think?

The direct costing method also has broad appeal for product costing and cost control purposes because of its close relationship to the "contribution approach," to break-even analysis, and to flexible budgets. Grouping all fixed costs together leads at once to break-even analysis for decision making (cost-volume-profit analysis) and to flexible budgets for cost control.

We have discussed the managerial significance of direct versus absorption costing in several of the cases. This note is intended only to clarify mechanical issues—not to propose an answer as to which approach is "better."

[1] Assuming no variable selling and administrative expenses.

**EXHIBIT 1**

Effects of Absorption and Direct Costing Alternatives

| | Standard Absorption Costing | | | | Standard Direct Costing | | | |
|---|---|---|---|---|---|---|---|---|
| | Jan. | Feb. | Mar. | Total | Jan. | Feb. | Mar. | Total |
| Sales at $1 per Unit | $1,000 | $1,000 | $2,000 | $4,000 | $1,000 | $1,000 | $2,000 | $4,000 |
| Standard Cost of Good Sold | 750 | 750 | 1,500 | 3,000 | | | | |
| Under (Over) Absorbed Overhead[a] | (500) | 250 | 250 | -0- | | | | |
| Gross Profit | 750 | 0 | 250 | 1,000 | 1,000 | 1,000 | 2,000 | 4,000 |
| Selling and Administration | 200 | 200 | 200 | 600 | 200 | 200 | 200 | 600 |
| Fixed Factory Overhead | | | | | 1,000 | 1,000 | 1,000 | 3,000 |
| Net Income (Loss) | $ 550 | $ (200) | $ 50 | $ 400 | $ (200) | $ (200) | $ 800 | $ 400 |
| | | | | | | | | |
| **Computation of Cost of Goods Sold:** | | | | | | | | |
| Beginning Inventory at Standard | $ 0 | $ 750 | $ 750 | | | | | |
| Current Manufacturing Costs | 1,000 | 1,000 | 1,000 | | | | | |
| Total Manufacturing Costs | $1,000 | $1,750 | $1,750 | | | | | |
| Less Ending Inventory at Standard[b] | 750 | 750 | -0- | | | | | |
| Cost of Goods Sold (Net) | $ 250 | $1,000 | $1,750 | | | | | |

(No cost of goods sold and no ending inventory under this method and this specific example)

[a]The variance or adjustment could follow the gross profit computation as a period loss or gain. The effect on net income is the same.

[b]Ending inventory is valued at total standard cost per unit times the number of units unsold. The difference between ending inventory and total manufacturing cost is therefore the "cost of goods sold" for the period.

323

# Managing Against Expectations (A): A Note on Profit Variance Analysis

Not surprisingly, a major function of accounting is facilitating accountability—measuring the performance of individuals in terms appropriate to their assigned responsibilities—ROI for "investment center" managers, profits for "profit center" managers, and costs for "cost center" managers. Not all aspects of a manager's performance can be captured in accounting measures. This is particularly true for measures of activity in just one period. Nevertheless, measures of periodic profit, cost, or revenue performance do provide a point of departure from which a more comprehensive performance assessment can begin. It is no accident that the last figure on an earnings statement, net earnings, has provided the basis for the now more ubiquitous phrase "the bottom line."

If a manager is charged with profit responsibility, the measure of how much profit was earned is clearly relevant in evaluating the manager's performance. Nevertheless, the statement, "the profit last month was $3,000," is, by itself, not very informative. There is a need for some criterion by which the $3,000 can be judged to represent good, bad, or indifferent performance.

In almost every case we have some criteria which are used implicitly, if not explicitly—the profit last month, the profit for the same month last year, the profit for a company or department of similar size. An argument can be made that the use of return on investment is an attempt to put profit performance on a more universally comparable basis. The concept of investment is applicable across companies and profit per dollar of investment has meaning in and of itself. Even with the use

Copyright © 1976 by the President and Fellows of Harvard College. Reproduced by permission. This technical note was prepared by Professors Neil C. Churchill and John K. Shank as a basis for class discussion. Distributed by the Intercollegiate Case Clearing House, Soldiers Field, Boston, Mass. 02163. All rights reserved to the contributors. Printed in the U.S.A.

of ROI, most financial statements prepared for internal use show figures for "this month," "year-to-date," "this month last year," and "year-to-date last year." Financial statements of publicly held companies also show figures for both the current and previous year, to provide a base point for evaluation of current performance.

## THE BENCHMARK

Although measures of past performance are widely used as benchmarks or as evaluation criteria, they are not the only criteria which can be used, nor are they always the best basis for evaluating performance. An alternative which requires more sophistication and managerial judgment is to use a measure of *expected performance*. Such a figure could be something as simple as last year's profit, last year's profit plus 10%, or last year's profit plus $20,000. It could also be, for a cost center, a carefully thought through set of standard costs at each possible level of activity. For a business as a whole, it could be a 1-year profit plan—a detailed profit budget.

Whatever the nature of the activity and however sophisticated the analysis, the essence of this approach is to establish a target level of expected results and then to compare actual performance with this expectation. Such a comparison provides a picture not only of what actually happened but also of how actual results differed from what was expected and by how much.

## MANAGING AGAINST EXPECTATIONS

The comparison of actual performance against target provides management with a guide as to which areas of activity warrant investigation and which ones seem to be going essentially as planned and thus can probably be safely ignored for the moment. This is a basic application of the technique of *management by exception,* which is an essential ingredient of any formal management system for allocating the time of managers to those areas that most need attention.

The efficacy of any system for managing against expectations depends, of course, on the appropriateness of the expectations used as the benchmarks for comparison. The more dependable the benchmarks and the more closely they fit the nature of the activity, the greater the reliance that can be placed on the difference (variance, in the accountant's terminology) between actual and expected results. With highly dependable benchmarks, such as engineered standards for routinely produced components, relatively small variances from standard can be cause for immediate investigation. On the other end of the scale, it would be rather inappropriate to compare the actual profits of a new division or product line with profits planned a year before and conclude that small differences are good and large differences are bad. The causal factors are not well enough understood and the methods for putting them together are not tested enough to allow such dependence on simple comparisons. Rather the detailed assumptions underlying the estimates need to be examined and compared to what really occurred before any conclusions can be drawn. In such cases, analysis of the difference between actual and expected results is but a *starting point* for developing an understanding of what really occurred, determining the implications for the company, and assessing the performance of those in charge.

## ANALYZING DIFFERENCES

There is a methodology for analyzing business activities in order to better understand the differences between actual and expected results. This methodology is often referred to as "analysis of variances." It involves nothing more than starting with an overall difference between actual and expected performance and then "peeling the onion," one layer at a time, to obtain more and more detailed explanations for the differences between what happened and what was expected to happen. With relatively imprecise or uncertain information on either what happened or what was expected, the "peeling" might stop early, focusing instead on a more informal approach. When more complete data are available, when expectations are held with more confidence, and when there is greater understanding of the underlying activity, the formal analysis can be more extensive.

Like any technique, analyzing differences must involve considerable judgment. Thus what is needed is:

1    A description, in accounting terms, of what happened and a description in the same terms of what was expected—even if the criteria being used as "expectations" is only what happened last year rather than a carefully thought through concept of what "ought to be."

2    A realization that the process is designed to produce insight. It will not produce *answers,* it should be applied with a healthy dose of management judgment.

The methodology of managing against expectations can best be explored through a series of increasingly more detailed examples, each of which involves more detailed accounting information and more analytic rigor. The same example will be used throughout the exposition, but previously undisclosed detailed data will be added at each succeeding level.

*Level 0*

The most crude form of a profit variance analysis is as follows:

| | | |
|---|---:|---|
| Expected Profits | $3,000 | |
| Actual Profits | 3,045 | |
| Profit Variance | $     45 | Favorable |

The first level of analysis (Level 0) identifies the fact that actual profits were $45, or 1.5% more than expected. Exploring the situation a bit further, we could expand the analysis as follows:

*Level 1*

|  | *Expected* | *Actual* | *Difference* | |
|---|---|---|---|---|
| Revenues | $10,000 | $11,025 | $1,025 | Favorable |
| Expenses | 7,000 | 7,980 | 980 | Unfavorable |
| Profit[a] | $ 3,000 | $ 3,045 | $ 45 | |

[a]We will use the terms "profits" and "earnings" interchangeably.

Here we see a substantial favorable variance in revenues of $1,025 (10.3%) which is largely offset by an unfavorable expense variance of $980 (14.0%). This illustrates one danger in stopping too soon—what appears to be a small total variance may actually be the result of larger but offsetting differences. We will deem as *Level 1* an analysis which compares, on as detailed a basis as desired, actual and expected performance for the various line items in the earnings statement. This is an important first step, but it is only a first step.

*Level 2*

The next level of variance analysis is to attempt to isolate the effects of changes in the level of business activity from the effects associated with changes in prices, costs or operating efficiencies. The most useful way to carry this out is to use the concept of a *flexible or variable budget*. This is simply an intermediate evaluation criterion of what our profit expectations would have been if we could have precisely predicted what the actual level of activity would be—as though we had perfect foresight with respect to sales volume and sales mix.

To our example we add the flexible budget column and expand the detail of expenses to separate variable cost of sales from the relatively fixed period costs. This latter step is not essential but simplifies the pesentation.

This way of looking at what happened indicates that profits were $50 greater than originally expected because of the higher level of sales activity. This is column (2) vs. column (1), where only the volume of units sold varies. Standard costs and standard prices are still used. The fact that actual profits were $5 less than the flexible budget of $3,050 indicates that at the actual activity level, price increases did not offset increases in costs. Prices were $675 above plan ($11,025 − $10,350), while expenses were $680 above plan ($7,980 − $7,300). Of course, price and volume are not independent; it is conceivable that more units could have been sold if prices had been raised less. If this had occurred, the favorable sale

|  | (1) | | (2) Flexible Budget (actual Volume and Actual Mix) | | (3) | |
|---|---|---|---|---|---|---|
|  | Original Expected Performance | | | | Actual Results | |
| Sales | 2,000 units @ $5 | $10,000 | 2,100 units | $10,350ᵃ | 2,100 units @ $5.25 | $11,025 |
| Variable Cost of Sales | 2,000 units @ $3 | 6,000 | 2,100 units @ $3 | 6,300 | 2,100 units @ $3.29 | 6,910 |
| Period Costs | | 1,000 | | 1,000 | | 1,070 |
| Total Costs | | 7,000 | | 7,300 | | 7,980 |
| Profit | | $ 3,000 | | $ 3,050 | | $ 3,045 |

ᵃThe $10,350 consists of 1,320 units of one product, at standard sale price, and 780 units of a second product, also at standard price. The resulting average price is not quite $5, because the actual mix of sales between the two products differs from the planned mix. This is analyzed in Level 3 below.

price variance would have been reduced and the variance due to sales volume would have increased. Even with this lack of independence, isolating volume effects from other factors is important in understanding and evaluating what has occurred.

To review so far, the Level 1 analysis compares what actually happened to some expectation of what should have happened. The Level 2 analysis elaborates the comparison, breaking the total difference into two parts by saying: "What would my benchmark have been if I had perfect knowledge of what the level of activity would be?"–the flexible budget. With this concept, the difference between the original expectation and the flexible budget can only represent sales activity differences since expected prices and expected costs are used in both measures. Differences between the flexible budget and actual results can only be due to cost and price differences since the level of sales activity (volume and mix) is the same in both measures. This separation of sales activity related variances from cost/price-related variances is both powerful in itself and fundamental to the analysis which follows.

*Level 3*

The cost/price and sales activity variances can each be analyzed further. For the sales activity variance, this involves a split into the part due to volume changes and the part due to a changed composition or mix of the items sold. For the cost/price variance, Level 3 involves splitting out the sales price variance from the cost variances and decomposing the cost variances by cost categories.

Sales Activity Differences

If the company sold only one product in one size, the sales activity variance of $50 calculated above would be due entirely to sales volume changes. If, however, more than one product is sold, the difference can be composed of both overall sales volume changes and change in the *mix* or relative amounts of the different products sold. Consider the following extension of our example.

| | Expected Sales | | | Actual Sales | | |
|---|---|---|---|---|---|---|
| Product | Units | Price/Unit | Revenue | Units | Price/Unit | Revenue |
| A | 1,200 (60%) | $4.00 | $ 4,800 | 1,320 (63%) | $4.40 | $ 5,808 |
| B | 800 (40%) | 6.50 | 5,200 | 780 (37%) | 6.688 | 5,217 |
| Total | 2,000 | | $10,000 | 2,100 | | $11,025 |

Using these data, we can decompose the sales activity variance into two parts by introducing a new intermediate column. This column shows expected profits with sales at 2,100 units but in the same proportions as originally expected (product A sales = 60%, or 1,260 units, and product B = 40%, or 840 units). These numbers would lead to expected profits of $3,200. This is shown as follows:

| | (1) Original Expected Performance | | (2) Revised Budget at Actual Volume with Standard Mix | | (3) Flexible Budget (Actual Volume and Actual Mix) | |
|---|---|---|---|---|---|---|
| Sales | 2,000 units @ $5 | $10,000 | 2,100 units @ $5 | $10,500 | 2,100 units | $10,350 |
| Variable Cost of Sales | 2,000 units @ $3 | 6,000 | 2,100 units @ $3 | 6,300 | 2,100 units @ $3 | 6,300 |
| Period Costs | | 1,000 | | 1,000 | | 1,000 |
| Total Costs | | 7,000 | | 7,300 | | 7,300 |
| Profit | | $ 3,000 | | $ 3,200 | | $ 3,050 |

| Product | | | | Units | Price/ Unit | Revenue | Units | Price/ Unit | Revenue |
|---|---|---|---|---|---|---|---|---|---|
| A | | | | 1,260 | $4.00 | $ 5,040 | 1,320 | $4.00 | $ 5,280 |
| B | | | | 840 | 6.50 | 5,460 | 780 | 6.50 | 5,070 |
| | | | | 2,100 | | $10,500 | 2,100 | | $10,350 |

If we compare column (2) with column (3), we get a difference due entirely to product mix that is $150 unfavorable. The variance due solely to sales volume (assuming no variation in mix), is $200 favorable. This is shown in column (1) versus column (2). The net of these two is the $50 F shown at Level 2. You should note that expected costs and expected prices are used in all three columns.

Cost/Price Differences

The sales price variance is just actual sales units X expected prices versus actual sales units X actual prices. This comparison, as shown in the Level 2 calculations, is $10,350 versus $11,025, or $675 favorable.

The expense differences isolated earlier were:

|  | Expected Costs (Flexible Budget) | Actual Costs | Cost Differences |
|---|---|---|---|
| Variable Costs | $6,300 | $6,910 | $610U |
| Period Costs | 1,000 | 1,070 | 70U |
| Total | $7,300 | $7,980 | $680U |

Further analysis of the cost differences can be made if additional information is available on the nature of the costs incurred.

Consider the following expected costs[1] for products A and B in our example:

Variable Cost per Unit:
Labor: .3 hr at $5/hr                                      $1.50
Materials and Supplies: .5 lbs. at $2/lb.                  $1.00
Other Variable Costs                                        .50
Total Variable Costs, per Unit                             $3.00

Other Expenses, Fixed, per Period                         $1,000

With this detail, the flexible budget at 2,100 units of activity would be:

Labor: .3/hr/Unit X 2,100 Units = 630 hr @ $5/hr          = $3,150
Material: .5 lbs/Unit X 2,100 Units = 1,050 @ $2/lb.      =  2,100
Other Variable Costs: $.50/Unit X 2,100 Units            =  1,050
Period Costs                                             =  1,000
Total Flexible Budget                                       $7,300

Let us further extend the example by assuming that the expenses actually incurred were as follows:

[1]In a typical company, different products would have different expected costs. Thus, the flexible budget for expenses would involve mix considerations as well as volume. For this analysis we will ignore the mix factor, believing it to be sufficiently well illustrated in the revenue section to permit its application to costs. We will consider products A and B as costing the same, but sold in different markets.

| | | |
|---|---|---|
| Labor: 580 hr at $5.50/hr | = | $3,190 |
| Material: 1,120 lbs. at $2.30/lb. | = | 2,576 |
| Other Variable Costs | = | 1,144 |
| Period Costs | = | 1,070 |
| | | $7,980 |

With this more detailed information, the variance analysis can separate out at Level 3 the labor, material, and overhead differences as follows:

| | *Flexible Budget* | *Actual* | *Difference* |
|---|---|---|---|
| Labor | $3,150 | $3,190 | $ 40U |
| Material | 2,100 | 2,576 | 476U |
| Variable Overhead | 1,050 | 1,144 | 94U |
| Period Costs | 1,000 | 1,070 | 70U |
| Total | $7,300 | $7,980 | $680U |

*Level 4*

The last level we will examine involves decomposing the sales mix variance by products and evaluating the impact of market position on sales volume changes. For cost/price variance, it involves decomposing the sales price variance by products and the cost variance by efficiency-in-use versus purchase price changes.

Sales Mix Variance

The overall $150 sales mix variance can be broken down by product as follows:

*Standard Profit Contribution Variance*

| | *Standard Profit Contribution* | *Average Profit Contribution at Planned Mix*[a] | *Variance* | *Actual Sales Volume* | *Mix Variance* |
|---|---|---|---|---|---|
| A | $1.00 | $2.00 | $1.00U | 1,320 | $1,320U |
| B | $3.50 | $2.00 | $1.50F | 780 | $1,170F |
| | | | | Total | $ 150U |

[a]60% × $1.00 plus 40% × $3.50 equals $2.00.

As can be seen in the example, the unfavorable performance is the result of selling fewer units of the high-margin product (product B) than would be expected at an overall volume level of 105% of plan. When several products are involved, the mix variance results are not as obvious as they are here.

Sales Volume Variance

In looking closer at the $200F sales volume variance, let us assume that the company has traditionally had an 8% share of the market and expects this to be the case in the current period, during which the market was expected to be approximately 25,000 units. This would produce the original expectation of $4,000 of profit contribution (25,000 × 8% × $2.00 per unit).[2] If the market increased to 28,000 units while the company's sales went up to 2,100 units, the company's market share was actually only 7½%. This interplay between the company's growth and that of the market it serves can be usefully analyzed as follows:

Change in expected profit due to market size change

= (expected total market − actual total market) × (expected market share) × (expected profit contribution per unit at expected mix)
= (25,000 − 28,000) × 8% × $2.00
= $480F[3]

That is, the profit should have gone up by $480 due just to change in the size of the overall market. If the company could have maintained its market share, its expected profit in a 28,000-unit market would have been $4,480. It did not, however, and the effect of the decrease in market share is as follows:

Market share variance

= (expected market share − actual market share) × (actual market volume) × (expected profit contribution per unit at expected mix)
= (.08 − .075) × (28,000 units) × $2.00 per unit
= $280U[4]

This is the profit lost because of a decrease in market share. The combined result from volume and share changes ($480 − $280) is the total sales volume variance of $200F shown at Level 3.

---

[2] Sales price of $5 less expected variable cost of $3, at the expected mix.
[3] Representing $1,200 of sales at expected prices, less $720 of expected variable costs.
[4] $700 in sales, at expected prices, less $420 in expected variable costs.

## Sales Price Variance

The sales price variance, as calculated at Level 3, was $675 favorable. This can be detailed as follows:

| Product | Expected Price | Actual Price | Unit Price Difference | Actual Units | Sales Price Variance |
|---------|---------------|--------------|----------------------|--------------|---------------------|
| A | $4.00 | $4.40 | +$.40 | 1,320 | $528F |
| B | 6.50 | 6.688 | + .188 | 780 | 147F |
| Total | | | | 2,100 | $675F |

## Cost Variances

On the cost side the analysis can proceed further by separating out the efficiency-in-use element from the purchase price element for each cost component. This separation is almost universally calculated in the following way:[5]

$$\text{Purchase price difference} = (\text{expected price} - \text{actual price})$$
$$\times \text{ actual quantity used}$$
$$= (P_E - P_A) \times Q_A$$

$$\text{Efficiency-in-use difference} = (\text{expected quantity} - \text{actual quantity})$$
$$\times \text{ expected price}$$
$$= (Q_E - Q_A) \times P_E$$

Thus, in our example we would have, by cost element:

$$\text{Labor price variance} = (\$5 - \$5.50) \times 580 = \$290U$$
$$\text{Labor efficiency variance} = (630 - 580) \times \$5 = \underline{250F}$$
$$\text{Total labor variance shown at Level 3} = \underline{\underline{\$\ 40U}}$$

This is the difference between the flexible budget figure of $3,150 and the actual labor cost of $3,190. Similarly for materials:

---

[5] This reconciles the total difference, as can be seen by multiplying out the two equations and adding them together:

$$\text{Purchase price variance} = P_E Q_A - P_A Q_A$$
$$+$$
$$\text{Efficiency variance} = P_E Q_E - P_E Q_A$$
$$=$$
$$\text{Total variance} = P_E Q_E - P_A Q_A$$

Material price variance        = ($2.00 − $2.30) × 1,120 = $336U
Material efficiency variance = (1,050 − 1,120) × $2.00 =   140U
Total material variance shown at Level 3                              $476U

We could summarize this analysis differently, by nature of the variance, as follows:

| | |
|---|---:|
| Efficiency variances | |
| Labor | $250F |
| Material | 140U |
| Subtotal | $110F |
| | |
| Purchase price variances | |
| Labor | $290U |
| Material | 336U |
| Subtotal | $626U |
| | |
| Other (variable $94, period $70) | 164U |
| Total expense difference | $680U |

Which method of looking at the cost variances is "better" depends on what actions caused them. Although labor efficiency was very good, the labor rate or "price" increase more than offset the benefits. If this was due to substituting more efficient but higher-priced labor for that normally used, then showing labor rate and efficiency variances together (or even not separating them at all) could be more useful. If, on the other hand, purchase price increases produced pressure to really use workers and material efficiently, then showing the data by type of variance is useful, for it reveals that expenses were $626 more than expected, due to price increases. After adding in the spending variances on other costs ($164) the total was $115 ($790 − $675) more than could be passed on via sales price increases. The methodology is the same; which format is preferable depends upon managerial judgment.

## IN SUMMARY

We started with actual profit performance of $3,045 in a period and found first that it was $45 more than expected. Then we looked a bit deeper and found that profit was $50 better because of increased sales volume but $5 worse because of increased costs of operation that were not passed on in higher sales prices. Pulling out all stops, we finally determined that the situation was much more complex.

The overall market grew by 3,000 units more than planned (28,000 units versus 25,000). This should have yielded a $480 F profit variance in the period. However, market share slipped ½%, which caused a $280U profit variance. Furthermore, the sales mix included a higher than planned proportion of the low-margin product and this led to a $150U profit variance. Cost performance was also unfavorable. Materials variance was $40U, labor variance $476U, other variable costs variance $94U, and period cost spending variances $70U. Considering all these negative factors, the overall profit variance was favorable by $45 only because of $675 in sales price increases. A much different picture is thus presented than that suggested by the simple statement that profits were $45 higher than expected.

This multilevel analysis is illustrated in summary form in Exhibit 1. Further levels could, of course, be added if desired. The overall market change could be decomposed into economy-wide factors and industry-specific factors. The market-share change could be broken down by products. The sales mix variance could be decomposed by geographic region or customer class. Sales price changes could be decomposed into "list price" changes and discount changes (either early payment discounts or quantity discounts). Cost variances could be broken into controllable and noncontrollable segments by responsibility center. The analysis can stop any time the next level does not produce useful enough management information.

The discussion has focused on a manufacturing firm with two products. The concept is equally applicable in retail, financial, or service organizations. The focus is a separation of sales activity related and cost/price-related differences from expectations. Decomposing the profit variance one level at a time is a very powerful management tool. Understanding the specific impact of the various factors is the first step in undertaking appropriate corrective actions.

*Level 0*

Expected Profit = $3,000
Actual Profit   = $3,045
Variance      = $   45F

*Level 1*

|  | *Expected* | *Actual* | *Variance* |
|---|---|---|---|
| Sales Revenue | $10,000 | $11,025 | $1,025F |
| Costs | 7,000 | 7,980 | 980U |
| Profit | $ 3,000 | $ 3,045 | $    45F |

*Level 2*

*Overall Variance = $45F*

*Variance due to level of sales activity*

| Original expected performance | $3,000 |
| Flexible budget | 3,050 |
| Difference | = $    50F |

*Variance due to cost/price changes*

| Flexible budget | $3,050 |
| Actual results | 3,045 |
| Difference | = $    5U |

*Level 3*

*Difference due to sales volume*

Original expectation $3,000
Expected profit at actual volume with standard mix $3,200
Difference = $200F

*Difference due to sales mix*

Expected profit at actual volume with standard mix $3,200
Flexible budget $3,050
Difference = $150U

*Sales price variance*

Expected sales at actual volume and mix $10,350
Actual sales $11,025
Difference = $675F

*Cost variances*

| Labor | $  40U |
| Materials | $476U |
| Other variable costs | $  94U |
| Period costs | $  70U |
| Difference = $680U |

*Level 4*

*Difference due to overall market changes* $480F

*Difference due to market share changes* $280U

Product A  $60F
Product B  $210U

Product A $528F
Product B $147F

Efficiency variances $110F
Purchase price variances $626U
Overhead variances $164U
Difference $680U

*Level 5*

• • •    • • •    • • •    • • •    • • •